THE END of EMPIRES

African Americans and India

Gerald Horne

TEMPLE UNIVERSITY PRESS
Philadelphia

Gerald Horne, Moores Professor of History & African-American Studies at the University of Houston is the author of many books, including *Black and Brown: African-Americans and the Mexican Revolution, 1910–1920, The Deepest South: The United States, Brazil, and the African Slave Trade, and Cold War in a Hot Zone: The United States Confronts Labor and Independence Struggles in the British West Indies* (Temple).

TEMPLE UNIVERSITY PRESS
1601 North Broad Street
Philadelphia PA 19122
www.temple.edu/tempress

Text design by Becky Baxendell
♾ The paper used in this publication meets the requirements of the American National Standard for Information Sciences—Permanence of Paper for Printed Library Materials, ANSI Z39.48-1992

Library of Congress Cataloging-in-Publication Data

Horne, Gerald.
The end of empires : African Americans and India / Gerald Horne.
p. cm.
Includes bibliographical references and index.
ISBN-13: 978-1-59213-899-9 (cloth : alk. paper)
ISBN-10: 1-59213-899-3 (cloth : alk. paper)
1. African Americans–Relations with East Indians.   2. African Americans–Racial identity.
3. African Americans–Intellectual life–20th century.
4. United States–Race relations–History–20th century.   5. India–Race relations–History–20th century.   6. India–History–Autonomy and independence movements.   7. Imperialism–India.
8. Decolonization–India.   9. United States–Relations–India.   10. India–Relations–United States.
I. Title.
E185.61.H82 2008
303.48'25407308996073–dc22

2008006410

122208P

The End of Empires:
African Americans and India

CONTENTS

INTRODUCTION

The hands on the clock were approaching midnight on 15 August 1947 as thousands of South Asians surged, chanting "Jai Hind"—roughly, "Long Live India." The man who was to become the first prime minister of a nation that is slated to become the planet's largest in the twenty-first century, Jawaharlal Nehru, was uttering the words that would resonate through the ages, referring to his nation's "tryst with destiny." Amid a riot of tints and shades, the nation's new tricolor flag was unfurled on the ramparts of the magnificent Red Fort in New Delhi.[1]

Yet amid the huddled masses, all were not of Indian origin. One in particular was an African American, William Nelson, born in Paris—Kentucky, that is—in 1895, a graduate of the famed, historically Black Howard University. He had been posted in South Asia by the American Friends Services Committee, affiliated with the Quakers, a Pennsylvania-based religious group.[2] His presence was not entirely accidental: For a long time, a lengthy umbilical cord had linked the largest "minority" in what was to become the world's most powerful nation and the largest colony of the once potent British Empire. It was not deemed hyperbolic when, after this epochal independence day, W. E. B. Du Bois, who once asserted that the "greatest color problem in the world is that of India"[3]—not Black America—avowed that 15 August was "the greatest historical date of the nineteenth and twentieth centuries."[4]

Nor was it a surprise when, a few years after his appearance in Delhi, Nelson heard from a young minister named Martin Luther King Jr., who

DR.W.E.B.DUBOIS

Figure I.1   W. E. B. Du Bois, founder of the NAACP, also saw African Americans as part of a global "colored" majority that decidedly included India. (*Courtesy Library of Congress; photographer unknown.*)

informed his fellow theologian that "in a real sense my visit to India was one of the most rewarding experiences of my life." Why? "I do feel," he stressed, "I gained many meaningful insights that will deepen my understanding of nonviolence and also my commitment to it." King asked Nelson whether he had accumulated during his visit "any books or pamphlets on untouchability [*sic*]," since King was "in the process of making a study" of the fraught topic of caste, which had obvious implication for the fate of African Americans.[5] Indeed, the future Nobel laureate conceded in 1959, "We found the problem of the untouchables in India to be similar to the race problem in America," although India was "integrating its untouchables faster than the United States is integrating its Negro minority." King also exemplified another trend that was to characterize relations between the two nations—using India as leverage for domestic change in the United States, and vice versa—as he warned, "Many Indians are concerned that unless America solves its race problem *soon*, America will lose prestige greatly in the eyes of the world."[6]

This infatuation with India was nothing new for King. As a student at Morehouse College in Atlanta, he had heard Howard University's President

Mordecai Johnson, just back from a trip to India, describe how the nonviolent *Satyagraha* of Mohandas K. Gandhi had brought about revolutionary changes in India society. King was so moved that, in the fall of 1950, he read extensively about Gandhi's life and work.[7] Then he took what he learned and applied it to Jim Crow in the United States.

The route of inspiration was not a one-way street leading from Black America to India. When Harold Leventhal, a member of the U.S. Army Signal Corps stationed in India (who later had a stellar career as a manager and promoter for Harry Belafonte, Odetta, and Bob Dylan), gained a coveted audience with Gandhi as World War II wound down, the saintly figure greeted him with a pressing query. "The first thing he wanted to know," recalled Leventhal years later, "was how Paul Robeson was."[8]

That King would seek to conjoin the destinies of Black America and India—or that Gandhi would be hungering for information about the tallest tree in Black America's forest—was not unusual. From the beginnings of the African's sojourn in North America, she had been linked to events in what was then British India.

This is a book that seeks to explore these conjoined destinies—though, admittedly, the major focus is on North America and the impact of ties between Black America and India there. Although it takes a glancing look at this relationship before the unfolding of the twentieth century, the primary emphasis is on the decades leading up to Indian independence in 1947. I suggest that African Americans and India shared a common experience of opposition to racism and imperialism during this period—albeit at varying tempos—that tended to bind them. I further suggest that this was part and parcel of a larger antiracist and anti-imperialist struggle that encompassed millions globally and that the 1945 defeat of Japan, a nation that had been a lodestar for Black America and India, along with the Cold War, which ensnared the Soviet Union (yet another nation that had been perceived as friendly to intellectuals in Harlem and Delhi), both set the stage for the retreat of Jim Crow and the erosion of colonialism.

This epochal process was of major strategic import for Black America. A minority in the United States that historically had been an orphan of sorts, virtually denuded of rights, Negroes had been compelled to seek succor and allies globally. As Du Bois—and, to a degree, Marcus Garvey—put it, there was a compelling need to be deemed part of a global majority of the "colored" fighting a common foe. However, after the forced retreat from juridical Jim Crow and the reluctant granting of formal citizenship rights to African Americans, this battered minority also felt the need to distance itself from previous allies—particularly an independent India that pioneered in forming the Non-Aligned Movement, which was perceived widely in Washington as all too close to Moscow. The question insufficiently contemplated, then as now, is what would be the fate of African Americans once the international equation (not least, the Cold War) that compelled these halting steps toward racial equality began to change?

Ironically, the heightened influence of Delhi that accompanied Indian independence and the mass diffusion shortly thereafter of Gandhi's ideals in a Black America about to be liberated from the worst excesses of Jim Crow did not lead to an expansion of this once important relationship. Today, the once bountiful bilateral tie has withered significantly.

Nevertheless, too much can be made of this latter point, since the crusading of a newly independent India on behalf of the plight of colonized Africa—a plight that was inextricably tied to the ravages of a slave trade that led to the creation of Black America—redounded to the benefit of African Americans, not least since independent African states quickly began to speak out against Jim Crow.[9] It was more than a half-century ago at a profoundly important meeting in Bandung, Indonesia, of nations that came to be called the "Third World"—mostly from Africa and Asia—that the cosmopolitan Nehru quite movingly spoke of the plight of Africa and, more particularly, of those who came to be known as African American. "There is nothing more terrible," he said with passion, "there is nothing more horrible than the infinite tragedy of Africa in the past few hundred years. . . . When I think of it, everything else pales into insignificance; that infinite tragedy of Africa ever since the days when millions of [Africans] were carried away in galleys as slaves to America and elsewhere, the way they were treated, the way they were taken away, 50 percent dying in the galleys. We have to bear that burden, all of us. We did not do it ourselves, but the world has to bear it . . . this Infinite Tragedy."[10]

These heartfelt words were also a reflection of the fact that, as the pivotal twentieth century unfolded, an Asian diaspora in North America increased substantially, which made leaders such as Nehru more aware of developments there. Thus, his words were expanded subsequently by Gary Okihiro: "We are a kindred people, African and Asian-American. . . . We share a history of migration, interaction and cultural sharing and commerce and trade. We share a history of European colonization, decolonization, and independence under neocolonization and dependency. We share a history of oppression in the United States, successively serving as slave and cheap labor, as peoples excluded and absorbed, as victims of mob rule and Jim Crow."[11] This shared history is particularly prominent in the richly braided relations that conjoin Black America and India.

The persistence of this conjoined experience became ever clearer when Jim Crow came under sharper assault—as India emerged as an independent nation. In 1955, Delhi's ambassador in Washington had an experience in that

Figure I.2 Jawaharlal Nehru, first prime minister of independent India, spoke eloquently of the plight endured by Africans and African Americans. (*Courtesy Library of Congress; photographer unknown.*)

citadel of Jim Crow—Houston, Texas—that sheds light on why his superior, Nehru, may have been so sensitive to the plight of Africans. For it was then that the management of a local restaurant placed the distinguished, but dark-skinned, ambassador in the less than commodious Jim Crow section for Negroes.[12] Over the decades, such commonalities bound ever tighter Black America and India.

When President Harry S. Truman welcomed Nehru to the United States in October 1949, he proclaimed, "Destiny willed it that our country should have been discovered in the search for a new route to yours." This signified how the settling and exploitation of North America was tied to India.[13] Early on, Africans in North America and India found themselves part of a similar economic circuit. As one study put it, "The textile industry of [the] whole of Western Europe was transformed during the seventeenth and early part of the eighteenth by two powerful influences . . . the African Slave Trade [and] the introduction into Europe of new stuffs, the cottons and muslins of India."[14] British traders had been attracted to the southeastern coast of India during the seventeenth century precisely because of the opportunity to obtain cotton textiles. These textiles initially were shipped largely to the Indonesian archipelago, where the East India Company used them to purchase pepper and spices that later were exported to London for resale in Europe, North America, or the African coast—the latter being a major site for the traffic in human beings. The point is that India and what was to become Black America were linked organically, just as London's colonies in South Asia and North America were connected.[15] Early on, comparisons between British North America and British India were rife, with some asserting that the latter was "more valuable."[16]

This Asian colony once exported calico to Great Britain, but after the advent of the cotton gin in the 1790s, the British began exporting cotton goods to India, thus destroying its counterpart in South Asia and becoming more dependent on African slave labor in the U.S. South. This cotton connection also indicated that Black America and India were exceedingly potent ends of an empire headquartered in London, part of a triangle trade of the new type. Thus, as one analyst put it, "India had been surpassed first by Britain as an exporter of calico, probably in the 1790s, and then by the U.S.A. as a producer of raw cotton in 1821: in the 1820s she became a net importer of cotton goods instead of a net exporter."[17] Actually, this changed relationship of London to India may have been affected by the loss of Britain's valuable colony in North America, for that loss increased the importance to the empire of South Asia.

The American Revolution underscored that African slavery was as important to the fortunes of the United States as India was to that of the British Empire. Thus, the concerted attempt in the run-up to Indian independence in 1947 to join the fate of India with that of the United States generally was not coincidental, for more reasons than one. As the pro–India independence intellectual J. T. Sunderland once put it, "England pays more heed to the public sentiment of America than to that of any other country, if not of all other countries combined. . . . [W]e know that it was largely the strong public sentiment of America in favor of home rule for Ireland that caused England to give Ireland freedom."[18] London's concern was justifiable. Near the same time that Sunderland penned these weighty words, the influential New York Times Book Review posted the telling question, "Why is there such an eager interest in all that concerns India?"[19]

Still, the engagement of the young republic with India served to reinforce calcified biases among Euro-Americans toward those with dark skin—yet another reason that this global relationship had such weight and longevity. North American merchants in India conducted most of their business in British-built ports, where, it was reported, "Race was an organizing principle. At Madras and Calcutta, there were forts where the Europeans lived and worked and a native [sic] section"—often shabby and dilapidated—"often known simply as 'black town,'". This must have been reassuring to Americans who were rapidly becoming accustomed to segregation. At Madras, one Yankee noted, no "'blacks' were permitted inside the fort," Such practices convinced "most Americans [that the] racial character of Indians [was] a factor in their subjugation by the British." Indeed, notes Susan Bean, "Remarks on the racial order of British India recur often in American journals throughout the age of sail."[20]

Opposition by African Americans to British colonialism in India was buoyed by the fact that there was a similar opposition among a sector of Euro-Americans, who continued to see London as an enemy in the wake of the 1776 Revolution and the War of 1812. Given such an atmosphere, it was easier for U.S. Negroes to express antipathy, which was no small thing, given that London often was seen in the immediate pre–1865 era as a firm opponent of slavery and the slave trade and thus in some senses preferable to Washington. Suggestive of the harshness of Euro-American opinion was Josiah Harlan, a staunch antebellum opponent of London whose stance was buttressed by his long and celebrated sojourn in South Asia, a journey that was celebrated in the film *The Man Who Would Be King*. In his influential writings, Harlan portrayed the British Empire as a "vast corrupt behemoth that had brought nothing but misery to the oppressed and plundered millions." London, he said, "has riveted the shackles of slavery upon the whole agricultural population of British India [and, in the process] inflicted famines, discontent, disaffection, rebellion, financial distress, fall of prices, reduced revenues, crime abounding . . . might against rights, cultivation declining, total absence of internal improvements, no public works, no roads, no canals, no dissemination of knowledge or improvements in education." These, he thundered, were "the consequences of a military despotism, . . . a government imposed upon millions and sustained by the sword, without a philanthropic motive, originating in cupidity, nourished and developed by tyrannous force, sealed in blood." And these were some of his milder reproaches of the empire, whose demolition he avidly advocated.[21] Yet despite Harlan's unmasked fury, the fact was that an unceasing river of cotton bound the empire, British India, the United States, and Black America.

By the mid-nineteenth century, the cotton industry was among the world's largest, drawing on the labor of perhaps twenty million workers. Prior to 1861, most of the world supply of raw cotton had been produced by enslaved Africans on plantations in the U.S. South and was spun into thread and woven into cloth by textile workers in Lancashire. Then the U.S. Civil War intervened, and as if on a seesaw, India again rose in importance. India had contributed only 16 percent of Britain's supply of raw cotton in 1860 and 1.1 percent of France's in 1857. By 1862, it contributed 75 percent to Britain and as much as 70 percent to France. As one journal put it, "The emancipation of the enslaved races and the regeneration of the people of the East [are] intimately connected." The Bombay Chamber of Commerce, which was in a position to know, opined at the Civil War's end that that the "emancipation of American slaves [was] a matter of paramount importance for the future of India's cotton industry, signifying a permanent change in the agricultural structure and trade of India."[22]

Likewise, Dwijendra Tripathi is not far wrong in observing that, by 1860, "cotton had become the nerve centre of England's industrial and economic life, [whereas] the role of supplies from substitute sources in frustrating the grandiose scheme of Southern policymakers has received insufficient attention." In other words, the ability of Britain to secure supplies of cotton in India—as opposed to the slave South—was a signal factor in buoying the effort by the progressive sector of the British working class to forestall intervention by London on behalf of the so-called Confederate States of America, whose success would have realized a central dream of the English elite: splitting and thereby weakening its emerging rival in North America.

India was pivotal in the foiling of the plot to divide the United States. This colony, says Tripathi, was "the most important feeder of the British manufactories during the war." India, he adds portentously, "contributed to shattering the Confederate design,"[23] which means that African Americans are forever grateful. In fact, as former U.S. Secretary of State William Seward asserted during the Civil War, "Fortunes were made by speculation in cotton almost as rapidly in Bombay as they were lost in New Orleans," suggesting how India was levitated as the slave South was submerged.[24]

The relationship between Black America and India was facilitated by their ties of singular intimacy. In 1762, a British expedition was sent from Madras to seize the rich Spanish settlement in Manila. The ships were staffed by a wildly heterogeneous body of workers, including African slave soldiers recruited by the East India Company (some of whom may have spent time in North America) and an even larger number of South Asians. In fact, not only Africans and Indians but Native Americans as well had been drawn into the orbit of the empire to serve its far-flung ambitions.[25]

South Asians began to arrive in the United States in larger numbers in 1851. For example, half a dozen Asian Indians marched in the East India Marine Society contingent for the Fourth of July parade in Salem, Massachusetts; they were said by New England chroniclers to have married Negro women and become part of the Black population of the city.[26] The presence of a large dark-skinned population in the person of African Americans meant that South Asians seeking refuge could find a home of sorts in Black America. However, the virtual equation of dark skin with bondage harbored dire consequences for South Asians. Some early migrants from India to North America in the late eighteenth century and nineteenth century, says Gordon Chang, "had been indentured, and in several cases others, because of their dark complexions had been forced into chattel slavery along with Africans."[27]

Granville T. Woods, for example, is a name routinely touted during Black History Month. Woods is highly regarded as a "Black" inventor; actually, he was born in 1856 in Australia, the place of birth of both of his parents, though his "mother's father was a Malay Indian and his other grandparents were by birth full-blooded . . . Australian aborigines, born in the wilds back of Melbourne." Although he was probably a "quarter black [sic]," says his biographer Rayvon Fouché, the "majority of both black and white societies viewed him as a Negro." Though his biographer asserts boldly, "I contend he was not an American Negro," today in the United States Woods is regarded as such, though it might be similarly plausible to regard him as "Indian."[28] Something similar might be said about the well-regarded Tuskegee Airman Virgil Richardson. He was born in Arkansas in 1916, but his mother's family traced its roots back to India. His mother's grandfather Joe Green Cotler had been brought to North America from Bombay by his mother, an indentured servant.[29] Paul William Quinn, a fiercely antiracist "Black" cleric in nineteenth-century Pennsylvania, was likewise a migrant from southern India.[30]

Richardson's diverse gene pool, which also included a modicum of African ancestry, should not be deemed shocking. Because of the profusion of Negro sailors in the United States,[31] African Americans had been sailing to South Asia for some years. Missionaries, too, flocked to the region, including Amanda Berry Smith of the African Methodist Episcopal faith, who was born to slaves in Maryland in 1837 but by 1881 was spreading the word of God in Burma. There Smith "held a meeting in the Methodist Church for colored men especially, [and a] nice company of these men gathered; some were from the West Indies, some from the West Coast of Africa, and some from Boston, Philadelphia, and Baltimore. One man from the West Indies, had been in Burma for twenty years." There were "about twenty of these men in all," Smith reported, and yes, she confirmed, "These were colored men; my own people." Further, she noted, "It seemed that these men were better off than [many of their compatriots in North America]. . . . [S]ome of them were engineers on railways, some conductors, some in government service, and they all had good positions, and made money. Some of them had nice families of children."[32] There seemed to be a special bond between African Americans and South Asians, or so thought former U.S. Secretary of State

William Seward. While traveling in Madras, he remarked that he heard a "Tamil lyric [that] was prettily sung by one class. Its plaintive strain recalled our Negro melodies."[33]

Because of the evidently intimate relationship between South Asians and African Americans, London felt compelled to monitor the latter, which was an important component of its former colony and now growing rival, the United States. When President Theodore Roosevelt deigned to have dinner at the White House with Booker T. Washington, London's influential *Spectator* seemed more concerned than some journals behind the "Cotton Curtain" in the U.S. South. Although the *Spectator* called the invitation a "noble and courageous act," it also sincerely wished that Roosevelt "had not invited Mr. Washington because . . . [a] recognition of the non-existent equality of the races is not the best way to kill the white prejudice against the black." Instead, the journal advocated as the "best solution to the problem" that the "whites and [the] blacks . . . avowedly form themselves into two castes like the Hindoos and Mussulmans of India, with no intercourse except in the common business of life."[34]

This apartheid-like sentiment reached an appreciative audience in a United States wracked with racist separatism. In such a manner, despite their frequent differences, London and Washington often reinforced each other. Still, peculiar strains characterized the relationship. In 1909, for instance, Roosevelt gave a major pro-empire peroration. Strikingly, he delivered the speech at an important African American church in Washington, D.C.,[35] reflective of the fact that those few blacks who could vote routinely cast their ballots for his party, the Republicans. Ironically, in the same year, African Americans, spearheaded by W. E. B. Du Bois, formed the National Association for the Advancement of Colored People (NAACP) to push for voting rights that could lead them to vote for pro-empire politicians and to push for civil rights that could lead them to assemble and petition on behalf of the dissolution of that same empire via independence for its chief asset: India.

To make sure that the colonized were quarantined from the putatively seditious messages carried by African Americans, London made it difficult for African Americans to visit India. Du Bois, an inveterate traveler, discovered this to his dismay when he sought to travel to the subcontinent in the 1930s. He found that it was next to impossible to obtain a visa, and once he did, he had to "pledge [to] limit his words and activities." Moreover, he lamented, "The accommodations offered by steamships often involve racial discrimination, while the cost of such trips is of course prohibitive to the mass of Indians and Negroes."[36]

Such barriers were strewn in the path of potential Black visitors to South Asia not least because there were so many parallels between the African

Americans and Indians. There was something to the point of making a linkage between the "Mussulmans," or Muslims, of India, who made up about 12 percent of that colony's population, and the situation facing the roughly 12 percent of the United States that was African American. This congruence sheds light on the profound influence that South Asian Muslims have had on the religious experience of Black America. Ghulam Ahmad of the Punjab was the leader of the Ahmadiyya movement that extended its tentacles into North America about the time of Booker T. Washington's infamous dinner. "While espousing heterogeneity," writes Michael Gomez, the movement "was in reality an Indian-led movement with a mostly African-American constituency." Not only were the "Ahmadis in North America . . . greatly dependent on the fortunes of Pan-Africanism and nationalism among the African-derived population," according to Gomez, but, in fact, the group now known as the Nation of Islam was influenced profoundly by Ahmadiyya and, it has been speculated, the "foreparents [of] Fard Muhammad [a patron saint of the sect] were from Pakistan, with possible connections to the Ahmadiya movement." A precursor of the Nation of Islam, which came into existence approximately seventy-five years ago, was the Society for the Development of Our Own, which had "10,000 [members in] fourteen chapters around the country." Those members included "individuals from India" along with "those of African descent."[37] (Of course, Ahmadiyya was not singular in its influence on Black American religious thinking. Fard, who is sometimes referred to as "Fard Muhammad," also reputedly worked with the ecumenical Theosophist Society in California, an entity that was deeply influenced by Hinduism, Buddhism, and South Asia more generally.[38])

According to its official journal, "The Ahmadiya Movement in Islam was founded in 1890 by Hazrat Mirza Ghulam Ahmad of Qadian, Punjab, India."[39] It dispatched missionaries not only to Black America but also to Africa, Australia, China, and Singapore. Like the Nation of Islam, it was quite successful in finding souls to save among those who were incarcerated.[40] Also like the Nation of Islam, it combined a scorching critique of Christianity with a searing analysis of the plight of Black America. In 1922, for example, Ahmadiyya's journal ran a lacerating story about the "thirty lynchings of Negroes by white Christians" that had been recorded in the first half of that year. "[S]ome [were] burnt at the stake, others [were] put to death. These are the wonderful acts of the meek lambs of Jesus," the journal added with biting sarcasm. "After all a tree is known by its fruits."[41] And in a final similarity to the Nation of Islam, Ahmadiyya was not necessarily embraced by other devotees of Islam. Although they did "claim to be the true followers of Islam" in their homeland (today's Pakistan), writes Surendra Nath Kaushik, they were "denigrated as apostates by fundamentalist forces,

[for] according to the critics, Mirza Ghulam Ahmad . . . by assuming the title of 'prophet' had flagrantly violated the principle of the Finality of Prophethood." The Nation of Islam was likewise accused of veering from orthodox and basic Islam.[42]

As emigration from South Asia to the U.S. West Coast increased in the early twentieth century, it was not difficult for developing anti–Asian biases to merge with pre-existing anti–African ones, giving Negroes and Indians a further reason to bond. It is no exaggeration to suggest that Jim Crow lubricated the path for bias against Asian migrants. At a meeting in San Francisco in late 1907, the Asiatic Exclusion League announced that "95 per cent of California's citizens are unanimous in their petitions and prayers for the rigid exclusion of all Orientals . . . that the Caucasian, Mongolian, Malay and Ethiopian can never dwell together in peace under the same fig tree." This was no idle threat: The league claimed "225 affiliated organizations," which did not include "Branch Leagues in Victoria, Port Townsend, Seattle, Bellingham, Nanaimo, Spokane, Everett, Tacoma, Portland, Anaconda and Denver."[43] To be sure, opposition to Asian immigration was not unknown in Black America. The fact remained, however, that white supremacy targeted these immigrants and Black America simultaneously, and more often than not, this drove the two into each other's arms—at times, quite literally.

As racist bias was rising, a large number of Indian Muslim men were moving in and out of, and settling in, U.S. port cities. By the 1920s, perhaps a quarter of the British maritime work force was of South Asian origin, and for various reasons these laborers saw more opportunity in North America than in the United Kingdom or India. In cities such as New Orleans and New York, a significant number of these migrants ended up living beside, working alongside, and starting families with African Americans, not least since color generally barred these men—and they were almost all men—from the Euro-American community. These men were primarily Bengali Muslims. According to Vivek Bald, by the 1930s dozens of them were working as peddlers in Jacksonville, Memphis, Atlanta, and Chattanooga, where, again, they became entangled with African Americans. Unfortunately, the desire for anonymity on the part of these men—who, after all, often entered the United States without proper documentation—and their frequent physical resemblance to African American men makes it difficult to trace their routes and numbers.[44] These keen resemblances were due in part to the fact that the African American population contained not only a modicum of Native American ancestry, but, as well, U.S. slave traders often had strayed far beyond the usual hunting grounds of West Africa to East Africa—which long had enjoyed a fruitful intercourse with India—and Madagascar, where Polynesians and Indians, too, had long resided. Thus, the gene pool of African Americans included traces and hints of South Asia.[45]

The developing relationship between South Asia and Black America was reflected in a 1922 U.S. Naval Intelligence report, which noted with some concern that "the present Hindu revolutionary movement has definite connection with the Negro agitation in America. And both of these movements have leaning, at least for political reasons, to Bolshevik Russia. Ganti [*sic*; Gandhi] the leader of the Hindu Revolutionary Movement, and Garvey, the leader of the American Negro Agitation, were class mates while they were studying in England and in India. Garvey has remained ever since the closest friend, most ardent admirer and the handiest co-worker of Ganti, even though they live thousands of miles apart. Both Garvey and Ganti are strong believers of socialism and the revolutionary methods for realizing it."[46]

This generally misleading report was not altogether misguided in the sense that the two movements in question—Indian and African American— did make common cause from time to time with regimes that were frowned on in Washington and London, not only the one in Moscow, but the one in Tokyo, as well. Revolutionaries in Black America also were inspired by their peers in India. Cyril Briggs, a nascent Black communist, once proclaimed, "Look what the Hindus, another colored race, are doing in India. All these things are factors that help us here, right here in Harlem."[47] Hucheshwar G. Mudgal, who was born in India before migrating to Trinidad, then to the United States, served as editor of Garvey's newspaper, the *Negro World*, during one of its most militant phases.[48] Likewise, Leonard Howell, a founder of the Rastafarian faith in Jamaica more than seventy years ago, "published his own book under the pseudonym Gangungura Maragh, Hindi for 'teacher of famed wisdom.'"[49]

Garvey's movement was not the only venue where Indians and Negroes could cross paths. Har Dayal, who was born in India and founded the influential Ghadar Party, became "secretary of the San Francisco branch of the Industrial Workers of the World [and] was friendly with socialists and anarchists," all of whom—and contrary to national practice—invited Negroes into the ranks.[50] The influential Indian migrant Dhan Gopal Mukerji arrived in California in the early twentieth century and became a student. He recalled that the cook at his fraternity "was a Negress. . . . [S]he gave me five dollars [when I arrived] and said, 'go and buy a pair of shoes and then come back to work.'"[51]

As the South Asian population began to proliferate in the United States in the early decades of the twentieth century, this kind of contact became more likely. More delegations were sent from Black America to India, especially those sponsored by Christian groups such as the Young Women's Christian

Association (YWCA) and the Young Men's Christian Association (YMCA), which were more difficult for London to bar. In 1928, Juliette A. Derricotte, secretary for colored student work for the YWCA, found herself in Mysore and was moved tremendously by what she witnessed. "I ache with physical pain," she informed the readers of the NAACP's journal, *The Crisis*, "when I remember the struggles of all India today, religious, caste, economic, social, political; how can I tell of the control which oil and rubber and jute have in the relations of East and West, or explain how back of oil and rubber and jute are the more fundamental and external puzzles of economics, race, and religion."[52]

The sympathy was mutual. K. A. Abbas arrived in the United States from India in 1938 and was in for the shock of his life. "I first became conscious of the Negro problem," he told his readers in Bombay, "when traveling from Los Angeles to New York [by train]." This became a journey toward insight as he was subjected to racist discrimination based on his skin color and found "the sense of white superiority lurking even in the most educated and advanced section of the American people with the only exception of Communists (whose rigid ideology admits of no racial bias)."[53]

It was precisely this increase in South Asian visitors to the United States that had a far-reaching impact on Jim Crow. The United States found it difficult to portray itself as a paragon of human-rights virtue and exemplar of democracy in the battle of ideas with Moscow, and other presumed ideological foes, when a significant percentage of its citizenry was clearly treated atrociously and others who happened to be dark-skinned were treated similarly. As a result, Jim Crow had to go.

But that issue was joined well after Abbas's fraught visit to the United States. During the time that he was enduring racism, Nehru, a key leader of the independence movement in India, was being told by a confidante of the "feeling of affinity that the Afroamericans have with us, and of this desire for closer cultural contacts."[54] A global consciousness was accelerating among African Americans, particularly during the Depression decade, fueled by a search for insight propelled by economic distress, the growing role of the Communist Party, and the spark ignited by Italy's invasion of Ethiopia. In April 1936, Robert O. Jordan, president of the Ethiopian Pacific Movement, based in Harlem, reminded Nehru, "We, the coloured people in the Western Hemisphere, are suffering the same as our brothers in India and we hope it won't be long before the dark people of the world will get away from the [yoke] of the white man." These were not just hortatory exclamations, he added, noting that in 1922, when Gandhi "started his campaign, the British government wanted to send the British West Indian regiment from Jamaica to go to India to fight, [but] the regiment adamantly refused to go to India."

This, he asserted, caused London to "disband . . . the British West Indian regiment." The episode was not an isolated one, either, he argued. "I can assure the Indian people," said Jordan with confidence, "that the dark men in the Western Hemisphere will not be an obstacle in the way of colored freedom."[55] Thus, argued one commentator, "A unique interest related to presumed membership in a dark-skinned brotherhood" united Black America and India.[56] Recognition of this trend led Gandhi to assert during the same year Jordan wrote to Nehru, "It may be through the Negroes that the unadulterated message of non-violence will be delivered to the world."[57]

In turn, for a number of reasons there were few national groupings anywhere on the planet who spoke out more vigorously against racism in North America than Indians. It was an inexorable response of Indian migrants faced with bigotry of the rawest sort. It was a way for Indians to deflect charges of backwardness in their homeland by pointing accusingly at the primitive and primal racism that obtained in the United States. And it was partially a reflection of the personal relationships that had developed between Indians and African Americans in the United States.

In the vortex of this last trend were Du Bois, founder of the NAACP, and Lala Lajpat Rai, who hailed from what is now Pakistan but spent a considerable amount of time in the United States in the first decades of the twentieth century. Du Bois, said Rai, was a "personal friend of mine,"[58] while Du Bois affirmed of Rai that "he was at my home and in my office and we were members of the same club." Du Bois also called Rai a man of "restraint and sweet temper."[59] This personal tie helped Rai to use his vast array of contacts in British India on behalf of the cause of African Americans, once requesting of Du Bois "any recent literature which you can send me about the treatment of Negroes in the United States and also about the activities of the Ku Klux Klan. I have a few new numbers of the *Crisis* from 1917 to 1920 from which I am going to quote profusely."[60]

This bilateral relationship between an oppressed national minority in a budding superpower and the world's largest colony exploded in significance during World War II. Both Indians and African Americans had been courted by Japan, and it was not preordained that either would support London and Washington in their battle with Tokyo.[61] As a result, ruling classes in the two imperial powers were on the defensive and highly susceptible to yielding to the claims of the oppressed. Against this backdrop, a prototypical gathering took place at the White House in September 1944. Black leaders including Walter White of the NAACP, Channing Tobias, and Mary McLeod Bethune had arrived to discuss with President Franklin Roosevelt the U.S. role in "urging the Allies to end colonial rule in Africa, India and the West Indies."[62] This was part of a remarkable upsurge in support among Black Americans for Indian independence, which helped immeasurably in pushing this inevitability toward realization. Again, this was a cross-cut saw, slicing in multiple directions. The famed General China, of the renowned movement toward independence in Kenya known popularly as "Mau Mau," recalled that it was in Calcutta that an "African-American soldier named Stephenson told him about the liberation of Haiti and he met Indian nationalists who asked him why Africans were not pushing off the yoke of colonial rule."[63]

World War II had trapped both the United States and the United Kingdom in a devolutionary spiral that led inexorably to the retreat of both Jim Crow and empire. This was particularly so for London. Indeed, when British rule in India finally ended in 1947, "80 percent of the Empire's subjects gained their independence at one stroke."[64] J. T. Sunderland observed in 1927 that, in a sense, India was driving the defense budget of London and shaping global events, in that "Great Britain demands to have the largest navy in the world and to control the seas. Why? Primarily in order that she may be able to keep India."[65] In 1901, Lord Curzon summed up the equation smartly when he asserted of the empire, "As long as we rule India we are the greatest power in the world. If we lose it, we shall drop straightaway to a third-rate power."[66] The post–1947 era suggests that he was not far from the mark.

The connection between India and African Americans continues to the present day, although admittedly, since African Americans began to gain full citizenship rights, their perceived need for global alliances has dissipated. When the hip-hop icon Tupac Shakur carved the word "thug" on his abdomen, he (and his admirers) probably did not recognize that he was etching this connection in his flesh. In nineteenth-century British India, "thugs" were "bands of robbers who strangled their victims as sacrifices to the goddess Kali."[67] The term, of course, was no longer tethered to its original meaning when Shakur performed his homage, but it did continue to signify India's continuing resonance in the English-speaking world. After all, India today contains more English-speakers than any other nation—to the point that "thug" could be transformed into a reigning symbol for the outlaw culture that some in hip-hop would like to project.

Since the halcyon days leading up to August 1947, the relationship between Black America and India has so lost resonance that even posing such a tie may seem odd or, at best, quaint. However, as the self-proclaimed "sole remaining superpower," the United States, continues to lose altitude and is dogged even more by real and imagined adversaries, its relationship with India grows in importance. Certain Washington hawks, for instance, would like to play India against China, just as Beijing was manipulated against

Moscow during the Cold War. At the same time, however, one leading Indian military figure has predicted "a U.S.–India armed conflict late in the next decade, where, increasingly, China is on the India side."[68] Simultaneously, fear of China has contributed to an entente between Washington and New Delhi that has accelerated inward investment in India to a point at which this nation is being touted as a possible superpower itself at some point in this century.

Whatever scenario plays itself out, it is clear that African Americans, who have become the bulwark of the progressive voting bloc in an otherwise conservative national electorate, will play a crucial role. Thus, as what has been termed a "U.S. empire" winds down,[69] it is equally clear that African Americans, the most left-leaning sector of the electorate,[70] must play a pivotal role in the process, guaranteeing their importance, once more, in the end of empire. More to the point, when in October 2005 U.S. Secretary of State Condoleezza Rice—in the presence of British Foreign Minister Jack Straw—referred bitterly to the "empire of Jim Crow" that she had experienced during her Alabama childhood,[71] she was, perhaps unintentionally, again conjoining the fates of those who had endured U.S.-style racism and those who had languished during the heyday of the unlamented British Empire.

This book primarily concerns the relationship of Black America to India before August 1947—with the accent on the former. Yet overall it concerns how African Americans, a principal "end" or raison d'être of the empire of Jim Crow, came to crusade against the principal "end" of another empire: India.

1

PASSAGE TO—AND FROM—INDIA

The relationship between Africans and India extends to the era of prehistory. Consider, for example, the inhabitants of India's Andaman Islands, a remote archipelago east of Bengal. These direct descendants of the first modern humans to have inhabited Asia are apparently descended from the first modern humans to have left Africa thousands of years ago. Their physical features—"short stature, dark skin, peppercorn hair and large buttocks"—are "characteristic of African Pygmies," according to one analyst. "They look like they belong in Africa, but here they are sitting in this island chain in the middle of the Indian Ocean," according to Professor Peter Underhill of Stanford University.[1] Such contemporary comments reflect similar comments made decades ago by the NAACP journal *The Crisis*. "The sympathy of Black America must of necessity go out to colored India and colored Egypt," *The Crisis* said. "Their forefathers were ancient friends, cousins, blood-brothers, in the hoary ages of antiquity. The blood of yellow and white hordes has diluted the ancient black blood of India, but her eldest Buddha still sits black, with kinky hair."[2] And, argued W. E. B. Du Bois, "The connection between Asia and Africa has always been close. . . . There was probably actual land connection in prehistoric times." The "culture of the black Dravidians," he wrote, "underlies the whole culture of India, whose greatest religious leader is often limned as black and curly-haired."[3]

In other words, the Indian mainland, which is within sailing distance of East Africa, also bears the earmarks of the continent where humans emerged. More than a thousand years before the foundation of Greece and Rome, the extremely dark-skinned Dravidians erected a powerful civilization in the Indus Valley. They traded with the region now containing Ethiopia and Somalia. However, their heyday was eclipsed when the "Aryans" began to rise in prominence and began to extend a caste order that was heavily invested in color—or, more specifically, in placing the darker-skinned at the bottom of society.[4] The "lowest servile caste, the Shudra, is characterized by the ancient Vedic literature as 'black' and 'dark complexioned,'" Michael Gomez observes, but "as there are many dark-skinned populations throughout the world, attempting to locate Shudra origins in Africa may be pointless."[5]

Such an effort would be similarly unavailing for the purposes of this study, not least because the bulk of African Americans have roots on the western side of Africa, not on the eastern side, which is closer geographically—and historically—to India. However, it is evident that the ancestors of far more African Americans than has been recognized hail from East Africa, just as European trading companies in the seventeenth, eighteenth, and even as late as the nineteenth century, transported a not insignificant number of enslaved Africans into Asia, particularly into India and southwest Asia. These companies were also shipping the enslaved from Madagascar to India and the East Indies.[6]

Then there were the "Siddis," who are the descendants of Africans brought originally as slaves and are found today in quite a large number in different regions of Gujarat, Maharashtra, Karnataka, Andhra Pradesh, and other parts of India. Their color, hair texture and other features suggest roots in Africa. This forced migration of Africans seems to have given a boost to the expansion of trade to India by the Arabs in the 6th century A.D., just as later the labor of enslaved Africans in North America was to give a fillip to the South Asian economy.[7]

With London ruling an India that countenanced slavery and North American colonies that were similarly oriented, it was not accidental that there were enslaved Africans who traveled between all three sites. This in turn suggests that there may be "African Americans" whose ancestors were born in India. London—whose tentacles extended from Africa to India—was instrumental in transporting South Asians to North America as indentured workers or slaves, where it is likely they intermarried with African Americans.[8] Many of Goa's slaves hailed from Mozambique, for instance, as did enslaved Africans in the Americas. A "Negro page boy was as common a sight in an English lady's household in Calcutta or Bombay as in London, about the middle of the eighteenth century," notes Jeanette Pinto, and the same was true for New York and Charleston.[9]

As revolutionary fervor increased in North America, more colonists found common cause with the people of India as fellow victims of colonial exploitation. In fact, remarks on the racial order of British India recur often in American journals throughout the age of sail. At the same time, India was at the fulcrum of a transcontinental trade arrangement, supplying textiles, sheeting and shirting and goods for the African slave trade, as well as provisions for plantation slaves. In turn, for the African trade India was pivotal in the supply of "dyed piece goods, for example, brown *gurrah* or blue *guinea*. . . . [A] sample of blue *guinea* cloth, made in southern India for the African trade, is preserved in a letter to Boston merchant Henry Lee."[10]

Apparently, some colonists in British North America resented the implication that their colonial status in the empire was akin to that of South Asians. Yet when the revolt against London commenced in the Thirteen Colonies, some colonists came to envisage India as an ally against British tyranny. Haidar Ali of Mysore, for example, became a cult figure: Philadelphia merchants named a ship after him. The fabled Boston Tea Party was reported to be tied to India. Increased shipments of tea from South Asia to Massachusetts were intended to relieve the East India Company of the serious financial crisis that had beset it in 1772: Tons of this tea wound up in North American waters, though lost on many was the intimate tie that linked the two continents of Asia and North America.[11]

Slavery was instrumental in the quadrangular relationship that prevailed between and among British India, British North America, Africa, and London. Many U.S. Negroes, skeptical of the cries of liberty coming from slave masters, often sympathized with the United Kingdom during the course of the revolutionary upsurge in North America. After the revolution triumphed, the continued presence of these Negro dissenters became somewhat uncomfortable, and many decamped to Sierra Leone. Among the first eight men to go there, as it turned out, was "John Lemon, a 29 year old Bengali hairdresser and cook who could read."[12]

This human connection between India and U.S. Negroes reflected a structural relationship rooted in the production of cotton. Certainly, the invention of the cotton gin had a sizeable impact on the industry, though it is equally accurate to point out that as early as the seventeenth century, artisans in India had developed a hand-cranked device with two rollers known as a *churka*, which the British then transferred with similarly sizeable impact to the Caribbean and North America.[13]

The United States—cut off from its traditional West Indies market as a result of the Revolutionary War—was compelled to look elsewhere for new and profitable markets. The British, preoccupied in a conflict with Napoleon, provided something of an opening for U.S. merchants who had an interest in South Asia.[14] As the nineteenth century began to unfold, more ships from the United States, which carried more than their share of African American sailors, began to trickle into India. In turn, more Indian influence became evident in the United States. No better symbol of this tendency was Rammohun Roy, who had a significant influence on Ralph Waldo Emerson, on Transcendentalism, and, by implication, on abolitionism. Articles about Roy appeared in at least 50 percent of the religious publications of the eastern coast of the United States, especially in New England, according to one estimate. Roy was so frequently discussed in the United States that all the major libraries contained copies of his work relative to the controversy on Christian dogma. Several editions of his writings were also published in New England.[15] However, Roy's sharp and stinging criticism of Christianity, which was not uncommon in India, was to become a flashpoint of contention between India and African Americans in the twentieth century.

The commonality of interest between British India and what used to be British North America—that is, the United States—was reflected in a rigid form of residential segregation. Madras, for example, was "divided into two parts, the Black and the White Town," recalled the traveler Henry Delamere. The so-called White Town, the residence of the Europeans, was "very handsome," in stark contrast to the site for those not deemed to be European. "White Town [is] inhabited by merchants and their dependents, military men and troops of the natives under our command," Delamere observed. "The Black Town is inhabited by Gentoos, Mahometans, Jews and Indian Christians, who are chiefly Armenians."[16] While visiting Madras more than two hundred years ago, Dudley L. Pickman of Salem, Massachusetts, noticed that "the whites have the Danish church, and one for the Roman Catholics, where blacks are admitted after the whites have finished their devotions." The "blacks (natives)," he asserted, using a term for South Asians that was routinely appended to African Americans, "have one of their own color for their preacher."[17]

U.S. travelers in South Asia found many things to remind them of home, which helped to reinforce the idea that South Asians should be treated as contemptuously as African Americans—a trend that would drive the two despised groups into each other's embrace.

William Maxwell Wood, while passing through what is now Sri Lanka in 1856, referred to the "indolent effeminacy of East Indian life." He observed, "Every house seems to be crowded with a multiplicity of servants, all of whom do more than one good stout house servant in the United States." The resultant indolence, he said, created a "demoralizing influence upon the young" that was "more than that attributed to slavery in our Southern States. No matter what pains European parents may take to prevent their children becoming indolent and dependent, the result seems inevitable."[18] At times it seemed it was easier for some Euro-Americans to perceive the crass exploitation that underpinned white supremacy when it was viewed abroad as opposed to at home.

This was particularly the case for Ceylon, which, as William Seward, a comrade of Abraham Lincoln, noted during his sojourn there, was a "distinct British province" whose "government [was] under the direct supervision of the Secretary of State for India."[19] The U.S. national Mary Thorn Carpenter spoke of the "babel of strange sounds and colors, all bewildering" in Colombo. "Fancy a town of one hundred thousand blacks," she mused. "All our servants are men; and are called, old and young, indiscriminately, by one general name 'boy,'" which was not unlike home. Like the slave South, "In the East you are not expected to do anything for yourself, never to stoop or cross the room; one call in corridor brings a black multitude to your door," Carpenter averred.[20] Fellow traveler Harry A. Frank agreed: "It is easy to account for the vagabond's fondness for tropical lands. He loves to strut among reverential black men in all the glory of a white skin; it flatters him astonishingly to have native policemen and soldiers draw up to attention and salute as he passes."[21]

But as tensions rose between London and Washington, culminating in the War of 1812 and near-misses in the run-up to the Civil War, there were sober reconsiderations in Great Britain of the feasibility of its heavy reliance on cotton from the United States to fuel its mills. At the same time, a Unitarian missionary in Calcutta in the late 1850s was becoming excited over the possibilities of growing cotton on the Ganges. He queried, "Could you not send me some good abolitionists to cultivate cotton in the great Daccan district?" India seemed so like the slave South that one U.S. national was "deploring the British use of the opprobrium 'nigger' to describe Indians." This mutual unease between the United States and Britain was reflected in the idea that London had striven to deepen its control of South Asia as a kind of reparation for its loss in North America. "She 'leaped like the old lioness she is . . . to the Orient for compensation,'" argued one North American. But in a rehearsal of arguments that reached a crescendo in the first few decades of the twentieth century, U.S. nationals sought to blunt the British critique of Washington's domestic failings by pointing to the obvious demerits of the empire's colonialism. "Ladies of England just now dropping tears by the bucketful for Uncle Tom and appealing to our ladies upon the iniquity of slavery," said one of these disgusted Yankees, "should rather march down to the India House and with their handkerchiefs bedewed with tears of tenderest sympathy, beseech the merchant princes to stop the sale of opium to four millions of crazed coolies." Still, other North American visitors could not help but revert to their own unique practices on arriving in India. After arriving in Calcutta in 1859, according to Bernard Saul Stern, one Yankee was stunned after being "surrounded by a group of nearly naked 'niggers.'" He was struck by the fact that "the masses of India [were] very dark in color" and "on one occasion [the visitor] beat a 'moonshee', a clerk, which precipitated a 'troublesome predicament." Inevitably these sojourners described Indians in ways that Negroes would have found familiar—for example, their alleged penchant for "invariably" being "late for appointments." This reflected the notion as Stern put it, that "Hinduism was especially repugnant to most Americans in the second half of the nineteenth century."[22]

Such ideas did not necessarily endear the United States to a gathering pro-abolitionist sentiment in Britain. In 1858 in Manchester, a bitter philippic was directed at the "most abject and hazardous dependence upon the Slave States of America." Indeed, it was stressed, "England's demand for slave grown cotton is the secret of American slavery." This was hardly necessary, it was thought, since "cotton *can* be grown on the banks of the Indus, by *free labour*, at a less cost, and with a greater profit, than it can be in New Orleans, or Mobile or Arkansas." One "10 [pound] note invested in the 'East India Cotton Company,'" it was announced triumphantly, "will do more to put an end to the slave trade . . . than double that sum contributed as a mere donation to an Anti-Slavery Society." India should be wielded as a weapon against the United States, it was emphasized, for "so long as cotton is selling for 500 dollars a bale and Negroes are worth from 1000 to 1500 dollars, all the preaching, and all the entreaty, and all the schemes for the emancipation of the American slave, will be as fruitless as 'The Whistling Wind.'" Thus, "as soon as cotton is grown in sufficient quantities, and at a fair profit, on the banks of the Indus . . . by free adult labour, that moment the 'slavery of the South' will cease to be either a necessity or an expediency and *America will be free!*"[23]

I. G. Collins, the author of the foregoing, who had served with Her Majesty's Navy fighting the slave trade, was firm in his belief that India was the key to liberating enslaved Africans in the U.S. South,[24] a view that was gathering momentum as the Civil War approached. Collins's view reflected the serious qualms that were being raised about the industry after 1857. The origins of the concern rest in the shortfall of the slave South crop of 1856 within the context of wider fears of over-dependence on one source of supply, anxiety as to Anglo-American relations, and the desirability of opening up new markets in return for raw cotton.[25] This fraught discussion led inexorably to brighter prospects for British India, suggesting once more its ties with the fate of the slave South. Even before this crisis in the 1850s, India as a site for cotton was not a new development. In 1835, the writer Edward Baines announced that "the birthplace of the Cotton Manufacture is India."[26]

As persuasive as Collins might be, and as popular as his viewpoint was becoming, his opinion was not universally held in the United Kingdom. Some in London were more interested in splitting the United States by backing the so-called Confederate States of America (CSA) than they were in wielding India against enslavement of Africans. They were influenced more by the perceived instability of India as manifested in the Sepoy Revolt of 1857—a monumental and historic development spearheaded by angry Hindu and Muslim troops. One U.S. journal compared the Sepoy uprising to parallel developments in the United States. "England took twenty-eight months to repress the Sepoy rebellion," said the *Christian Recorder*, which was "about as great an undertaking as to put down a rebellion among the Negroes of a South Carolina county."[27] This comparison between a slave rebellion and the Sepoy Revolt was not unusual. "Just as [with] the uprising of black slaves in the Caribbean and North America," says the historian Denis Judd, "the white, male response to the menacing, 'uppity nigger' of the Bengal Army was an explosive and lethal mixture of fear and loathing. At the heart of this uncompromising reaction was a horror of the sexual violation of white women by black men."[28] Such comparisons were driven by real considerations, for as early as 1804 London considered the idea of exchanging West India regiments—close cousins of African Americans in the Caribbean—with the Sepoy regiments of the East India Company.[29]

Actually, when the epochal Sepoy Revolt erupted, the "dire agony of Cawnpore was shared by American gentlemen and ladies," according to the Reverend William Butler. "Indeed," he continued, "they took precedence to their sorrows, for the group first 'led as sheep to the slaughter', before the murder of those from the intrenchment [*sic*] was perpetrated, included the Rev. Messrs. Freeman, Johnson, M'Mullin, and Campbell, with their dear wives and children." Butler himself "narrowly escaped the fate which befell these brethren and sisters." Stunned and embittered by his harrowing experience, Butler brought a familiar, racialized conclusion to his U.S. audience, expressing unalloyed hostility to Hindus and Muslims alike, who he contrasted invidiously with Christians. "The North American savage," he opined, "need no longer be considered the master of human cruelty, as the red man has found his match in the Sepoys."[30] Ineluctably, parallels had been drawn between those with dark skin in Asia and in North America, a comparison that served to bind the reviled.

Perhaps London could learn a few lessons from the U.S. South in how to strangle the rebellious. Looking at the complex situation, Washington quickly concluded that, perhaps, the CSA had more in common with the United Kingdom than with the United States, although, as it turned out, the stunning Sepoy Rebellion may have helped to reinforce a pre-existing belief that abolitionism itself could unleash an overall challenge to white supremacy as deadly as what had riled Reverend Butler.

The fate of Indians was an aspect of the larger question of U.S.–U.K. relations in the context of cotton. From roughly 1820 to 1860, a de facto alliance existed between Lancashire and the U.S. South. Then, from 1850 to 1900, Britain represented the exploitation of India as a market and as a source of supply for raw cotton in the service of the virtually Anglo-Indian city of Manchester, which represented a direct challenge to its counterpart in New England. As early as 1820, Britain was the single largest consumer of raw cotton in the world and remained so until the end of the century, when it was surpassed by the United States. At the same time, the United States had surpassed India by 1821 as the planet's leading producer of cotton, a reflection of the toil of enslaved Africans and a reflection of how that toil affected South Asia. This tie between the United States and African Americans and London and India became so close during the upsurge of Anglo-American trade in the first half of the nineteenth century as to inspire Sidney Smith's sardonic observation in 1843: "'the great object for which the Anglo-Saxon race appears to have been created is 'the making of calico.'"[31] The larger point was that enslaved Africans in the U.S. South had reason to hope that, if cotton production increased in India, there would be less of a need for their compatriots in Africa to be shackled and dragged across the Atlantic to toil for nothing.

As for London itself, the Sepoy Revolt may have added to a pre-existing concern about the undesirability of being so heavily dependent on gross exploitation of those with dark skin. In Britain, there were some 2650 cotton factories containing over 3,000,000 spindles and 350,000 looms operated by 440,000 persons. The British cotton mills were producing 2800 million yards of cotton cloth and 200 million pounds of twist and yarn for exportation. Seventy-seven per cent of the raw material for this gigantic industry came from the United States alone, according to Dwijendra Tripathi. About one-fourth or one one-fifth of England's population depended for its bread on the cotton industry, one-tenth of England's wealth was invested in it and nearly half of her export trade was made up of manufactured cotton goods. By 1860, cotton had become the nerve center of England's industrial and economic life, and this nerve center rested unsteadily on the reluctant backs of thousands of enslaved Africans in North America.[32] Correspondingly, Washington had to be concerned that this reliance predisposed London to intervene in the Civil War on behalf of the CSA.

British India was thinking similarly—which is why during the Civil War's early stages one correspondent remarked on the "absolute necessity for fortifying the port of Bombay," since "we may be at war with the Northern United States within a month. The whole world is politically smoking and may burst into a flame at any moment."[33] This inflammatory notion had occurred to the local Chamber of Commerce in Bombay. The eminent gentlemen of the chamber were "viewing with anxiety and alarm the present defenceless state of Bombay." Respectfully but strongly, they decided to "urge upon the Government the absolute necessity of protecting a port in which [were] centered the greatest interests of Western India and which [was] so essential to the commercial prosperity of Great Britain, by vigorously prosecuting the permanent fortifications of the Harbour." This "proposition" was put to a vote, which carried unanimously. But as the opinions of I. G. Collins suggested, British India might have had as much to fear from the CSA as from the United States. Thus, said one India-based journalist about the vote, "It was gratifying to see the American merchants and among them, Mr. Healy, Consul for the United States, raising their hands in favour of the proposition."[34]

Certainly, the CSA, which was heavily dependent on King Cotton, was not heartened by the U.S. consul's remark about the "unprecedented fluctuations in the prices of cotton in this market—caused by the Civil War in the United States."[35] Reverend Butler, fresh from his escape from the clutches of the Sepoy rebels, retained the presence of mind to realize that the U.S. Civil War "woke up the dormant intellect of ten thousand homes in the depth of India, and led men to inquire and study, and so far stimulated education, and showed its value, as no foreign event for hundreds of years previously had done." Moreover, he declared, the "'cotton famine' raised so wonderfully the value of their staple and the Hindoo farmer began to receive two and even three, rupees for the same quantity of cotton for which he obtained only one the year before." Hence, "men opened their eyes and began to study geography" and other weighty matters.[36] The more perspicacious African Americans realized that events in faraway India were helping immeasurably in determining their destiny.

India's role as a challenger to the United States in the cotton market raises the possibility that the competition was an impediment to the pretensions of King Cotton and the CSA, and thus hastened the downfall of African slavery in North America. As Tripathi has put it, "In marshalling his might and forces King Cotton failed to take into account the impact of the shot from Britain's distant mercenary. The factors that resulted in frustrating the Confederate hopes were intricate and interwoven, but India may claim a legitimate share in thwarting a design which would have permanently divided the United States of America."[37]

As early as 1862, a consul at a Spanish port wrote, "The importation of wheat raised by the cheap labour of India into Europe by steamship through the Suez Canal has become a novel competition against the American farmer and Russia in supplying European markets with wheat; and it must naturally exercise an influence over prices in every quarter where even a momentary demand may arise for foreign supplies." A U.S. consul in India informed the State Department that wheat "was and would be grown cheaper in India than in the United States" and that this Indian export would "'keep down the prices of American and all other wheat' in the markets of the world. . . . [N] umerous anxious inquiries by the State Department at the same time indicate the seriousness with which the United States viewed India's bid to share the wheat market of the world," though, with the beginning of the twentieth century, the danger began to retreat. If India could threaten U.S. hegemony in wheat, why not in cotton? And what would that mean for the thousands of African Americans whose fate depended on the production of this crop? Would not this serve as an incentive for African Americans so situated—or least, for their representatives—to find out more about India? Certainly India's rising prominence in the cotton industry restrained those lords of the loom in Manchester who might otherwise have been inclined to support the lords of the lash in the so-called CSA.[38]

For as one British analyst announced ominously as the result of the Civil War remained unclear, "Our great staple manufacture and one chief source of our national wealth and commercial power has grown up, as everyone knows, in almost entire dependence of a foreign country for the supply of raw material of that manufacture." The immense danger of such a dependence" would not cease even if the CSA prevailed. "War with that foreign country was always a possible contingency," it was said pointedly. "Somebody or other was always warning us, and telling us to have more than one string to our bow and especially to look to our own Indian territory."[39] The existence of India was a formidable barrier to the ultimate success of the CSA and the very existence of African slavery. Suggestive of this close tie is the fact that at Lincoln's death the Calcutta Consul received various condolence notes from Indian nationals. The father of the famed poet Rabindranath Tagore, along with a number of his fellow Indian compatriots, expressed admiration for the North because of Lincoln and his policy toward the Negroes.[40]

The ebb and flow of the cotton industry crested during the Civil War. "India," says D. A. Farnie, "had become in 1861 the main focus of the aspirations of all who hoped to end Britain's slavish dependence upon the USA." Bombay was seeking to replace New Orleans as "the center of gravity of the cotton trade." But the United States recovered remarkably with the war's end, which helped to "frustrate official hopes to maintain India as a source of supply of raw material." But other forces were intervening—for example, the opening of the Suez Canal, the organization in 1870 of the New York cotton market for futures trading, and the re-laying of the transatlantic cable in 1872 and the resultant extension of the commercial influence of New York that further served to re-establish the United States as a source for cotton—a development that was an extension of the labor of African Americans who, after the initial hope of the Civil War, were driven back into cheap, bestial labor in the wake of Reconstruction's suffocation. This resurgence of the United States was buffeted by a drop in prices in partial response to increased production not only in India but also in Egypt, Turkestan, China, and elsewhere and the development of a global market in cotton. Part of this expansion was also the extension of cotton production in the United States more deeply into Texas, which led to a tripling of the volume of U.S. cotton exports from 1872 to 1891.[41] Thus, again, the well-being of African American sharecroppers and agricultural workers was being shaped by events thousands of miles away.

This debate about the Civil War and its aftermath should not obscure the parlous state endured by those few South Asian immigrants who somehow made it to the United States. They were not necessarily greeted warmly, since, as Joan Jensen has put it, "For the most part, Americans, like Europeans, did not oppose British colonialism in India."[42] In the post–Civil War decades on the West Coast, even those of Japanese origin—who came to be regarded as the staunchest opponents of London's rule in South Asia—were not treated benignly, or so recalled Tuly Singh Johl. As he remembered it, these fellow Asians taunted Indians as "English slaves" and because of their height "referred to them as 'poles.'" Thus, "Indians kept to themselves or joined Mexican-American or black communities. Some Indians who had difficulty finding jobs in cities claimed to be Mexican or black, believing the prejudice to be greater against Indians." They were referred to as "nigger kind of fellers." This deployment of the ultimate epithet against Indians reflected how their fate was conjoined with that of African Americans. "The attempt to admit blacks to politics, it seemed to reformers, had already failed, and they had no intention of making the same mistake with Asians," Jensen says.[43]

The realization that the fortunes of the United States were bound to those of South Asia inevitably brought a stream of visitors from the former to the latter. Also inevitably, these North Americans brought with them a suitcase full of assumptions based on their experience at home. Such was the case for Andrew Carnegie, a baron of industry who arrived in Lucknow in 1879. "Who can assure us," Carnegie asked rhetorically, "that these bronzed figures which surround us by millions may not again in some mad moment catch the fever of revolt? This is the anxious question which I find intruding itself upon me every hour." Carnegie was conscious of the failed attempt to bring more blacks within the ambit of the United States by annexing Haiti's neighbor, Santo Domingo.. "It is a dangerous game, this, to undertake the permanent subjugation of a conquered race," he said, "and I do not believe that after General Grant sees India he will regret that the foolish Santo Domingo craze passed away." As it had for other Euro-Americans, a passage to India made this multimillionaire more attuned to the workings of white supremacy, which could not be comforting to African Americans. "As a European walks the streets," Carnegie remarked, "he is salaamed by every native he chances to look at. He moves about, one of superior race and rank. As he approaches a crowd, to look at a passing sight, a clear lane is made for him" as if he were parting the Red Sea. "All this spoils a man for residence at home," he concluded, "where 'one man is as good as another a good deal better.'" Like other Euro-American visitors, Carnegie was able to grasp more carefully the nettle of white supremacy abroad than at home, as he was a stern critic of British rule in India, though he did not link his sentiment to his other heartfelt point that, "during the Civil War in the United States, cotton cultivation in India . . . reached an extraordinary development."[44]

But Euro-Americans were not the only sojourners in South Asia. African Americans were also making their way to India and its environs. Thus it was that Amanda Berry Smith arrived in Bombay in late 1879, eventually winding up in Burma, where she was surprised to encounter a number of African American and West Indian migrants. A tall, smooth-skinned woman with a well-proportioned body that she chose to clothe in a simple, Quaker-like dress and scooped bonnet, Smith stayed in Bombay for a few months before traveling to Cawnpore (then called Allahabad) "to see the heathen idol worship." Like many of the African Americans who made it to India before 1947, Smith was a Christian missionary bearing an ideology that was often contemptuous of the major faiths of the land: Hinduism, Buddhism, and Islam, in particular. "How sad to see the different idols they worship displayed on their flags and in every possible shape and way," she cried. "My heart ached, and I prayed for the Lord to send help and light to these poor heathen." In Bangalore, she found "superstition and idolatry, and infidelity so rampant it seems the very air one breathes is impregnated with them." However, she was sufficiently alert to notice that, in India, "there are generally two roads; a native road and an English road." The English roads, which she was allowed to traverse, she noted, were better.

Berry Smith encountered a complement of Black workers in Rangoon. She had "hoped to distribute about eleven Bibles" but found herself flummoxed because she could not speak adequately the indigenous languages. "How much good anyone with a missionary spirit could do here in [Burma] or India," she reflected, "especially if he or she had an aptness in acquiring the language." Language may not have been the decisive factor, since even the English-speaking black workers "often" had decided to "give up all hope in Christ." These were "my own people," she exclaimed. "Some of them had left good Christian homes and started out Christians themselves. But they get into these ports, and there are no colored churches or missions to go to, and they fell lonely."[45]

Smith, in sum, did not see fit to challenge British rule in India. If she had, she might have been expelled. Similarly, when Pandita Ramabai visited the United States around the same time Smith was traveling through South Asia, she chose not to challenge the unique "racial" folkways of her hosts. She was "arguably among the most notable women India has ever produced," according to Robert Eric Frykenberg, and wrote about the United States during her tour in a way that has evoked Tocqueville. Her tour was a sensation. She traveled thousands of miles throughout the continent, yet she confessed that her critics had accused her of "speaking only good of the United States and of excluding everything bad"—though there was plenty in the latter category to peruse. Yet she also confessed, "I have not found fault with the people of the United States to the extent so many think I should have." Her critics may have had African Americans, then enduring the nadir of their existence in this land, foremost in mind when contemplating her reticence.[46]

2

THE COLOR LINE

The twentieth century, as Du Bois famously suggested, was the era of the "color line," and in the United States this hued tripwire ensnared African Americans and Indians alike. As Indians began streaming to U.S. shores, particularly to the West Coast, they began to experience a form of discrimination that became pervasive and that mirrored what U.S. Negroes had endured for centuries. In fact, the alliances that developed between Southern U.S. politicians driven by Negrophobia and those in the western United States with similar concerns about an influx of Asians created a powerful axis that came to propel U.S politics for decades. These alliances created objective conditions for the rise of another axis: that between their victims—South Asians and African Americans.

Just as cotton served to conjoin the fate of these alliances, developments in the silver market played a similar role. In the late nineteenth century, as South Asian migration to North America began to accelerate, there was a global collapse in the value of silver, a trend driven in no small part by new discoveries in the United States. Sterling silver, whose value was based on gold, was less affected than the Indian silver rupee, which dropped in value by more than half, curbing investment and helping to induce a deep depression and thereby spurring migration across the Atlantic. This was the capstone of other disturbing trends that had characterized what had been a trying nineteenth century for South Asians. There were the aforementioned strains in the cotton industry—particularly in Bengal—which fomented a precipitous drop in the population of Dacca. This was followed by the ruin of weavers and other craftsmen, such as potters and metal workers. British planters, who mirrored their counterparts in the U.S. South by routinely referring to "beating their own niggers," figuratively drove South Asians to North America in search of more benign climes.[1]

Unfortunately, South Asians were greeted in this hemisphere in a way congruent with racial epithets that were so casually tossed their way in their homeland. The Asiatic Exclusion League (AEL) had deep roots in the Golden State of California a century ago and was explicit in stating that it was not concerned only with those of Chinese, Korean, and Japanese origin. In 1910, the AEL noted that the South Asian migration to California was "of recent origin" in that "previous to 1907 no mention [was] made of Hindus separately but are probably included under the caption 'Other Asiatics' in the tables." In that critical year, 1907, "1405 East Indians arrived," the AEL reported, and "for the six months ending [in] December 1909 no less than 600 Hindus . . . entered the port of San Francisco."[2] Gary Hess has noted that between 1820 and 1972, "some 70,140 immigrants from India entered the United States," but there was certainly a bump in their numbers at the time the AEL was being organized.[3] According to one account, almost five times more Indians arrived in the United States in 1907, than had come in 1906, and in 1908 there were even more, while 1910 saw the largest number ever to enter the United States in a single year. This was no ecstatic encounter. Bhai Parmanand, a missionary who arrived during this wave, affirmed that the United States was "no happy land for the coloured." The intellectual activist Har Dayal likewise was struck by the fierce attachment of the United States to white supremacy, a policy that was driven in no small part by antipathy to the Negro. "This cursed pigment . . . erects a barrier between the Hindus and other civilized races everywhere," he exclaimed. The "white races . . . [do] not enjoy 'some innate superiority.'" The arrival of enormous numbers of South Asians on U.S. shores focused national attention on migration from South Asia and, in turn, generated a responding consciousness on the part of Indians who soon began plotting the overthrow of British colonialism from the streets of San Francisco.[4]

Actually, driven not least by the periodic famines that characterized British misrule, nearly seven thousand men from the Punjab alone immigrated to the United States during the peak immigration years of 1907 to 1911, and a heavy percentage made their way to the Pacific Coast. Their presence helped to generate further anti-Asian sentiment, which was already buoyed by the presence of sizeable populations of Chinese and Japanese origin. Euro-American labor leaders often perceived Asian Indian immigrants as the new so-called "Asiatic Menace." It was easy to conflate this newer presence with the pre-existing Negro "menace" because the South Asians also tended to be dark-skinned. Thus, it was no surprise that, like U.S. Negroes, Asian Indians were subjected to gruesome medical experiments as they captured the attention of white supremacists.[5]

Indeed, rather quickly South Asians were described in terms eerily reminiscent of how African Americans were portrayed. Governor William D. Stephens of California sputtered that "the Hindu . . . is the most undesirable immigrant in the state. His lack of personal cleanliness, his low morals and his blind adherence to theories and teachings [so] entirely repugnant to American principles makes him unfit for association with American people."[6] Such bigoted expressions were endemic in the Pacific Rim. The Indian intellectual L. L. Rai noted that British Columbia had a rule that Indians could come there only if they took a ship directly from India, which then was thought to be an "impossibility" and thus a putatively non-racial barrier to their arrival. But an affluent Indian chartered a ship and took it to British Columbia as World War I was erupting, sparking a major row and confirming the obvious point that discrimination within the empire was rampant. "If the colored man comes, the white man goes," was the conventional wisdom—so the former had to be prevented. "The dread of the Asiatic is the dominant fact in the world today and it will largely govern the politics of the twentieth century," Rai noted with prescience.[7]

Politicians in California who were sincerely interested in keeping their jobs could not easily ignore such anti-Asian sentiment. As Punjabis began flooding into the state, a journal arose appropriately called the *White Man*. It was a "monthly magazine devoted to the movement for the exclusion of Asiatics" that was "for racial segregation." But what was striking about the journal was not its white-hot rhetoric but its white-skinned supporters. Labor organizations that endorsed and subscribed to the *White Man*, the magazine reported, included the "Seattle Central Labor Council, Portland Trades and Labor Assembly, Denver Central Labor Council, San Francisco Central Labor Council, San Francisco Building Trades Council, [and] San Francisco Council of Painters." The publishers planned to print "30,000, possibly 50,000, of [the initial issue]," which indicated that their message was gaining traction. Even the advertisers subscribed to the magazine's principles. The American Tailoring Company of San Francisco, for example, blared the fact that it was "an American firm run by Americans on American principles"—that is "STRICTLY WHITE LABOR."[8]

One of the "chief reasons" for the Asiatic Exclusion League's 1908 name change from "'Japanese and Korean' to . . . 'Asiatic'" was "the knowledge that we have of the great number of Hindoos that are looking toward the Pacific Coast, especially California, as a field for exploitation." It was via western Canada that the Indians began to flock to the United States, the AEL stated:

"A batch of 100 Hindoo laborers" arrived in British Columbia, but "upon landing they seemed to disappear as if the earth had swallowed them." They made their way to Bellingham, Washington, "but the disturbance . . . caused by the displacing of white mill hands by Hindoos caused them to flock to California by the hundreds, and their presence in the southern part has caused such apprehension among the people of that section that Senator [Frank] Flint contemplates introducing a bill for their exclusion."

Though their numbers were just in the hundreds, their presence was the proximate cause of "incipient riots in Bellingham, Everett, Danville, Seattle, Portland and other places . . . caused by the employment of Hindoos at a wage far below what is required by a white man to support himself, let alone support a family." There were only "2500 to 3000" Indians in the region but, that number was sufficient to cause the AEL to "induce the Hindoos to go to the Hawaiian Islands to work on the plantations," though they later found, to their dismay, that "Hindoos are not wanted in Honolulu." For the "police on the water-front" viewed "with much concern the large importations of Hindoos and assert that it means trouble in the future, possibly more serious than the Chinese or Japanese ever yet received." Why the hostility to Indians? The reason would have sounded familiar to African Americans. "Europeans are preferable to Hindoos," it was announced. "We believe the American continent should be preserved as the exclusive heritage of the whites."[9] No, it was stressed, "there is no community of thought, nor of feeling, nor of sympathy . . . between the white American and the Asiatic[,] there is no common tie whatsoever. . . . [T]he character of an Oriental population degrades the idea of labor, as did the chattel slavery of [the] South."[10]

Of course, this anti–Indian and anti–Asian hysteria was not confined to the U.S. West Coast. British Columbia in many ways preceded—and energized—the generation of this sentiment, with one Canadian advising that "it demands no explanation to say that the Chinaman and Hindu [are] dangerous and competitive factors," although they were "negligible factors compared with the . . . audacious incursions of the Japanese." This overriding feeling is what helped to unite those of African and Asian origin, since what the writer stressed emphatically was the "importance of conserving British Columbia for the benefit of a purely white population."[11]

Besieged though they were, articulate African Americans objected more than once to this demonizing of Asians. "The Asiatics have been regarded as people worthy only of contempt, to be robbed at will at the point of the sword, their lands divided at the pleasure of the Powers in interest," said the *Colored American Magazine* in 1904. "This condition [was] made possible, especially in the case of India and China, by the venality and effeminacy [*sic*] of their rulers." It was "not suspected anywhere that the Asiatic worm, so long trod upon by Europe, would or could turn. It was placed in the same category with the African worm," but the anticolonial stirrings in India were leading to second thoughts. Moreover, an alliance that would stir the United States within decades—that between India and Japan—was already beginning to stir consciousness, for, the *Colored American Magazine* reported, "Japan has the world thinking [of the] 'yellow peril' " and, allied with the leading British colony, it could transform the planet.[12]

At this juncture, the Asian—or "Asiatic"—population was viewed as akin to a V-shaped formation of flying geese, with the Japanese leading the way. That is, the major threat to white supremacy was seen to emerge from Tokyo, then spread like an oil spot to others, particularly South Asians, whose tie to the British Empire—at least, theoretically—provided them with an entry point into North America via Canada.

Worse, according to advocates of white supremacy, was that African Americans were seen as joining this formation. African Americans themselves were beginning to look to Tokyo as a beacon of opposition to white supremacy, a trend that also developed in India. *Voice of the Negro*, a popular journal, covered Japan's war with Russia avidly and did not hide its bias, A "Russian triumph would be a triumph for color prejudice," *Voice of the Negro* stated, "for Russia regards the darker peoples of the earth as inferior." In this respect, the journal said, in a way designed to clinch the argument, "Russians are not unlike our southern neighbors."[13] Booker T. Washington exclaimed, "There is no other race outside of America whose fortunes the Negro peoples of this country have followed with greater interest or admiration [than Japan. In] no other part of the world have the Japanese people a larger number of admirers and well-wishers than among the black people of the United States." His Indian counterpart Jawaharlal Nehru hailed Japan's 1905 victory over Russia as a "great pick-me-up for Asia," while his comrade in the independence struggle Subhas Chandra Bose declared that "Japan's victory over Russia . . . was the harbinger of Asia's resurgence. That victory was hailed with great joy not only by the Japanese but also by the Indians."[14] This brutal war was "taken to be a struggle between Europe and Asia," and Asia's "victory proved that the European superiority was a myth," according to R. P. Dua. According to an Indian student then matriculating in Tokyo, "So great was the interest of our people in Japan, that our weekly papers turned into daily ones and the press had sometimes to publish extra issues."[15]

Consequently, the *Colored American Magazine* was reflecting a gathering hysteria when it reported on some Euro-Americans who were centered mostly on the West Coast. These elements were petrified at the prospect of a rising Asia challenging white supremacy. This was not a fringe element but a rising movement that held influence in Sacramento particularly. Nor would it be proper to see this as solely of local concern, for that would not explain why in early 1911 Governor Hiram Johnson, who had a reputation for being "progressive," contacted Secretary of State Philander Knox, the man responsible for the nation's global diplomacy, after "Assemblyman Hall introduced Assembly Bill No. 486 providing for segregation of pupils in our public schools and excluding Indians, Mongolians, Chinese, Japanese, Malays and Hindus."[16] Assemblyman Hall was responding to the Democratic Party's 1900 platform, which proclaimed its support of the "continuance and strict enforcement of the Chinese Exclusion law, AND ITS APPLICATION TO THE SAME CLASSES OF ALL ASIATIC RACES."[17] Eight years later, this potent command was seen as in need of bolstering, so the party exhorted, "We are opposed to the admission of Asiatic immigrants who cannot be amalgamated . . . or whose presence among us would raise a race issue," adding, "we favor the total exclusion of all Asiatic laborers from this country by extending the provisions of the Geary Act to Japanese, Koreans and all other Asiatics."[18] Certainly, this bar encompassed the mostly dark-skinned South Asians.

It was not just labor that was being targeted but potential property owners, as well. Complementing the activity of the AEL, the Alien Land League arose, which was able to persuade legislators to back a bill mandating that "no alien shall acquire title to or own real property."[19] The racial chauvinists who made up the Patriotic Order of Sons of America complimented Governor Johnson and state legislators for "their part in the preparation and passage of the Alien Land Bill; and [their] hearty support of the same."[20] As one angry white man put it, "To the whites of the West Coast, the Japanese are quite as impossible in even the most distant social connections as the Negroes are to the whites of the South." In a sense, it was worse out west, because "the Japanese [was] infinitely superior to the Negro" and thus provided stiffer competition.[21] Be they of Asian or African origin, be they Indian or African American, their equality was an idea that racial chauvinists on the West Coast and in the South opposed.[22] Remarkably, this chauvinism was a Pan-Pacific movement that encompassed the region stretching from Vancouver and San Francisco to Wellington and Canberra.

In the bright spring of 1913, an august panel gathered in Sacramento to discuss the specter of Asia. Giving the moment added gravity was not only the presence of Governor Johnson but, alongside him, Secretary of State (and perennial presidential hopeful) William Jennings Bryan. They sat in rapt attention as one California legislator declared the Pacific Coast "the frontier of the white man's world." The "peril" to the region, the legislator said, was so "serious [that] steps should be taken to guard against it. It is the Negro problem over again made more perilous because back of the Orientals are two great nations, one in the process of formation, the other already one of the great world powers." What was even more frightening to these forces was that, although it was easy to guess the identity of one of these powers—Japan—it was unclear who the other was. Was it China—or India?

Again suggested was, a conflation of Asians and Africans that was being led by the nose by Tokyo. Another concerned legislator asked, "Is it not a fact that when the people first requested a law as to the Japanese, the Japanese worked on the railroads and that the Hindus of today only followed the Japs [*sic*]?" The terse and blunt response was that the "feeling was not as much against the Hindus as it is against the Japanese." "Well," said the legislator, "I do not want [either group] here." A fellow lawmaker demanded that a "Monroe Doctrine [be] applied to California with reference to Oriental . . . immigration" and, lest the term be misconstrued, he added, "by Orientals, we mean the Hindus also." If something is not done, he warned darkly, "We will have race quarrels, race riots and race troubles." A nation that had recently endured anti–Negro conflagrations that had swept from Atlanta to Springfield, Illinois, could only wonder what plundering and pillaging Asians in California might bring.

Some legislators recommended that California emulate the State of Washington, which had enacted anti–Asian legislation in 1909, or Arizona, which enacted such legislation when it gained statehood in 1912. Even the Socialist Party, which was thought to stand for the interests of workers irrespective of color, was said to declare for an anti-alien land law along with the Democrats.

But amid the hellfire and brimstone, voices of dissent cautiously piped up. Mention was made of the state's 1894 constitution, whose Article I, Section 17, limited certain rights to "foreigners of the white race or of African descent," which might hamper including Negroes in racist bans. Then the silver-tongued, portly Secretary of State Bryan poured cold water on the festivities by stating that he was present "to speak for the President who represents this nation before the world, and to tell you what he has already told you, that he earnestly advises against the use of any language that would offend any people who have dealings with us." Already, the threat from Tokyo—which exploded in 1941—was being considered. And beyond diplomatic concerns was the similarly hefty matter of labor. As one politician reminded, "The white man cannot and will not work in the delta . . . for the reason that in the growing of asparagus and potatoes, the Asiatic is best fitted to the work at present. It is the constant stooping and moving along on their knees that the white men will not submit to, and cannot. Somehow his nature and temperament will not stand for it."[23]

The AEL begged to differ. In the pivotal 1912 election, the backers of the pro–Jim Crow Virginian Woodrow Wilson presented him as a Southerner who would understand West Coast racial attitudes. Many voters who left the Republican Party for the Democratic Party expected Wilson to take a strong stand against Asian immigration and had a hard time accepting the importance of Tokyo's ascension.[24] These diehards thought they had sensed the way elite winds were blowing when Theodore Roosevelt seized the occasion of the African Diamond Jubilee Mass Meeting in the Metropolitan Episcopal church in Washington, D.C., to declare, "In India we encounter the most colossal example history affords of the successful administration by men of European blood of a thickly populated region in another continent." This, he exhorted, was a "greater feat than was performed under the Roman Empire." It was, in his words, quite simply "one of the most notable and the most admirable achievements of the white race during the past two centuries."[25] The less well-known Sydney Brooks, writing during the same era as Roosevelt, concurred ruefully as he lambasted those who "seem to regard all government of Oriental peoples by the white races as an abomination."[26]

Of course, Roosevelt's rancid ruminations did not represent the entire range of elite opinion on British India. There was simply too much anti–London sentiment with roots stretching back to the American Revolution. Not only Bryan but also Mark Twain, William Randolph Hearst, and Andrew Carnegie would have expressed skepticism about the beneficence of British colonialism. Yet it proved difficult to accept ideas of "racial" superiority with regard to African Americans and reject their implications when it came to British India.[27] This was the problem encountered by supporters of Indian independence in the United States. This also suggested that this problem could be circumvented in part by deepening ties with African Americans in a rising tide of the dark-skinned.

Although powerful and persuasive, the reasoned voices of diplomacy found it hard to compete with rank calls to chauvinism, calls that apprehension about Tokyo could not stanch, not least because they were buoyed by prevailing anti–Negro sentiment that had no such powerful counter. The AEL placed the matter in a portentous context that did not ignore these feelings: "Once America looked toward the Mediterranean as the forum where the world's questions were solved. . . . [T]oday America is beginning to look outward [to the "Pacific]." Then in bold letters that were meant to signify an even bolder pronouncement, the AEL declared: "IF THE OCCIDENTAL MAN IS TO HOLD HIS NARROW STRIP AND SOLVE THE QUESTIONS THAT FACE HIM, HE MUST SET HIM AGAINST SHARING THAT STRIP WITH OTHERS." But the AEL could hardly ignore what was roiling the rest of the nation—namely, a "recent decision of the United States Supreme Court upholding the right of states to legislate constitutionally against co-education of the white and black races, thus strengthening California's case against the co-education of the whites and Chinese and other Orientals."[28] Lest there be any doubt, it was made clear that "other Orientals" most specifically included the "large numbers of Hindus and Sikhs" who were "being recruited to the United States and were quietly but effectively forming large colonies in various parts of California."[29]

And as with Negroes, according to the AEL, Asians posed a "racial danger to our people [that consisted of the] avowed purpose of Orientals to amalgamate with the Caucasians by miscegenous [sic] marriages."[30] Again, the perceived threat emerging from Indians and African Americans was being conflated. As the ultra-bigoted journal the *White Man* spluttered in 1910, "The association of white women with Mongolians, Hindus and Negroes is racial pollution. Race aversion is mutual. If up-to-date proof is required, we cite the outcome of the Jeffries–Johnson prize fight." (The reference is to the controversial boxing match between the African American Jack Johnson and the Euro-American Jim Jeffries.) There were, the journal stated, "nearly one hundred killings as an aftermath; a national crusade against prize fighting, while we secretly pray for a white man who can slaughter the Ethiopian."[31] That "women comprised [a mere] one percent of California's South Asian immigrant population in 1914," as Jaideep Singh Alag noted, only exacerbated the cascading hysteria that created bigoted synergies yoking Indians and African Americans alike into a tightening noose.[32]

In 1889, an event occurred in the Punjab that proved significant for Black America: Mirza Ghulam Ahmed founded the religious movement that came to be known as Ahmadiyya. Like the U.S. group that was to be called the Nation of Islam, Ahmadiyya was regarded as heretical by many Muslims, because Ahmed called himself a prophet even though a basic precept of Islam was that Muhammad was the final prophet. Less than a century after Ahmadiyya's founding, a successor state to British India, Pakistan, made it a criminal offense for those of Ahmadiyya to call themselves Muslim or to use Muslim practices of worship to propagate their faith. As late as the fall of 2005, murderous attacks continued to be made against this minority, which had 10 million members globally.[33]

Like a number of foreign nations that historically have seen Black Americans as ripe for recruiting,[34] Ahmadiyya early on dispatched a mission to the United States that targeted them. This helped to forge a new racial emphasis, which led to a new vision of a global Pan-Islamic alliance in which Indian nationalism and Pan-Africanism were linked in potent multi-racial synthesis of anti-imperialist and anti–Christian religious and political ideas. Early on, according to Richard Turner, a direct relationship existed between Ahmadiyya and Marcus Garvey's UNIA, and Ahmadiyya had more than a cursory

Figure 2.1 As the boxer Muhammad Ali (top row, far left) looks on, Elijah Muhammad, leader of the Nation of Islam, addresses the assembled. Nation of Islam members were among many in Black America who were influenced by Islamic pilgrims from India. (New York World-Telegram, *Sun Newspaper Photograph Collection, Library of Congress.*)

influence on the nascent Nation of Islam. It was Ahmadiyya that published the first Muslim newspaper and the first Quran in English in America—and most of the Islamic literature that would be available to African American Muslims until the 1960s By 1940, Turner notes, "The Ahmadiyya movement had almost two million followers worldwide and somewhere between 5000 and 10,000 members in the United States," with "the majority of its American converts [being] black." This cohort included numerous jazz musicians, such as Ahmad Jamal, Yusef Lateef, Art Blakey, Dakota Staton, and Mc Coy Tyner, whose cultural capital and purchase adumbrated a further spread of Islam in Black America.[35]

To a degree, the migration of Ahmadiyya to Black America was a poisoned chalice in that the movement was perceived in South Asia as "the hand of Great Britain." This idea was given fodder when Ahmad "declared forbidden" the idea of warring against London, which in return "showered the choicest of favours" on his group. It became "a privileged, influential and prosperous community," and, according to Surendra Nath Kaushik, there was "some truth in the allegation that the British rulers had promoted the growth of the Ahmadiya [*sic*] sect among the Muslims."[36]

To be sure, Ahmadiyya was not the only religious influence emanating from South Asia. In the 1890s at the Parliament of Religion in Chicago, "Swami Vivekananda" was introduced to a large audience and "suddenly found himself famous," not least among African Americans. This "popular Hindu Monk," said one local journal, "looks so much like . . . Othello." But he was not treated like a celebrated and renowned person when he arrived in Baltimore. Instead, he was treated like any other person of color in that he was "refused admission to every first class hotel to which he applied but one." African Americans in Baltimore "seem to have regarded the Swami [as a fellow] 'cullud [colored] person . . . like themselves."[37]

Yet despite the swami's ministrations, Hinduism—the majority faith of British India—never seized the imagination of Black America as did Islam. (However, it remains true that when the talented and creative African American musician Alice Coltrane, widow of the similarly religious and famed saxophonist John Coltrane, opened a Vedantic meditation center in 1975, it was further testimony to the continuing magnetism of the swami's beliefs.[38] By the time of her death in 2006, she had established a forty-eight–acre ashram in Southern California where dozens of full-time residents pored over the Vedic scriptures of ancient India, along with Buddhist and Islamic texts.[39]) Negroes were a minority and about the same percentage of the population—12 percent—as Muslims in British India. Ahmadiyya, the leading edge of this wedge, foreshadowed a tack adopted quite profitably by the soon-to-emerge Nation of Islam by conducting some of the most sustained anti–Christian propaganda that had ever been witnessed in North America. This line of attack, questioning severely why African Americans should assume the faith of those who not only had enslaved them but had enslaved them in the name of this religion, was to become even more prevalent when more Black missionaries and conferees began flocking to South Asia beginning in the 1920s. The racism that was imputed to Christianity was contrasted sharply with its presumed absence in Islam.

Black Americans, no doubt, paid rapt attention when Ahmadiyya reported in 1921 that "our good Missionary has secured 10,000 more Muslims for the Ahmadia Order" in West Africa. They may have been similarly moved when Ahmadiyya clucked sympathetically about the "sad news we come across every now and then about the conflict between the Blacks and the Whites in this country. It is a pity [that] no preaching of equality or Christian

Charity has so far been able to do away with this evil." In contrast, "In the East we never hear of such things occurring between the peoples, [for] in Islam no Church has ever had seats reserved for anybody. . . . Islam is the only religion that has ever destroyed color and race prejudices."[40] The "true salvation of the American Negroes," said Ahmadiyya, was not Christianity. The "Christian Profiteers brought you out of your native lands to Africa and on Christianizing you forget the religion and language of your forefathers—which were Islamic and Arabic. You have experienced Christianity for so many years and it has proved to be no good. It is a failure." Was there an alternative? Yes, the *Moslem Sunrise* proclaimed: "Join Islam in the Ahmadia movement, founded by Ahmad of India, the Prophet of the day and be blessed." Readers were directed to the journal's headquarters in Chicago at 4448 Wabash Avenue.[41]

This anti–Christian message juxtaposed with the reputed contrast of egalitarian, antiracist Islam was Ahmadiyya's repetitive theme. It was tailored to appeal to a burgeoning African American population that had descended en masse on major Midwestern cities, where they faced a variety of the brutal white supremacy that had been their ignominious lot in the Deep South. In this context, Ahmadiyya was not only sailing against the prevailing winds of U.S. society; it was also projecting words that could only resonate in Black America. "Crescent or Cross?" asked Ahmadiyya rhetorically. "A Negro may aspire to any position under Islam without discrimination. Apart from a confederation of the African tribes or peoples of African origin, the possibility of which is an awful nightmare to the white man, he lives in fear and trembling that El Islam may become the religion of the Negro." The *Moslem Sunrise* claimed that "within recent years 53,000,000 natives have been converted to Mohammedanism in Africa," not least since—this theme again— "under Islam a Negro may aspire to and attain any position in mosque or state, and Islam knows nothing of segregation and discrimination." Making explicit what was surmised, the journal declared in 1923 that "the spreading of El Islam cannot help but benefit the [Marcus Garvey's] UNIA." For akin to Garvey, "Great Britain, France, Spain—in fact all the white powers—fear Mohammedanism. None of them can afford to offend El Islam. With millions of Moslems in India, China, Arabia, Persia, Afghanistan, Turkey, Negroes would find valuable allies who would bring pressure to bear upon the white world, convincing them that a peaceful solution to race question would be best to all concerned."[42]

Negroes were not ignoring this message. February 1921 found an "American gathering" in the Auto-Workers' Hall in Detroit to hear a Dr. Mufti Muhammad Sadiq lecture on Islam. The turbaned, bearded speaker, adorned in dark robes, spoke to an audience composed overwhelmingly of suited Negro men[43]—a group that was to form the backbone of the soon-to-become Nation of Islam that was also to emerge in the Motor City. Perhaps not coincidentally, by 1923 a number of South Asian students took advantage of a trade school opened at Detroit by the Ford Motor Company and had formed a not inconsiderable community there that was strategically sited to influence similarly dark-skinned African Americans.[44]

This gathering was not sui generis. "American Moslem ladies" seemed to be as taken with Islam as some African Americans. In a 1923 portrait published in the *Moslem Sunrise*, these women displayed the Islamic fashion of covering their heads with shawls or hats. Ahmadiyya also had garnered vigorous recruiters among Black Americans—for example, "William Patton of the Lamarsay Shop in St. Louis, M[issouri] . . . an energetic Moslem who is trying his best to bring others to the fold of Islam."[45] Soon an indigenous form of Islam was to arise in Black America that came to be called the Nation of Islam, though when it did, few recognized that its path had been lubricated by a force that hailed from the Punjab.

A. Philip Randolph's radical journal, *The Messenger* was keeping a close eye on Ahmadiyya. "Islam is bidding for converts among the Negroes of our large American cities," the paper reported in May 1927. "Mr. M. M. Sadiq of India came to America early in 1920 as a representative of the Ahmadiya Movement, an aggressive sect among the Moslems." While visiting the movement's mosque in Chicago, *The Messenger*'s correspondent observed that "attendance varies from 25 to 40," and "Mr. Kahn, the lecturer, is listened to with interest, [as] his severe criticisms of the West bring the largest response from his hearers." The prime culprit here was religion. "Christianity is held responsible for all the vice and crime of western civilization. Mohammed was greater than Jesus," as the journal reported, and the "idealism of Islam is contrasted with the baser elements of the West." *The Messenger* was not unmoved by this discourse, adding tellingly that Ahmadiyya "has possibilities of growth among the Negroes of our cities, two-thirds of whom are not being reached by the Church."[46] Soon thereafter, the paper felt compelled to run a series asking starkly, "Orthodox Christianity: does it handicap Negro Progress"?[47]

The severe interrogation of Christianity that Ahmadiyya foreshadowed was also reflected in the Black Nationalist and Pan-African movement led by Marcus Garvey, which attained stunning popularity in Black America during the World War I era. This interrogation took many forms—for example, in an editorial call for a "United Asiatic Christian Church" that added, "The native Christian churches in Africa will ultimately unite under their denominational unions."[48] Later and quite querulously, Garvey's *Negro World* said that "the Jews were taught to distrust the Greeks even when bearing gifts. Will the Africans and Asiatics be taught to distrust the White Christians when bearing the Bible in one hand and the Cross of Jesus in the other? The Africans and Asians are beginning to look at the question in that way."[49] This supposed perfidy of Christianity belted the planet, it was asserted. "The conditions of the natives under the administration of the Union of South Africa is bad enough in all conscience, but conditions in New Guinea are far worse." The "clear case against the government of Australia for conniving at the enslavement and torture of the native blacks" was further evidence of this religion's insidiousness: "Such things [should] be impossible anywhere in Christendom, but they are not. Some or all of them prevail, or have prevailed, whenever the whites have conquered and rule the blacks. We have had much of it in our Southern States; we have some of it now in our [Northern] States."[50]

With metronomic repetition, Garvey's *Negro World* asserted, "The African World has declared that the white man's religion has ceased to be good enough for the African, because it has been used to enslave and rob him."[51] The "Hindu," said the newspaper, also "rejects the white man's religion"—code for Christianity. "A young Indian took me to task recently for my interest in Christian missions," wrote a correspondent, "'Can't you see,' he said, 'that we've had enough of a 'white man's earth not to yearn for a 'white man's heaven'. The fact of the business is that we don't trust your [religion] any more than your political and economic pretensions.'" Well, this "Hindu" concluded triumphantly, "'You can't police our souls. And we can refuse to accept your religious exclusion laws.'"[52]

Such sniping at Christianity was accompanied by high praise of Islam in a manner that paved the way for the budding Nation of Islam. "A Negro may aspire to any position under Islam without discrimination," it was proclaimed. Meanwhile, "the majority of the converts to Christianity in India and Africa are of the lower caste. . . . [T]hey belong to that type which toadies to the white man." This "spreading of the El Islam cannot help but benefit the UNIA," the paper affirmed, since "with millions of Moslems in India, China, Arabia, Persia, Afghanistan, Turkey, [and so on], Negroes would find valuable allies who would bring pressure to bear upon the white world."[53] The "uproar" created by Islam "is alarming Europe," chortled *Negro World*. "Great Britain, France and Italy are watching the Moslem drama. It may have vital consequences to all of them and to every white power with a foothold in Africa or Asia."[54] There was a "battle royal on between France, Italy and Great Britain," the paper claimed, "to hold what they have and to extend their influence over the Islamic people. . . . [R]eaders of the *Negro World* are interested in this question of domination of the Islamic people because so many of the darker races belong to the Moslem religious order."[55]

India and Islam were being embraced, not least because both represented major centers of population and thus actual or potential force. *The Crusader*, which styled itself as being of the left, agreed with its nationalist cohort on this score. "We believe," said an August 1921 editorial, "that it is essential to the early success of our cause that the Negro seek cooperation with the Indian nationalists, the Turkish nationalists, the Persians, the Arabs and all other peoples participating in the common struggle for liberty and especially with those peoples whose struggle is against the great enslaver of the darker races—England." Indeed, the paper urged, "Since it is by the British Empire particularly that we are subjugated, we must seek the destruction of the British Empire. And since it is to best to fight with allies than without them, we must seek co-operation."[56] Shortly thereafter, in a reciprocal gesture, S. N. Ghose wrote "on behalf of the fighting forces of India" soliciting funds for the Indian Independence Fund.[57] That *The Crusader*, which was allied with nascent Communist Party members, was in sync with Garvey's Black Nationalism, which was thought to be an ideological foe of the left, suggested the growing influence of India and Islam.

The NAACP also took note of this development in *The Crisis*, noting the remarks of a prominent cleric that the "great question for the future is whether the dark continent [Africa] is to be Moslem or Christian." Perhaps, *The Crisis* added strikingly, "The psychos [sic] of the Negro responds to Islam better than to Christianity. One point in the former's favor is that it regards the Negro convert as equal to Berber or Arab, Turk or Persian. Islam does not draw the color line. The Prophet of Mecca was in one sense the supreme democrat." Citing the words of the historian Arnold Toynbee, the journal asked rhetorically: "Why can the Moslem beat the Christian missionary, when the Christian has beaten the Moslem soldier, merchant and administrator? Confessedly because the Moslem takes the colored convert to his bosom, while the Christian keeps him at arm's length and imparts his creed without opening the doors of his home."[58]

It might be overly simplistic to deposit this burgeoning Negro critique of Christianity—and simultaneous boosting of "El Islam"—at the doorstep of a movement that originated thousands of miles away in the Punjab. After all, the ancestors of some Africans in the Americas hailed from heavily Islamic regions of Africa, and the heavily Islamic Egypt long had been a resonant and crucial point of reference for a growing cohort in Black America.[59] But it would be even more of an error to assume that Ahmadiyya's message went unheeded in a Black America that was writhing in a parched desert of discrimination and longing for some answer—any answer—that could point toward a meaningful exit from its plight.

3

REVOLUTION?

A s South Asians began flooding into the United States in the second decade of the twentieth century, they were stunned by the virulent white supremacy they encountered. Of course, crass exploitation at the hands of those of "pure European descent" was not a new experience for many of these migrants, but in North America the phenomenon was magnified because they were now a minority in a strange and unusual land. Moreover, as bad as their treatment was, the more discerning among them recognized that there was a group that fell even beneath them on the social scale: African Americans. "When I came here for the first time," said Du Bois's comrade and friend, the Indian intellectual and writer L. L. Rai, "I was shocked by [the] treatment of the Negro."[1] This startling form of maltreatment combined with a lingering anti-London sentiment that helped to generate one of the most significant Indian independence movements before 1947: Ghadar (or Ghadr or Gadar), centered in California.[2] Ghadar members were overwhelmingly Sikhs, and the "centres of their activities were Sikh temples," though "most of the leaders were educated Hindus or Moslems."[3] Ghadar's rise in the United States also reflected how exile in North America eroded sectarian barriers among Sikhs, Muslims, and Hindus, who were hardly distinguished by the broad sweep of white supremacy. Ghadar was a powerful anticolonial symbol, but it was not the only such expression of Indian discontent found in North America at that time.[4]

As Ram Chandra, a leading member of Ghadar, put it, the journey of those who formed the revolutionary organization began with a voyage of

South Asians to British Columbia, where, despite their presumed relationship to the empire, their entry was barred. "We were left alone to brood over our dismay," said Chandra in 1916. But there was another element that was disconcerting, he said: "No, we were not alone. They had appointed a Negro over us, and he kept a close watch. My wife took it very badly. . . . [N]ext to our cabin was a Filipino. He had, of course, permission to go about as he pleased. My Negro guard mistook him in the dubious glow of the twilight for me. The victim protested . . . but my guard would not let go his hold on him. He was quite sure it was a ruse." What was the point of Chandra's recounting this anecdote to the broad audience of the *New York Times*? "The moral of the story is this," he announced. "All [are] welcome to Canada—Japanese, Chinese, Negro, Filipinos— . . . but not the people of India."[5]

Because South Asians were barred from Canada's western coast, Northern California quickly became the epicenter of their migration to the United States, and San Francisco, a fog-bound and gray cosmopolitan city redolent with modernity, just as rapidly became the headquarters for Ghadar. At the same time, being the United States, California was not exactly devoid of the cruder forms of white supremacy. "Hindus," San Francisco's *Literary Digest* announced in the early post–World War I era, were "too brunette to vote here. . . . [W]e have already in this country all the race problems we can handle. We want more and will not have them."[6] The writer Herman Scheffauer made explicit why so much animosity was being whipped up against the new arrivals. "The American," he had said a few years earlier, "far removed on the globe, finds it difficult to accept the Hindoo as a brother of the blood. Between him and this dark, mystic race lies a pit almost as profound as that which he has dug between himself and the Negro."[7]

The analogy being drawn between the Negro and the South Asian was not simply an articulated strategy of the enemies of both. Ram Chandra, editor of the *Hindustan Gadar*, pointed out in early 1918 that it was "Lincoln the sixteenth President who broke the shackles of the downtrodden race and set the Negro free." That, he suggested, was why Washington, DC, should be sympathetic to the downtrodden Indian. "Does color or mere geographical position act as a barrier to justice?" he asked. "Did the color of the black race congeal Lincoln's sympathy or stay his hand?" Even so, he said, foreshadowing a refrain that was to become more prominent in the 1920s, "[T]he Hindus belong to the Indo-Aryan Caucasian race."[8]

Chandra, a leader of the California-based Indian independence movement, was born in 1886 in India, knew Du Bois's comrade Rai, and, like Rai, had spent time in Lahore. Like other Indian revolutionaries, he decamped to Japan for a while—to Kyoto, in his case. "We had a good time in Japan," recalled his wife, Padmanati Chandra, years after his death. But Chandra's desire was to get to the United States, she said. "It was the land of the free. Abraham Lincoln, George Washington," and others who somehow came to be seen globally as avatars of freedom and liberty. Also like Rai, Chandra sought to knock down sectarian barriers: Ghadar, which he helped to found, included South Asians of various stripes including Nepalese and Bengalis. Chandra's ability to speak Punjabi and Urdu facilitated this process.[9]

Chandra was one of a number of like-minded South Asians who found themselves in Northern California, one of the more enlightened areas of the United States. Paradoxically, however, San Francisco also was part of a land that countenanced white supremacy and anti-London sentiment, even though the British Empire was a guarantor of the same idea of "racial" superiority. Such contradictory currents created a favorable climate for the rise of the kind of militancy that Ghadar came to symbolize. On or around 12 December 1913, Ghadar came to fruition in Berkeley, home of the flagship campus of the University of California. Ghadar was further marked by the prevailing atmosphere of the time, which was not unsympathetic to the anarcho-syndicalist and pro–Negro Industrial Workers of the World. Also involved in Ghadar's founding was Har Dayal, "the greatest intellectual exponent of the anarchist philosophy in San Francisco."[10] Certainly, Ghadar's voice was not the only one calling for independence, but it was generally "more militant than most of the nationalist element back in India at that time." Shedding light on why this was the case was the fact that "hostility towards the prejudice of North America whites was transferred into hostility against the British," as one analyst has put it.[11] Punjabis in the U.S. West were routinely insulted and despised; people who defined themselves as white often "refused to sit at a table" with Punjabis, just as happened with U.S. Negroes. The "consoling explanation," according to Randhir Singh, was that "Americans hate slavery—and [Punjabis] are slaves." Such outrages propelled resistance. In March 1913—months before Ghadar came into being—120 "Indians" formed the Hindi Association of North America.[12]

Some might argue—not without justification—that the "freer" atmosphere in the United States (compared with the colonial prison that was British India) drove many South Asians away from religious and ethnic sectarianism and toward unity and revolt. Actually, the opposite is just as likely: that the contrast between the white supremacy that actually existed in the United States and prevailing notions about the liberty that was supposed to be found in the Land of Lincoln was so great that South Asians resolved that the only way out was full-scale, non-sectarian, and united revolt. Har Dayal, writing on the "meaning of equality," argued that "race introduced the first inequalities in Hindu society. The distinction between the Aryans and the aborigines was the thin end of the wedge that finally destroyed the unity of Hindu society itself." This, he said, brought a "double evil" of caste superiority and bigotry that was comparable to the kind of white supremacy with which he had become all too familiar in California.[13]

Hence, Ghadar in San Francisco played an instrumental role in developing non-sectarian strategies drawing upon their U.S. experiences that were deployed to repulse British colonialism. When London claimed that colonialism was necessary because Indians were backward, superstitious, and so on, Ghadar pointed out that such rationalizations were similar to those used to justify oppressing Negroes in the United States. Ghadar further noted that such forms of exploitation were coming under increasing assault from enemies of U.S. imperialism who sought to repel the United States' heartfelt expressions of superiority.[14]

Ghadar was not merely a propagandist organization—or so alleged L. L. Rai, the consummate Indian intellectual activist. When he arrived in the United States about ninety years ago, he encountered a "large number" of Indians who were "being supplied with money by German government agents." They "were contemplating and planning an armed insurrection in India, so timed as to be useful to Germany in her European campaign."[15] In 1918, the U.S. Attorney in San Francisco spoke about the "Hindu plot" that led to a trial that "covered a period of some five months." There it was shown, he said, that the "Hindus of the Pacific coast were organized for the purpose of effecting a revolt in India. The Hindus were given German money and arms and ammunition which they endeavored to ship to India."[16] This occurred as anti–Berlin sentiment was reaching a fever pitch as a direct result of Germany's war with the United States. Berlin had long sought to take advantage of racism in the United States by appealing to its victims—notably, African Americans and Native Americans—and this alleged conspiracy with South Asians was seen as being of a piece with this strategy.[17] Such an approach—national chauvinism aside—roiled racial tempers in the United States. "John" of the "American Independence Union" informed the notorious Franz Bopp, Germany's U.S. Consul and presumed author of the conspiracy against British rule in India, of the "disgrace you brought on the German cause. . . . [T]he American people could easily have been brought to understand in the beginning of the European war, that Germany is making a white man's fight for commercial freedom"—but instead, "John" said, the devious Bopp had to foil this rationale and disrupt white unity.[18]

Men like "John" had a hard time understanding why Germany would seek to ally not only with dark-skinned South Asians but also with the despised U.S. Negroes. As the investigation of the so-called Ghadar Conspiracy deepened, Washington had reason to believe that U.S. Negroes were also part of the wide-ranging plot. That, at least, is what emerged from the government's interrogation of Franz Kasper Schnitzler, a German national who arrived in Manila in 1915. The investigators suspected that Schnitzler wanted to use that Southeast Asian capital—headquarters of U.S. colonialism in the region—as a base of intrigue against British and U.S. imperialism. "Who is the man, R. L. Clay?" he was asked. "He is an American Negro" was Schnitzler's terse response. When Clay was brought in for questioning, the U.S. authorities found that he had been born in Des Moines, Iowa, although he had been in Manila since 1907, when he arrived with the U.S. Army's 10th Cavalry. He was discharged in 1910, married an indigenous woman, and fathered two children before settling down to what appeared to be a life as an "ordinary engineer and machinist." Clay told the interrogators, "I have been knowing Mr. Schnitzler for a long time, and so I went to him last month and asked him if I could get work in his sawmill," but his interrogators were reluctant to accept his innocent responses since he had been found on a small sailboat that had entered Manila after it was reported that it had come from Peleleh in the Dutch Celebes.[19] The sailboat's crew, the investigators reported, included "Tulikowski, German, Senn an East Indian, Clay an American Negro and one Filipino sailor," along with "three . . . automatic revolvers with 134 rounds of ammunition and one (1) Winchester .351 automatic rifle with 35 founds of ammunition." A great deal of money was also found on board, which only heightened suspicions and frayed nerves further.[20]

When a crew member was asked, "Who was running the ship?" the response was blunt: "the Negro."[21] This episode was taken quite seriously in Washington. A representative of London had told U.S. Secretary of State Robert Lansing that a "party of German Americans and British Indians who had left the United States with the object [of] stirring up revolt in India" had arrived in the Philippines. The group had chartered a sloop called the *Henry S*, which was owned by a "local German American," and, the representative said a "hostile expedition was being planned and fitted out" when they were detected.[22]

Clay disagreed vigorously, portraying the events as innocence personified, although his explanations were not reassuring, not least since he "could understand" Tagalog and Japanese, which was viewed as suspect. "We met a ship," he said, "and we tied up alongside the ship and took some boxes from the ship . . . about between [*sic*] 100 and 120 boxes." Then, he continued, "we met another ship at night and we unloaded the boxes." But, he insisted, he was just a functionary following orders from a fellow crew member. "He told me to keep quiet about everything that happened on the trip," Clay said. "He instructed me in the hotel in Jolo not to tell the Customs authorities [any-thing]; . . . he also told me to tell them that he [had] brought two cans of gasoline from the Japanese cruiser." This raised the specter of collaboration

between Tokyo and Berlin in the midst of a world war that already had ensnared London on the opposite side of the barricades from Germany and was
about to drag in Washington.[23] Clay might have been well advised to keep his
counsel, for the more seemingly exculpatory statements he made, the more
he seemed to confirm suspicions about what appeared to be a far-ranging
conspiracy. "One officer advised me not to use the engine," Clay said. "That
same day a Japanese cruiser came, and stopped outside the three mile limit
[to confer with the crew]."[24] But Clay's attempt to minimize his own role was
being steadily undermined by his comrades. The engineer on the ill-fated
vessel, Isidro Avillado, blamed Clay for their detention: A mechanical problem apparently had led to the boat's detection, and this, Avillado insisted,
was Clay's fault. "There was nothing wrong with the engine," Avillado
charged, "but the nigger that had charge did not know how to run it and ru-
ined the engine."[25]

The wide-ranging investigation of Ghadar by the U.S. authorities reflected a deepening unease in Washington—and London—not only about a
German-orchestrated plot but more so about the specter of a coming
V-shaped formation with Japan at the point and Indians and African Americans at each shoulder. The U.S. Attorney in Northern California informed
his superior, the Attorney-General in Washington, D.C., that "most of these
Hindus [referring to those deemed to be part of the Ghadar Conspiracy
against British India] embarked from a port in Japan to this country and the
idea of [their] attorneys no doubt is to have them sent to Japan in case of deportation."[26] One of the "Indian revolutionaries" interrogated—"Verman"—
was "27 years of age and came to the United States in May 1913." Deemed
relevant was the fact Verman he had "remained two nights in a Japanese
Hotel . . . having purchased a ticket direct from Japan to San Francisco. He
had a passport from the American and the British Consuls in Kobe, Japan."[27]
Bhagwan Singh also was thought to have been tainted by Tokyo. He was
"about 30 years of age; heavy set and fleshy; smooth shaven, and has something of the appearance of Japanese. He probably passed for a Japanese or a
Persian."[28] Also uncovered in the U.S. investigation was a "most secret" dispatch from Berlin to Washington noting that "the Japanese Hideo Nakao is
traveling to America with important instructions from the Indian committee." That was not all. The dispatch also said, "I advise giving Nakao up to
fifty thousand dollars in all for the execution of his plans in America and . . .
Asia." Thus, in early 1917, as Washington marched inexorably toward joining
London in war against Germany, the U.S. authorities thought they had reason to believe that Germany, in response, was seeking to stir discontent
among Indian revolutionaries in North America in a manner that could ex-
plode in San Francisco.[29]

Most unsettling from Washington's point of view was the role of Japan, which already had begun to tug at the loose thread of the U.S. suit—African Americans—in a manner that could be terribly destabilizing. A U.S. official noted agonizingly about a Ghadar publication in San Francisco, that "there is not an issue . . . in which there are not virulent diatribes against the British government, both as a race of white men and as rulers of India." Evidently, Indian revolutionaries' exposure to the foul racial air of the United States had helped to convince them that not only colonialism but also white supremacy was at play in British India. This could only prove disquieting for a nation founded on this unsteady principle—and could only serve to be appealing to African Americans.[30] In that light, the San Francisco stockbroker John Hilliard found it worth noting, on 14 December 1917, that "Dr. A. Farid, an Egyptian, was arrested yesterday in connection with the Hindu plotters."[31]

Certainly, like Africans, African-Americans, Japanese, and others who were not of "pure European descent," Indians had reason to be concerned about the sour sweep of white supremacy. Their increasing presence in California was engendering a highly negative reaction. Thomas J. Vitaich, a thirty-one-year-old business agent for the San Joaquin County Central Labor Council and a resident of Stockton, California, for seven years, was enraged by the presence of Indians in his new hometown. "They are employed to quite an extent in the [potato and asparagus] fields" and have proved to be "very undesirable as residents," Vitaich said in sworn testimony. "They have no sense of morals," he said, claiming that he had "noticed them in an intoxicated condition, at which time they are very boisterous and noisy. . . . I have observed in theatres and street cars that the American people do not care to come within reaching distance of them. . . . The odor from their bodies is decidedly offensive." Vitaich was ardent in his conclusion: "We are emphatically opposed to a further influx of Hindus into this community."[32]

The prosecution of the Ghadar "conspirators" thus appears to have been driven not only by the opposition to colonialism and white supremacy expressed by these migrants (and what that entailed for African Americans) and by their ties to Berlin and Tokyo, but also by the impact South Asians generally were having in California north of the Tehachapi Mountains. Stockton's Chief of Police Fran B. Briare swore that the South Asians were "filthy in appearance" and "clannish," with "general immoral habits" and an "unsanitary way of living." they were "very undesirable resident[s] indeed," he concluded.[33] William Johnson, Sacramento's police chief, concurred, adding that the "Hindu is unruly, boisterous and quarrelsome when intoxicated" and sodden with "filthiness."

These descriptions were remarkably similar to how African Americans were routinely described. Johnson also charged that, like their fellow "colored" people, the South Asians seemed to have a penchant for consorting with Euro-American women. "They have at different times hired white girls ostensibly for housekeepers," he said, "but we have found it necessary to remove the girls for other reasons."[34] An immigration official from Bellingham, Washington, was similarly outraged when "some members of the Hindu colony . . . made insulting advances to some women." Bellingham had "too many Hindus," he said, and thus "they should be asked to move on." Many South Asians did move farther south, but apparently not rapidly enough, since, the official reported, "the Hindus asked permission to spend the night in the city jail fearing violence, [then were] escorted to the city limits where they were requested to move on." And as was said of Negroes, South Asians' supposed similar appearance made punishing them problematic: "A number of [petty theft] cases would have been prosecuted but for the fact that the similarity of dress and complexion among the Hindus made it difficult to identify a certain one among a number."[35]

George E. Gee, secretary of the Yuba County Trades Council in Northern California, also described Indians in terms reminiscent of African Americans. They have "no more sense of morals than an animal," Gee said. The "white race does not care to assimilate" with them because the migrants are "regarded by the common laborer and average citizen in general simply as vermin." Of course, he noted, it would not be easy to rid the land of them because they were employed principally by the region's powerful sugar-beet growers and were doing labor that was scorned by others.[36] This constituted no bar to M. C. Polk, a city surveyor in Butte County, California, who claimed that "five ordinary white laborers could have done the work [of] fifteen or twenty Hindus in probably half the time." Moreover, said Polk, the "Hindus" are "generally obnoxious," and "white people in general are annoyed by their actions."[37]

Similarly objectionable, according to Amy Dudley, was the allegation that "the common people of India" were "ignorant of English and therefore know nothing of Kipling. The educated classes, however, dislike Kipling intensely," while "Kipling detests Hindoo intellectuals."[38]

Given the fetid atmosphere of bigotry, the toxic fumes of war, frightening allegations of Japanese and German subversion of the United States, and justifiable trepidations about the fate of white supremacy and the like, the South Asian defendants faced an uphill climb. Gopal Singh arrived in San Francisco on 2 February 1917 and was indicted on 17 April, then convicted of violating the neutrality laws. He was sentenced to a term of a year and a day, then deported on the day of his release.[39] Compared with Ram Chandra—whom many viewed as the mastermind of Ghadar—Singh escaped unscathed. At the conclusion of his well-publicized five-month trial, which did a great deal to catapult Indian independence to the forefront of consciousness in the United States, Chandra was "assassinated by another Indian defendant who was immediately shot and killed by a U.S. marshal."[40]

The NAACP's publication *The Crisis* was not pleased with the disposition of this case. As one writer reported in late 1919, "Within the past three weeks more Hindus have been arrested for deportation to India. The men are D. K. Sarkar, in New York, and Bhagwan and Santokh Singh of Seattle. These, with Gopal Singh, arrested for transportation some months ago, Taraknath Das, now in Leavenworth Prison, and some others, if sent back home, will be in effect condemned to death. For that has been the fate of their fellows in agitation at the hands of the British government." This was terribly unjust, the writer said, because "they have been struggling to free their country from the rule of the stranger."[41]

The Messenger, the journal produced by A. Philip Randolph, who became a staid labor leader but began as a militant socialist, was irate. These "helpless Hindus sought nothing but justice in American courts," it said, yet "after the trial by a prejudicial judge and jury was over, they found themselves within the prison walls." Moreover, "The British government spent over $2,500,000 to convict the Hindus. . . . [I]n fact, almost all the witnesses to testify against the Hindus were British subjects brought from British territories." *The Messenger* was furious about the subsequent "deportation of Hindu political refugees," who were dispatched to an uncertain fate. "The Hindu politicals came to this country to enlighten and educate the public mind of this land about the intolerable miseries and sufferings, oppression and outrages, persecution and prosecution that are being perpetrated upon the people of India by a government which has more than once threatened the very existence of this great republic." The crass exploitation of South Asia was reminiscent of the worst days in Black America. "While the people cry for food, the English government exports wheat and rice to England for the maintenance of the English army and the manufacture of liquor to keep Europe intoxicated," claimed *The Messenger*. Then, "when last April the unarmed people rose in 'bloodless' revolt, innocent men, women and children were bombed from aeroplanes, mowed down by machine guns, annihilated by armored cars, bayonets and bullets."[42] Where was the justice?

The Messenger was published in New York City, which, with its influx of "West Indian" migrants, was becoming something of an outpost of the British Empire. It was thus hard to ignore the journal's report in 1922 that "the military authorities of the British government [had] ordered the West Indian regiment, stationed on the island of Jamaica, to board ship for service in India," but the regiment, "composed entirely of Negroes, refused to the last man to take up arms against the Hindu people in their struggle for freedom."

The Messenger deemed the soldiers' actions as even more appropriate since "the subjugation of the Hindus is carried on by British imperialism with 'we must come to the aid of the backward races' as its motto—the same excuse as that used here to justify exploitation of the colored man."[43] This was not the only concordance to which *The Messenger* called its readers' attention: Haiti, then under brutal occupation by the United States, was "America's India," the journal opined, but, not coincidentally, "like India, Haiti is revolting."[44]

Unfortunately for London, a "New Negro" seemed to be developing in Black America in the World War I era. This phenomenon was propelled in no small part by West Indians who recently had migrated to Harlem. This "New Negro" was more assertive and militant than her older predecessor, and—as the travails of the West Indian regiment suggested—this could have real meaning for the empire and its crown jewel in South Asia.

The complementary nature of the struggles in Asia and Black America was revealed repeatedly in the first decades of the twentieth century. This complementarity was generated in no small part by the increased presence of South Asian migrants in the United States and the stirring example provided by Ghadar. There were other aspects also. When the African American heavyweight champion Jack Johnson began pulverizing opponents of "pure European descent," for example, the "cry 'don't show the fight pictures' [extended] as far as India." And when London "heard that similar enthusiasm [for Johnson] had been shown by Indians and Ceylonese" it worriedly "consulted an authority on Anglo-Indian affairs" for advice. As a result, footage of Johnson's fights was barred from being shown in "large parts of the Empire, this time including India and Ceylon."[45] Thus, influence did not travel solely in one direction; nor was it exclusively physical. As a student in prewar Europe, for instance, the African American intellectual Alain Locke was influenced by "Indian . . . revolutionaries and socialists conversant in Marxist doctrine,"[46] which helped to catapult him into the front ranks of opinion molders in Black America.

Just as Tokyo was a beacon that tended to bring South Asians and African Americans together in common opposition to white supremacy, the emergence of the Soviet Union and the socialist ideal after World War I brought these two blocs together in common opposition to imperialism. The mainstream Black writer Ira Reid credited Socialist and Communist Party writers in various journals with having "promoted interest in the problems of Negro peoples throughout the world"—including South Asia. When the Moscow-oriented left organized the global "International Congress against Colonial Oppression and Imperialism" in Brussels in 1927, one of the people present was Nehru.[47] He may have had the opportunity to bump into William Pickens of the NAACP, who also was present.[48] It is known that Nehru encountered both black and white Americans at the congress, which was part of the main benefit derived from his 10 exhausting days in Brussels.[49]

In 1929, the NAACP gushed, "To this great future movement of the majority of mankind, there approach two allies: Russia, with its attempt to organize a government for the benefit of the workers, rather than for the benefit of the present owners of capital; and on the other hand, India, with its movement toward political autonomy." Just as some saw a link between India and Japan, the NAACP saw a link between India and the Soviet Union. "If white Europe insists on seeking to curb Russia [and] to keep India as a field for exploitation and in political swaddling clothes," *The Crisis* said, "the spirit of economic revolution among all the peoples of Asia is going to be tremendously increased."[50]

Still, despite the NAACP's—and the left's—yeoman efforts, it was probably the Jamaican Marcus Garvey and his Universal Negro Improvement Association (UNIA) that strove most strenuously to link the cause of Indian and Negro freedom. With UNIA chapters ranging from Harlem to the dankest precincts of the former slave South and from the Caribbean to Africa, Garvey represented a major headache for the British Empire. Like Ghadar, the UNIA saw itself as a vanguard nationalist force. Also like Ghadar, the UNIA—which, after all, was born in a real sense inside the empire—held London to be its major antagonist.

In the spring of 1927, Dr. B. V. Ghayanaa of the Hindustan Ghadar Party was invited to speak at a mass meeting at the new "Colored Elks' home" in Oakland, California. People "from every district in Oakland and suburban vicinities were attracted to [the] hall," said the *Negro World* newspaper, as "passenger machines of every description surrounded the block facing the meeting place. They came on foot, street cars and otherwise." Ghayanaa held the large, interracial audience "spellbound," the paper reported.[51] In fact, such gatherings of the Negro faithful listening enthralled to Indian orators was not unique. The "Indian philosopher" Imayat Khan, for example, had appeared at a Manhattan hotel in late 1925 "garbed in a flowing black robe, caught at the middle with a single loop or button," as Garvey described him. "Hailed by his friends as a mystic and seer of the first order," Khan "talked with a quiet earnestness which was irreconcilable to any suspicion of insincerity or fraud. He is forty three years old and the graying fringes of his coal black hair and beard lent him something of the look of a patriarch saint," he exulted" as Khan mesmerized those who had assembled to hear him.[52]

Garvey himself continually linked the two causes, asserting at one point, "If it is possible for Hindus and Mohammedans to come together in India, it is possible for Negroes to come together everywhere."[53] In sum, the example of Ghadar—which, after all, arose in California within sight of Garvey—was serving as an example for his own Pan-Africanism. "As Provisional President of Africa," he announced audaciously in early 1922 to a New York audience that applauded him vigorously, "I pledge the support of all the Negroes of the world who support the principles of this organization to the cause of India's freedom."[54]

Being a product of the British Empire, Garvey (and his followers) realized that London's power ultimately rested on the shoulders of India. Thus, the *Negro World* kept close tabs on South Asia, not least since it was thought that incidents there often foretold developments in the Caribbean and, by extension, Black America. Thus, in early 1924 the paper announced portentously:

> There is so much discontent with civil and economic conditions of the British colonies, in the West Indies, in Africa, in Asia, among the natives as to lead to the conclusion that, as far as the natives are concerned, British rule has reached [the] parting of the ways. . . . In East India the civil and economic distress of the people is so great that the atmosphere is surcharged with economic possibilities. . . . [D]iscontent among British colonials is co-extensive with the British commonwealth of nations, and is based on the same grievances, making a common cause for all those concerned and a concert of action that would affect in one way and another a very large part of the peoples of the globe. . . . [A]n international convention of these disaffected British colonials is something that may be expected in the future. It is needed.[55]

Yes, the paper said in a later issue, "Readers of the *Negro World* [are] vitally concerned in everything that relates to Great Britain"—and, by implication, its foundation, India—"because there are so many Negroes under its flag in the West Indies and in Africa."[56] In fact, "Any betterment of their condition which the Indians may be able to get out of the London Conference should ultimately redound to the benefit of the Negro subjects of the Empire in the West Indies and Africa, as their grievances are much the same."[57] "Indians and Africans have [the] same fight," said the *Negro World*, "and so long as the white races insist upon this racial supremacy and will sacrifice every other interest to it, there will be no peace in the British Empire."[58]

Because it was transnational, the UNIA played a leading role in easing the tensions that often emerged between Indians and Africans as a result of complicated interactions in East Africa, Trinidad and Tobago, British Guiana, and elsewhere. Thus, in early 1926, the *Negro World* described how "Indians protest[ed] persecutions in Africa. A deputation from South African Indians . . . arrived in Bombay [and announced they had] come to seek the intervention of the Government of India and the Indian nation for the unjust and cruel persecution to which Indians are subjected in South Africa."[59]

Mohandas K. Gandhi had earned his political spurs in South Africa. Perhaps as a result of his fearless crusade there, he was treated heroically by the UNIA to the point that his being compared to Garvey—by Garveyites—reached the level of triteness.[60] The two were called "the world's greatest humanitarians of the colored races."[61] They were portrayed as the twin bedevilment of the empire, whose "disintegration" was "becoming more pronounced." The "people of India deserve the sympathy of well-thinking people everywhere," the *Negro World* editorialized. Gandhi's "work and that of Marcus Garvey in arousing the Negroes of the world to their social, civil and economic values and to more self-determination in ordering these, is very much alike and just as necessary."[62]

As suggested, the plight of the Caribbean and British India were seen as similar. Side-by-side editorials in 1926 proclaimed, "Britain refuses protection to its Negro subjects" and "British bleed India white. [A]s in India, so it is in the West Indies and British Africa—the natives are driven to hard tasks at starvation wages and are taxed the limit they can be made to pay, while the British ruling class receive the highest salaries possible and have their expenses, for the most part, paid by taxing the native."[63]

Embroidering on this parallel between the Caribbean and India, another commentator referred to the "big four of the human race," in which Garvey and Gandhi were grouped with "Lenine [*sic*] and Wilson."[64] In 1923, they were grouped with Eamon de Valera of Ireland "as martyrs in jail for ideas"[65]— and, coincidentally, the staunchest of opponents of the British Empire. On another occasion, Gandhi was praised as "India's 'new Tolstoy.' "[66]

"How much longer will England keep its foot upon the neck of India?" asked one *Negro World* commentator. Tellingly, as other Negroes had, this commentator suggested that the exploitation of India was the most dire on the planet, exceeding even what had befallen Africa:

> England's despoilment of India constitutes the supreme crime of all ages. It is the acme of infamy. The oppression of the children of Israel by the Egyptian Pharaohs, the Babylonian King and Roman Emperor fade into insignificance when compared with what the people of India have suffered at the hands of John Bull . . . . Europe never dreaded Alaric the Visigoth, nor hated Attila, as India dreads and detests John Bull, "The White Beast from over the Black Water."[67]

India, by the way, was posited by the same commentator as being part of the "Black World."

The United States, then straining to surpass the United Kingdom as the reigning power, could smirk and smile at these double-barreled assaults on the British Empire but could hardly be comforted by the similarly potent attacks on Washington. "America has no civilization," said the "wealthy Indian" Byram Chiceje, a Parsee and Bombay merchant, during a visit across the Atlantic in 1925.[68] The *Negro World* was upset with the "expulsion of the Indian patriot," Shapurji Saklatvala, a "Parsee" and "Communist member" of the Parliament.[69] He "declared that he hated the Union Jack" and "was out for revolution," but close readers of the newspaper could easily conclude that his opprobrium was not limited to London.[70]

Worse than that, Washington could hardly be comforted by the Garveyites' prediction of the V-shaped formation of "non-Europeans" led by Japan and bolstered by India and—behind the gates—African Americans turning violently on the United States itself. In early 1924, one analyst predicted that a "vast colonial uprising against the 'white yoke' extending from Morocco to China is looming up on the horizon of history. . . . [T]he struggle will be long and one of the bloodiest in history," with its "center" in India. "Connected closely with the worldwide colonial uprising," the commentator concluded, "will come a war between Japan and the United States."[71] The "events in China, Morocco and India," said a *Negro World* writer the following year, "are apparently the preliminary stages of the unparalleled war to the death between the white and colored races with the Pacific as the central background."[72] Of course, it was thought, Indians and African Americans would not be found fighting alongside London—or Washington.

The NAACP, which otherwise was confronting the UNIA at the point of a dagger, reflected this striking interest in Nippon. "Japan has no notion of sitting quiet under American racial distinction," *The Crisis* reported in late 1920. It raised concern about "American anti-Japanese legislation" and the "question of racial equality in the League of Nations," which Tokyo was pursuing avidly on its own behalf but which had obvious implications for African Americans—and India.[73] *The Crusader* was decidedly to the left of the NAACP, but it, too, crowed that "Japan seems likely to be added with Africa, to the Mohammedan world. This possibility is not a pleasant one for the white Christian robber nation." As others had done, *The Crusader* warned that "Mohammedanism is fast driving Christianity out of Africa by reason of the latter's failure to live up to the ideal of the Fatherhood of God and the Brotherhood of Man."[74] And *The Messenger* acknowledged that, because of the "Japanese problem," "western and southern politicians" in the United States would seek to unite on the basis of white supremacy and, respectively, anti–Negro and anti–Asian bias: "We may look for Hiram Johnson and Phelan of California to join hands with Tom Watson and Hoke Smith of Georgia."[75]

Such developments had not escaped the attention of the U.S. authorities. In late 1921, the U.S. Office of Naval Intelligence (ONI) in San Francisco—Ghadar's headquarters—was informed that the

> racial hatred of the black race against the white race is rather universal even though it does get very little chance to express itself; and probably the depression strengthens in a way the tension and scope of the hatred, although presumably under cover. Furthermore, it communicates with "colored races" other than the black. The Japanese agents are playing an important part of the role, and evidently there are Hindus who are busily engaged in aiding the novel and disastrous propaganda. And, too, the ultra-socialistic doctrine enters into the actual work of the propaganda. The informant met a certain Mr. Farr in a lunch place run by a Korean in San Francisco on Pacific Street near Kearney [Street]. This Farr person was evidently a rather well-educated Negro; he wore a yellow flannel shirt, which seems to suggest that he was in the U.S. Army (many of them now wearing them by mere habit). Though he claimed to be a negro, his manner of talk which had a little accent—not the Southern accent that is common to all Negroes, but the accent similar to that of an American-educated Hindu. He is rather small but stout. His facial color and the shape and structure of the face is also more like a Hindu than an American negro.

This "Hindu"—or was he an "American Negro"?—was also wearing the "red, black and green" of Garvey's UNIA,[76] redolent of the congruence that was growing between militant India and militant Black America.

If the naval intelligence is to be believed, San Francisco was becoming the locus of an emerging alliance between Black America, India, and Japan. And if this is accurate, it may very well reflect the atmosphere that gave rise to Ghadar and simultaneously reflects the pervasive influence of these South Asian revolutionaries. In 1922, the ONI concluded that the UNIA leader George Farr was being "financed by local Japanese interests." During a visit to the Emmanuel Gospel Mission, an ONI agent found that "the music, dancing, [and] the crowd were all frivolous. The congregation was composed largely of the mixed foreign population, Mexicans, Hindus, etc., and a number of Negroes." The multiracial assemblage was bent on "anti-Caucasian agitation," as protests abounded, the agent reported—notably, from "Hendric, a Hindu" and the "Negroes." He wrote: "Both the Hindu and the Negro preach among the Negroes, Hawaiians, Mexicans and Hindus, the doctrine of the supposed necessity of the union of all colored races against the whites. And they also preach: '[A]ssert yourself, fellow brothers; hit the white man twice if he hits you.'" The agent called the Emmanuel Gospel Mission "really one of the worst things that was ever born in the name of Christ's religion." Its "Hindu" leader, ironically, was "very strong against Christianity" and alleged that the "whites and the Christians are hardly human but . . . devils." He also spoke French, the agent reported, and knew "a number of Japanese."[77] Apparently, the church was evolving in a manner that was hardly embraced by those of the Christian faith who ruled in Washington and on Wall Street.

The point here is that Black America and India—both writhing in externally imposed wretchedness—were coming to view each other as comrades in arms with much in common and more to gain by a deeper alliance. This could not be comforting to London—or to Washington.

4

NOT QUITE "WHITE"

Bhagat Singh Thind immigrated to the United States in 1913 from the Punjab, in northwestern India. He served in the U.S. Army during World War I and was discharged with the rank of sergeant. He was active in Indian groups in the United States that backed independence for his homeland. Thind then applied for citizenship in Federal District Court in Oregon and, in a well-reasoned statement accompanying his petition, he explained that he was "white" within the meaning of the naturalization statute. After all, he argued, "white" could not refer to skin color, because many dark-skinned Europeans had been ruled eligible for naturalization and because inhabitants of India who, like Thind, came from the northwest were regarded as "Aryan" or "Caucasian." He concluded triumphantly, "I am, therefore, a pure Aryan."

The court was convinced by his words and, over the opposition of the naturalization examiner, granted him a certificate of naturalization. Undeterred, the U.S. Attorney filed a motion demanding that the court cancel the certificate, but the motion was denied. The government appealed, and ultimately the case reached the U.S. Supreme Court. Thind implied that he belonged to the Kshatriya caste, part of the Hindu elite, although he was a Sikh and thus outside the caste system, which—in an elongated sense—placed him well within the long-standing African American trend of "passing."[1]

Justice George Sutherland of the U.S. Supreme Court—who happened to have been born in Buckinghamshire, England—was not persuaded by Thind's argument. In a way almost designed to validate the idea of a commonality between those not of "pure European descent," he relied heavily on a case involving a man of Japanese origin. Takao Ozawa was born in Japan but moved to the United States as a young man in 1894 and grew up in California. He attended high school in Berkeley, then attended the local University of California campus. He sought naturalization while residing in Hawaii in 1914, but the district attorney for the district of Hawaii opposed his petition. He pursued his cause for eight years before reaching the U.S. Supreme Court, where he boasted about speaking English at home and living continuously in the United States for twenty-eight years. He openly rejected his Japanese ancestry and embraced his "American" identity with enthusiasm as he, too, sought to paint himself as "white"—again, compared with those of Mediterranean Europe. The high court acknowledged that Ozawa "was well qualified by character and education for citizenship"—then rejected his claim.[2]

Thind's fate was sealed. Sutherland was not moved by his military service or by other qualities that it was felt would bring him citizenship. "It may be true," sniffed Justice Sutherland, "that the blond Scandinavian and the brown Hindu have a common ancestor in the dim reaches of antiquity, but the average man knows perfectly well that there are unmistakable and profound differences between them today." Sutherland sought to undermine the very notion of "Aryan" and dismissed the "ill-chosen name of Caucasian." Also dismissed was the idea that "the high-class Hindu regards the aboriginal Indian Mongoloid in the same manner as the American [*sic*] regards the negro, speaking from a matrimonial standpoint." Like Ozawa's, Thind's claim was dismissed.[3]

Thind's claim was untimely in that it arose as the terrorist Ku Klux Klan (KKK) was surging, buoyed by a raging fear among many Euro-Americans that the postwar climate was all too favorable for African Americans, given the Negro's staunch military service. It was in a sense understandable that South Asian immigrants would seek to cloak themselves in the protective fabric of "Aryan-ness," because this seemed to be the surest path to naturalization, and the alternative was allying with the melanin rich, who were despised. Besides, at this precise moment nativist passions were rising, as reflected in the rush to impose restrictions on immigration and circumscribe the specter of miscegenation.

Predictably, Thind's defeat led to a campaign to denaturalize Indian Americans. Another outgrowth of this process was its effect on U.S. women who had married Indian men. As Ozawa's defeat was propelling that of Thind, Congress passed a law that deprived women of their U.S. nationality if they were married to aliens who were ineligible for citizenship.[4] There were dissenters. Senator Royal Copeland, speaking in 1927 at the Mecca Temple in Manhattan, stated boldly that "Hindus are white." In remarks reprinted by the India Freedom Foundation, he declared with some exasperation, "Every school child is taught that five races or peoples exist. They are the Caucasian, the Mongolian, the Malay, the Ethiopian and the American." The United States was moving to assimilate those who were Jewish, so why not Indians? Copeland endorsed Senate Bill 4505m which proclaimed, "A person shall be deemed to be a white person . . . if such a person [is] Hindu, Gypsy, Arabian, Hebrew, Syrian."[5]

The problem with this discourse for South Asian migrants was that the effort to establish them as some version of "white" compromised their ability to connect with their natural allies—African Americans—in the hope that avoiding the alliance would win friends among Euro-Americans. But how could this approach work when the United States that Euro-Americans administered was moving to the right?

Moreover, the specter of African American men ravaging Euro-American women influenced the passage of the Mann Act, which objectively criminalized miscegenation, and South Asian men were viewed similarly. A notorious case arose concerning Dinshuh P. Ghadiali, a "Parsee healer" who was convicted under the Mann Act for the "transportation of Miss Geraldine McCann, then 18 years of age, from Portland [Oregon] to Malaga, [New Jersey, and] back." Ghadiali was sentenced to five years in prison. Combining stereotypes, prosecutors argued that the "defendant exercised over the girl an influence which, in effect, if not in fact, amounted to mesmeric control." Henry Ford's wildly bigoted *Dearborn Independent* "bitterly attacked" Ghadiali, and his trial was deemed sufficiently important for the British Embassy to monitor it.[6]

As Ghadar surged in strength, and as a major threat to British rule in India seemed to be based in the United States, London had to pay more attention—which brought its attention to a lecturer named Bhagat Singh Thind. Apparently, the former U.S. military man was not pleased with his rejection by the forces of white supremacy. According to the British Embassy, one of Thind's most common declarations while lecturing in St. Louis was that "Japan became civilized overnight after the war against Russia and . . . the same will occur in the case of India as soon as the British yoke has been thrown off."[7] In the ultimate put down, Thind compared British rule in India to Belgian rule in the Congo. Indians were "subjected to [the] same treatment as slaves," said Thind, who was identified as part of Ghadar.[8]

With his long beard and turban, Thind certainly did not resemble the typical veteran of the U.S. military. His modus operandi for his lectures was to combine a caustic anti-British philippic with gauzy words about psychology and spiritualism. One of his topics, according to the British Embassy, was "jazz mania. Its cause and cure and the psychology of relaxation."[9] In a "confidential" missive, the British Consulate in Detroit, a city that also was a hotbed of Muslim and Negro militancy, noted that Thind had remarked that "an Indian is a Caucasian" yet was not "allowed to go to Canada, to Australia, to New Zealand."[10]

Thind's misfortune became a cause célèbre for Indian intellectuals in the United States, chief among them Subhindra Bose, who taught at Iowa State University. The "Supreme Court of the United States . . . has at one stroke branded the whole people of India with the mark of racial inferiority," Bose fumed. "The New World is to be apparently a 'white' world." As he saw it, "racial discrimination has become an obsession with the authorities and almost every important Asian question in America is to be settled not on merits but by color tests." Reaching a fever pitch of indignation, Bose exclaimed, "While the Indians are deprived of American citizenship, the right of owning land or even leasing it for a single year, the Viceroy's government is busily engaging in granting to Americans in Hindustan every sort of economic rights and privileges" (though, he admitted, these measures would have to go a long way to erode "imperial preference"). But that was not Bose's issue. He suspected that an important reason behind the opposition to the Hindus in America was religion. But even there he saw rank hypocrisy, since, he declared, "the inward religion of the Hindus is not and never has been a proselytizing religion, [while] Americans have been sending shiploads of missionaries to India to force their religion down our throats."[11] Among those missionaries were a large number of African Americans, he could have added, just as he could have noted that it would be difficult for South Asian migrants to receive justice in the United States at a time when the KKK was holding sway.

Bose was born of Hindu parents in Calcutta in 1883. Although he went to sea and arrived "penniless" in the United States, his "father was a high official of an Indian prince." Bose lived for a while in Philadelphia before arriving at the University of Illinois, where he received his doctorate. He was well versed in the discourse on the "rising tide of color" and appeared in one of his most prominent photographs with a Japanese woman.[12] He was irate about how Thind's case reflected the onslaught of white supremacy. "What does the court mean by the phrases 'European parentage' and 'European origin'?" he asked. "Was the greatest French romantic novelist Alexander Dumas, the grandson of a black negress [of] European parentage? . . . Thackeray was born in Calcutta and Mr. Rudyard Kipling in Bombay. Are they in the opinion of the Supreme Court of European birth and origin?" Incensed, he wrote, "Almost every line of the decision breathes of narrow race prejudice." Furthermore, "[t]he ruling of the Supreme Court is retroactive. All Indians who have been previously admitted to the rights of citizenship will be denaturalized," which, he said, would have "humiliating implications." There were "about 2000 Indians—chiefly Sikhs—residing in California," yet "Californians" had "worked themselves into hysterics "about an alleged " 'Hindu invasion' or a 'menacing spread of Hindus' in America." This nonsense was proliferating while there could not be "more than 3000 Indians all told" in the United States and although "Indian immigration to the United States [was] comparatively of recent date." The first Indian immigrants "came to America in 1899," he asserted, and "they numbered only fifteen."[13]

Bose's outrage was justifiable. Less so was the rebuke of him by J. T. Sunderland, a leading opponent of British colonialism in India. "I confess it with shame," Sunderland said, "that in some respects the United States government has not treated India well, [but] is that helped by gathering together a list of our worst sins and crimes and evils and sending the same to the Indian people?" One was less likely to witness such vacillation among African American activists, which served to underscore their value overall.[14] Sunderland, in contrast, sought to make amends, however, by asserting that "an injustice to an even greater number of Hindus has been done by the decision rendered . . . by one of the [decisions] of the United States Supreme Court, that high-caste Hindus do not belong to the white race."[15]

Such a state of affairs, in any case, was at once radicalizing South Asians' hostility to the empire and heightening their antipathy toward white supremacy, which tended to bring them closer to African Americans and their concerns. This was notably true of one of the greatest sons India has produced to date: Du Bois's close comrade L. L. Rai.

"My grandfather was a shopkeeper," Rai said in his memoir, originally penned in Urdu, while "my father was born in 1845 on the day when the British defeated the Sikhs in the battle of Mudki." Rai's father was also a Muslim who "then became a believer in the Vedanta," which predisposed his son to be a bridge between the two largest faiths of his homeland. (His mother, Rai said, was "an orthodox Pauranic Hindu.") Rai's father also taught him Arabic and a "good deal of Persian," although, he acknowledged later, "When I came to Lahore, Islam lost its charm," and he "became attached to Hinduism and Hindus"—an attachment that he called "nationalistic." Rai also recalled that he was married in 1877, at twelve and a half, a development that may have opened his eyes further to the need for change in traditional cultural practices.[16] He became sympathetic to socialism and later was elected president of the "first All India Trade Union Congress in which he declared: 'militarism and imperialism are the twin children of capitalism.' "[17]

But before that momentous occasion, Rai spent a considerable period of time in the United States. For three and a half year, he lived in the same room with N. S. Hardikar, a fellow South Asian, who later recalled that Rai "was like my parent, treating me like his son" and that he acted as a "task master. He could not tolerate laziness." The two men "together cooked, swept, cleaned vessels, washed clothes and did other household work ourselves." Rai was "meticulous at matters of home science," according to Hardikar, and "no room in the house was allowed to have the smallest dirt and, everything—books, letters, clothes, cooking vessels, etc.—were to be perfectly clean and each was to be kept in its proper place. He would lose temper whenever he found anything out of place. He would shout 'get out you fool.' " Because Rai was twenty-five years older, Hardikar often felt compelled to comply.

Hardikar hailed from Hubli in South Asia and had attended medical college in Calcutta from 1909 to 1913. Rai, he recalled, "used to say that men, particularly those in foreign countries, should know arts like singing and playing musical instruments during after-work leisure hours," which suggests that he also knew how to enjoy himself. Rai lived in the United States from December 1914 to December 1919, and "during these five years he also made a short visit to Japan."

Besides traveling and singing, Rai "carefully went through all the Hindi, Urdu and English papers regularly." He was "an extraordinary reader," Hardikar recalled, and "he felt the need to keep in close contact with events in America" and therefore "read local magazines with keen interest. . . . [Y]ou could always find books in his hand to read or writing materials. . . . [H]e would go to bed past midnight and again wake up at night and read books." He was a "victim to insomnia and so he could not sleep," Hardikar noted, perhaps because he was overly stimulated by his simultaneous exile and presence in a land where he was a virtual outcast. "At times he would tell me, 'I am restless. I cannot sleep. What shall I do?' " Hardikar recounted. "I used to wake up and massage his limbs and try to induce him to sleep." A relentless student, Rai was a "regular visitor to the Columbia University Library and New York Public Library."[18]

Hirsute, dark-skinned, and, at times—especially early in life—sporting a turban, Rai was a distinct presence in New York City. He was "slight in stature but extremely dignified," said the Irishman N. F. Dryhurst, who translated Kropotkin in his spare time. Rai, who was routinely referred to as "the most dangerous man in India," spoke "clear and beautiful English," which certainly eased his path in North America. "He lived extremely simply and dressed no less simply," said the writer Francis Hackett. Adorned in a "light homespun coat which became like a badge of his unpretentious character"—a character marked by his ability "to laugh"—Rai was "subtle and sensitive" and sufficiently alert to his culture that "he could not or would not eat beef."[19] A fellow exile from the Punjab, S. Nihal Singh, who resided in Chicago, noted that "America had a pronounced effect upon Lalaji. He had acquired the Yankee twang. He delighted in employing slang." It was "[not] that he was no longer a good Hindu," Singh said, but "he certainly was not the religionist he had been"—reflective, perhaps, of how the U.S. experience leveled sectarian differences among South Asians, a leveling that may have been induced in part by the fact that, irrespective of their status at home, they were treated as shabbily in the United States as Negroes. "More than once," said Singh "Lalaji and I discussed the advantage of abolishing all religion from India."

Rai's countryman Dr. N. R. Dharmavir expressed the consensus when he described Rai as "serious . . . not exactly jolly" but "full of innocent wit and humour." Further, according to Dharmavir, Rai "spent lavishly in helping Indian refugees and students in foreign countries," as he "cared little for money" for his own needs, a trait exemplified by his "ill-fitting suits." Rai "earned plenty of money and gave it away" and was a perpetual worker, often from "2 or 3 A.M. until mid-day."

Rai also liked to discuss politics and literature. "The Irish, you know, are even worse than the English to us in India," he said. Not that he was particularly accepting of the excesses of the Irish. "He told us," said Francis Hackett, "how he had settled down to read [Kipling's *Kim*] in a railway carriage and how after the first forty or fifty pages he was so disgusted he threw it out the window. 'And the worst of it was,' Rai said laughing, 'it was a borrowed book.'"

Rai expressed subversive ideas in the fourteen books he wrote, a diversion of sorts from his role as a brilliant lawyer who had been President of the Bar Association of India. Befitting a man of action, said Professor Diwan Chand Sharma, Rai was "greater as a speaker than as a writer. His speeches cast a spell over the audience." He spoke in a "deep ringing voice," with "effective diction." Combined with his "impressive personality [and] his knowledge of history," this versatile student of "Mazzini and Garibaldi," this "Sun Yat-Sen of India," this "lion of the Punjab" was also "one of the founders of the Punjab National Bank of Lahore."

Rai fought with Nehru occasionally, but generally he was viewed as a sweet and even-tempered man. His smooth disposition and intellectual candlepower did not prevent him from being persecuted by London. He was twice imprisoned, first in 1907 and again in 1921, after returning from the United States. He was "arrested without a warrant," recalled J. T. Sunderland. "He was refused a trial or any defense, he was not even permitted to know the charge preferred against him and under those conditions he was hurried away secretly to a prison in Burma." This occurred both times. When S. Nihal Singh visited Rai the second time he was jailed, he found the cell to be "small, bare and uncomfortable. It was quite clean, however, and rather well lit. There were some books," one of the few amenities, since the food was "coarse and poor." Singh's wife "wept when she saw the kind of food that our friend was compelled to eat." Later, Singh visited the cell of S. E. Stokes, a former missionary from the United States who had joined the movement. Consistent with the diktat of white supremacy, said Singh, Stokes "was treated much better than Lalaji. His cell was larger and more airy. His food was of superior quality." And remarkably for the times, "He actually complained to me of this differentiation."

Such maltreatment led to Rai's premature death in 1929. Yet during his lifetime, as one Lahore journal put it, "No other man in modern India had so much to do with so many departments of human activity for such a long period of time." Rai "was not in fact one man," the journal asserted expansively, "but half-a-dozen rolled into one. His death has created not one gap but a dozen or more."[20]

African Americans then reeling under serial pogroms and repetitive lynchings and desperately in need of allies could hardly disagree. For it was the at times turbaned, often mustachioed, and always brown-skinned Rai who wrote a book on the United States that focused incisively on their distressed plight. He had "first become aware" of the depressed plight of African Americans during his 1905 journey to the United States. He felt that their situation was "comparable in some respects to those of the depressed classes or untouchables in India." So inspired, he spoke with the eminent scientist, George Washington Carver, and in Atlanta visited the intellectual beacon that was Morehouse College.[21]

"Materially helped with letters of introduction [from Du Bois]," Rai wrote, "President [John] Hope of Morehouse College and his wife showed [me] great courtesy and kindness," as did "Mr. and Mrs. Booker T. Washington." As it turned out, Rai was one of the last foreign leaders to speak with the Wizard of Tuskegee. "One of the things that prompted me to pay a second visit to the United States of America," he announced, "was my desire to study the Negro problem on the spot." The "Negro is the PARIAH of America," he added, and being that India was not bereft of outcasts, he, like Martin Luther King Jr. generations later, thought that studying the predicament of another nation would provide insight to his own. "There is some analogy between the Negro problem in the United States of America and the problem of the depressed classes in India," Rai said, calling it "remarkable" that the "original Sanskrit term denoting caste should be an equivalent of the English word 'color,'" and that the "caste system in India owed its origin to probably the same considerations and causes as are to be found at the bottom of the caste feeling in the United States." The situation in the United States was so dire that even the "gifted Negro writer, Dr. Du Bois . . . (although fair in color) would not be admitted into any restaurant, hotel or theater, in the capital of the Union Government."

He also found it remarkable that in India and in the United States, the discrimination against people of different color (between the Varnas of the Hindus) should be manifested in almost identical ways—that is, that over and above political distinctions, color should be a bar to "inter-dining and inter-marriage." Another congruity he found was that "the worst features of the code of Manu find their parallel in American life," though Rai concluded sadly, "To me it seems that the Hindu Aryans of India never applied the color bar so rigidly as the Christian whites of the United States of America." More astonishing, he thought, was that "Christian writers who dare not raise their voice against the color line in the U.S.A., have no hesitation in sitting in judgment on Hindus." He held up the wildly popular film, *The Birth of a Nation*—a film that he denounced unequivocally because of its racist portrayals—as a case in point: "To me, this is a better and surer index of Christian feeling in this country than any number of books written by Christian missionaries."

Finally, Rai said that he could not understand why otherwise "charming hostesses" who were "very kind to me, personally expressing a great admirations for Hindus and Hinduism, flew into a sort of temper at my even remotely suggesting that the Negro was not having a square deal in this country." Thus, he concluded sadly, "the prospect of the disappearance of caste feeling in America, in the near future at least seems . . . very meager. . . . [The] so-called labor unions are nothing more than closed castes based on contract and mutual understanding but not on birth." The United States was "doubly caste-ridden," he thought. Although the Hindu was "also Caucasian by race," he mused, his "colors and habits and manners [are] so different than [those of] the Europeans," even Jewish Americans were "not prepared to acknowledge that his racial origin is the same as theirs." The Japanese had to be tolerated, however, because they were citizens of a country that had "recently whipped one of the great powers," an abject lesson for India. As for China, it was not more than "America's protégé" and thus in a different category from India and Japan.

Above all, a central point of Rai's book—and a major rhetorical device used by South Asians before 1947—was to rebut negative assessments of India that were deployed to undermine its case for independence by pointing to glaring flaws in the budding superpower that was the United States—notably, its treatment of African Americans—then argue that if the United States could be independent despite its obvious shortcomings, then India could also.[22] This contrasts sharply with the approach taken in Thind's case, where there was an attempt to embrace "whiteness" and, by implication, turn a frosty shoulder to African Americans.

A few years before his untimely death in 1929, Rai wrote, "One would have thought that the Americans would be the last people to declare Hindus to be unfit for *Swaraj* [self-rule] and democracy because of the existence of a class of untouchables among them. Americans never abdicated their right of self-government or allowed other people to question it, in spite of the existence among them of a larger proportion of 'untouchables' and a severer form of untouchability than that in India." When rebellious colonists wrote their "famous Declaration of Independence," he added sardonically, "slavery was an established institution in their country. It is less than seventy years ago that the American Civil War, costing hundreds and thousands of lives and millions of dollars, was fought because of this institution. Even today," he added strikingly, "the untouchables in India are neither lynched nor treated so brutally as the Negroes in the United States are." He filled page after page with a searing indictment of the United States, describing a nasty brew of lynching, disfranchisement, and outright meanness. "In reality the Klan is not merely a lynching secret society," he said with an acuity that has escaped many in this terrorist group's homeland. "It is the embodiment of the exclusive spirit in America. It is America's Protestant Nationalism of a very aggressive type." For Washington (and London) to "sit in judgment on us in the matter of the treatment of the 'depressed classes'"—or, worse, to deprive India of self-determination on that basis—"is like the pot calling the kettle black. Yet the United States of America is considered to be the freest country in the world. Free indeed! Even the lynching of the Negroes goes on accompanied by unmentionable cruelties and barbarities worthy of the modern 'civilization.'" And let us not begin to discuss the Congo, he added.[23]

The invocation of the plight of the U.S. Negro to cast severe doubt on the "civilization" that was said to be embodied at its highest level in the United States was a device used frequently and not by Rai alone. In August 1917, an "Asiatic Gentleman" told *The Crisis* how "deeply affected" he was by its accounts of racist riots in the Midwest. "During my visit to this country within the last three years," he said, "I have seen many evidences of blind race and color prejudice of the worst possible kind, but the present has exceeded all precedents. To think of women and girls maltreating, beating with shoes, dragging and otherwise belaboring their sisters of the colored community, simply because of their color, is something for which even I was not prepared." Although he had "never had much faith in the veneer of civilization and universal brotherhood and love for democracy, which the people of European descent put on," the writer said, these pogroms exceeded his already low standard of what he expected from that group. He found it similarly outrageous that "the Press has taken no editorial notice of the outrage."[24]

The NAACP was quick to capitalize on such sentiments, frequently sharing information abroad condemning depredations committed against African Americans, then publishing the results of its handiwork. "America's lynching fame spreads over the world," *The Crisis* reported in 1923. "We find in a Hindu newspaper, the *Swarajya* published in Madras, an account of the riot in Rosewood [Florida] and the following comment." *Swarajya* excoriated the United States, avowing that such practices expose a "great blot on American civilization." Notwithstanding its "vaunted advance in culture and civilization," the paper said, the United States was plainly deficient. "The whites cannot bring themselves to treat them [U.S. Negroes] as equals."[25]

Such critical commentary on the maltreatment of African Americans was becoming an irritant in relations between London and Washington.

Although Rai was not alone in holding such opinions, he may have been the most articulate and determined critic. It was he who, in late 1927, asked Du Bois for "any recent literature which you can send me about the treatment of Negroes in the United States and about the activities of the Ku Klux Klan. . . . [S]end me some telling pictures of the cruelties inflicted on your people by the whites of America."[26]

Rai, in sum, was a prolific writer and publisher on behalf of Indian independence, and it remains striking how often he referred to pressing racial matters in the United States to advance the cause for India. In the process, he was contributing mightily to the erosion of oppression of African Americans, a development that—perhaps not coincidentally—helped to push forward an ally of India on the anticolonial front. Even when London was invoked, the United States somehow managed to wend itself into the discourse. Thus, Rai said in 1920, Britain claims that "she is ruling the people of India for their benefit, [but] in the days of American slavery the slaveholders of the South made exactly the same claim regarding the Negroes."[27]

Such ideas were characteristic of many independence fighters who had spent time in the United States, for many South Asians had found it hard to ignore the cruel dilemma confronted daily by African Americans, not least since their skin color often meant they were treated as heinously as Negroes. The *Independent Hindustan*, published in San Francisco, for instance, was in the thick of attacking Lothrop Stoddard's *Rising Tide of Color*, an exemplar of the kind of racial hysteria that was emerging from the more febrile corners of white supremacy in the United States. Stoddard, it said, was "obsessed with the idea that Asians, being imbued with cosmopolitan spirit, may take the black man in their sides. There is no racial or cultural affinity between the black and the brown, yet they may form an alliance." In any case, the paper said, the "white man" or the "white race" was a "myth, for the tinge of white color can be found in almost every part of the world."[28]

Here as elsewhere, Rai seemed be leading the way, for it was he who set the pace in assailing Stoddard, characterizing his viewpoint as "white race über alles" and adding tellingly, "Of the different non-white races of the world he is fairest toward the yellow and the brown and the most unfair toward the black."[29] Stoddard, Rai argued, exuded "confused thinking" laced with "utter nonsense. . . . [T]he fact that all civilization originated in Asia [is] nowhere mentioned [in his book]." With rising fury, he declared, "These race arrogant European writers forget that the present would have been impossible without the past; and that white civilization is built upon or founded on brown or yellow and red cultures, maybe on black civilization also." If one "were to count the periods of political hegemony in history," he wrote, "it would be found that the yellow races, the Mongolians, the Tartars, and Turks, the Huns and the Scythians have been much longer in political power than the so-called Nordic races. Europe has been longer under Asiatic rule than vice versa." He concluded, "The coloured world is becoming conscious of the great wrong which is being done to it by the white races and they are very unhappy at the thought. It may be that they are biding their time."[30]

Rai had the advantage of operating in a context of ongoing affinity between Black America and India. As Earl Robert Schmidt put it, the "American Negro and his status were known to a few South Asians previous to the American Civil War through the contacts between South Asian intellectuals and missionaries. *Uncle Tom's Cabin*, Lincoln's Emancipation Proclamation and the Negro in American cotton production were the facets that aroused more South Asian interest in this problem." An American company "known as the Ethiopian Serenaders toured India in the 1870s. Outside of this group and possibly several Negro evangelists and entertainers, American Negroes seldom came to South Asia until World War I, when many came with the units of the United States Army which was stationed in India and Ceylon." However, Schmidt notes, "Some colored Spanish-American war veterans settled down in South Asia on [U.S.] pensions." This increased contact promoted a mutual concern about each other's problems, as between Black America and India. And Indians' interest in African Americans was intensified when Indians themselves "were taken for Negroes," as Rai at times was. "Stories about these affairs were drummed into the South Asian public's minds by these Indian students in America who acted as reporters for the various news sheets of South Asia in America," Schmidt says. Riots in Atlanta around the turn of the century sparked their concern, and the rising role of the "Negro in American sports quickened South Asian interest." Such developments caused Indians to compare the "Negro advance with general South

Asian uplift," although, "it was only in the 1920s that the progress of the American Negro was used as a measuring stick to compare with the progress of India's untouchables."[31]

Exemplifying his pioneering role, Rai was using such a "measuring stick" even before the Roaring '20s erupted. And it was Rai who, in his newspaper *The People* (Lahore), continued to apprise his audience of all manner of flaws in the U.S. racial fabric. "Modern America seems to have gone almost mad in its advocacy of the cult of the Nordic Race," said one writer in *The People* in mid-1925. The "Negro Race especially is made fun of on every possible occasion. Either the Negro is servile in his attachment to the white man, or else he [is] treacherous and cunning and wicked." Then, typically, the writer connected this defamation to British India: "The extraordinary thing is this, that the very people in Europe who have built up so meticulously this new caste system, are themselves the loudest in proclaiming the inhumanity of the caste system in India. Yet I seriously doubt whether India, even in her darkest moods of internal depression and decay, ever built up such fanciful barriers as these modern Europeans are doing in the hey-day of their success."[32]

The United States was repeatedly flayed because of its racism in order to discredit Britain. Another writer in Rai's journal apprised readers of his trip to the heart of darkness that was the U.S. South. "When one gets a few hours' train journey below Washington," he said, "one is shocked to find that there are separate coaches on the trains, separate sections on the trams, separate waiting rooms and booking offices, etc. for Negroes." Even in the presumably more enlightened North, he reported, "there seems to be an unwritten law that the Negro must not have well-paid jobs." Shockingly, "Property owners are in terror lest the introduction of Negroes should send down the value of their property." The writer also portrayed Negroes as noble in the face of such repression, perhaps providing a lesson to those chafing under London's rule: They have a "reputation in most places for honesty and good humour," he wrote, although "it cannot be expected that [Negroes] will tolerate indefinitely the existing bar to social advancement," not least since "little fights are taking place all over the country with the object of securing for the Negro the right to enter this or that institution or profession." An article adjacent to this one linked the fate of South Asians and Black America by describing the racist problems encountered by "Indians in South Africa."[33] Yet another writer noted that that, if Indians gained rights in South Africa, "the Negroes who are the original inhabitants of the country can claim them also," conjoining the fates of the African and Asian once more.[34]

Reviewing a book on Black America by the U.S. intellectual Scott Nearing, A. C. N. Nambiar wailed that African Americans were "treated as outcasts. The colour line is even more rigid in the United States than the caste line in India." Black women were routinely "outraged," even right after their weddings. Nambiar's long and detailed look at the brutal quandary facing African Americans was more pointed and detailed than those found in most U.S. publications—meaning, in this case, left-wing and African American publications—since the mainstream press rarely ventured into this thicket. "This is civilized America," wrote another *People* commentator with more than a whit of sarcasm, "that is today lecturing on Oriental savagery and Bolshevik atrocities."[35] The United States was a nation where the "cult of the superiority of the White Race seems to have revolutionized all branches of thought as much as did the Darwinian theory. The race doctrine now governs American immigration policies and deeply affects here foreign relations." The odious though influential KKK was mentioned as evidence of this disturbing trend.[36]

"It is a terrible and unequal fight in which the coloured people of the United States are engaged," lamented Rai. "Their enemies are more numerous, immensely more powerful, wealthy and resourceful, yet the American Negro never despairs." More than this, African Americans were "fighting the battles of all coloured peoples on earth"—a category that pointedly included India—"and [are] sure of victory." U.S. Negroes had allies in India, however, for it was while he was in Bombay in 1926 that Rai bumped into his friend, N. M. Joshi, general-secretary of the All-India Trade Union Congress, who handed him the "latest issue of *The Crisis.*" The magazine, Rai pointed out, was edited by another friend, W. E. B. Du Bois. "[I am] a coloured man myself," Rai pointed out, and, like Du Bois, "a member of a disinherited and dispossessed race, we had something in common that made us feel attracted toward each other." Hammering home a repetitive theme, Rai not only denounced U.S.-style racism, but he ascribed it in part to the majority religion of that land—a direct slap at those who criticized caste and Hinduism. He remarked, for example, that "the U.S.A. is a land of Christians who subscribe millions, perhaps billions, of rupees for the conversion of the heathens to the faith of Christ: but how far it is from Christ may be imagined from the awe-inspiring, blood curdling details of Negro lynchings which take place in that land of liberty and freedom every year. Humanity revels in hypocrisy all the world over. . . . [I]t is the same in India, and in the U.S.A. and Great Britain.[37] Such anti–Christian sentiments coming from such close allies served to predispose African Americans to lend a willing ear to Ahmadiyya missionaries and the nascent Nation of Islam.

Yet despite it all, the African Americans persevered. "The immensely rapid progress of the Negro race" was astounding, Indian readers were told. "No other people in the world have achieved such an advance in so short a time during the last century."[38] Europeans had "carried them in thousands from Africa to till the Virginia fields and incidentally to sow the seed of a great colour problem for himself in modern America," according to Rai, with the kind of "arrogance" that equally characterized the Europeans' arrival in South Asia. These invaders "proceeded upon the assumption that the white man was born to possess the earth and that the coloured man was born to be his hewer of wood and drawer of water, used if he needed him and thrown aside if he did not need him." But things were changing, said Rai with assurance, as "we talk less unctuously about the 'white man's burden' and are concerned much more about the white man's fear," a fear that skyrocketed after Japan defeated Russia in 1905.[39]

Perhaps because his voice was so strong and penetratingly transnational, Rai was treated harshly when imprisoned by the colonial occupier, which led to his premature death in 1929. He went down fighting as he "headed a march of several thousand prisoners" in British India "carrying placards and black flags toward the railway station," where he was "struck twice on the chest" and died.[40] His comrade Du Bois was inconsolable. "When a man of this sort can be called a Revolutionist and beaten to death by a great civilized government," he said, "then indeed revolution becomes a duty of all right-thinking men. As a matter of fact, the people of India, like the American Negroes, are demanding today things not in the least revolutionary but things which every civilized white man has so long taken for granted that he wishes to refuse to believe that there are people who are denied these rights. I hope that the memory of [Rai]," he concluded with a tinge of sadness, "will be kept green in India." In her eulogy, Du Bois's fellow NAACP pioneer Mary White Ovington returned to a defining theme of Rai's all too brief life: his solidarity with African Americans. "My interest in the welfare of the coloured races," he had said, "particularly the coloured peoples of the United States has never slackened." But, he had added conspicuously, "I am sorry that the prospects for a colour clash in the near or remote future are in no way slackening. . . . [T]he only silver lining to these clouds are the efforts which you so ably represent in the United States."[41]

There may have been something to this. The unrelenting sledgehammer blows against white supremacy wielded by the NAACP and its allies—particularly its South Asian allies—were not without effect. After the U.S. courts concluded that Thind was not quite white, Senator Copeland sought legislation to provide Indians with the right to be U.S. citizens and, as Rai put it, "Declare[d] that Hindus are whites. . . . Geographical boundaries do not coincide with racial distinctions. . . . [T]he Hindu has the skull, the features, the hands, the figure, and above all else, the intelligence of what we call the American. He is as truly 'Nordic' in the final analysis as the blond citizens of Norway and Sweden.'"[42] Writing from exile in New York, Sailendra Nath

Ghose endorsed Copeland's initiative in the name of the anticolonial struggle because it would strengthen the position of Indians in the United States.[43]

There may have been something to this, too. U.S. elites could hardly be indifferent as African Americans, then South Asians, began to flock to the banner of Tokyo, perhaps seeking to lessen the harsh white supremacy they endured in the United States. When in 1927 S. G. Pandit won his naturalization suit in Los Angeles as a "free 'white person,'" it may have convinced those who were wavering that the United States, despite its reputation, was not the heavyweight champion of white supremacy after all.[44]

However, it was difficult—ultimately—to reconcile the contrasting approaches of Thind and Rai—that is, aspiring to be taken as Aryan by the former and savaging white supremacy by the latter. Yet this may have been in effect a "good cop–bad cop" routine that ultimately proved useful in compelling at least a tactical retreat by the avatars of racial bias. The fact remains, however, that even today, Thind's descendants in North America would be deemed "not quite 'white'"—with all the penalties that entails—which suggests that Rai ultimately proved to be a more resolute ally of African Americans laboring in the antiracist trenches.

5

BLACK AMERICA AND INDIA

I t was his "favorite book," said the prolific Du Bois, referring to his riveting novel *Dark Princess*.[1] The book was a fictionalized version of the
V-shaped formation attacking white supremacy, with Japan at the point
and India and Black America on each side. A Japanese figure apprises the
African American protagonist, Matthew Towns, of the "Great Council . . . of
the Darker Peoples" that was to "meet in London three months hence. We
have given the American Negro full representation." The other leading figure
is an Indian woman, who says of her Nipponese comrade, "He is our leader,
Matthew, the guide and counselor, the great Prime Minister of the Darker
World." Apparently, the prime minister agreed with her brutal assessment
that the "strongest group among us believes only in Force. Nothing but
bloody defeat in a world-wide war against whites will, in their opinion, ever
beat sense and decency into Europe and America and Australia. They have
no faith in mere reason, in alliance with oppressed labor, white and colored;
in liberal thought, religion, nothing! Pound their arrogance into submission,
they cry; kill them; conquer them; humiliate them."[2]

This bracing vision of bloodlust was a keen reflection of the brutalities
visited on Indians at Amritsar and on African Americans at Tulsa and elsewhere. Du Bois envisioned the key victim of colonialism coming together
with the most victimized of capitalism—India and Black America, in other
words. Reading a draft of this novel and offering a critical response to it was
one of Rai's last acts before he died after being beaten by British police during
a labor demonstration,[3] thereby providing added poignancy to Du Bois's

angrily violent perspective. "I remember you with great pleasure," Du Bois told Rai, adding about his manuscript, "I shall be glad to have your criticism."[4]

Du Bois, however, was not constructing this viewpoint wholly from his vibrant imagination. He was also reflecting an extant viewpoint that was gaining currency in Black America as African Americans' predicament became ever more desperate. In one of the novels by his friend Jesse Fauset, the protagonist "passes" as white and bears no special love for blackness. Yet when she goes to hear a speaker, she is filled with pride when she notes his South Asian ethnic heritage. It seems that his color serves as a bridge to her ultimate reconciliation with blackness.[5]

But beyond the pages of fiction, actual events were driving Du Bois's taut narrative. Both Du Bois and Ghadar had close ties to Berlin, which features in *Dark Princess*. Du Bois was educated there, and the revolutionary organization received support there. The novel speaks of uniting Pan-Africa with Pan-Asia, which was of no minor concern to Du Bois's friend L. L. Rai. When the leading protagonists of *Dark Princess*—a Black American man and an Indian woman—marry and have a child, this symbolizes this hoped for unity of Africa and Asia against their common foe. The male protagonist toils as a train-car servant and subway digger, which evokes the important role of the All-India Railway Federation in the political economy of India.[6]

With perfect pitch, Du Bois neatly summarizes a fraught historical moment composed of the movement toward Indian independence and its intimate tie to Black radicalism in the United States and the connection of both with global trends emerging in Tokyo, Berlin, and Moscow. At this time, the Communist International was grappling with an approach to these incendiary issues, and Du Bois, a keen observer, sought the tool of fiction to excavate the meaning of these matters. *Dark Princess* reflects how the sweep of events was impelling a "race man" like Du Bois on an even more radical road.[7]

Du Bois was in an advantageous position to ascertain what was occurring. After returning in 1919 from a Pan-African conclave he had organized abroad, he spoke to a large audience in Harlem, where he was flooded with questions. Evidently, among his interlocutors were radical Marxists. Asked if he was in favor of the Egyptian and Indian rebellions against alien rule, Du Bois answered that "he was not in favor of anything foolish; that there were over 350,000,000 people in India and if they wanted self-government they could easily take it." This response was insufficient, *The Crusader* reported, since "he forgot to say what they should do in the event of the British opposing their taking over the government of India."[8] *Dark Princess*, with its envisioned pivotal role for Tokyo, provided a critical clue to his answer to this inquiry, although Du Bois was not unique in looking longingly across the

Pacific. A. Philip Randolph's *The Messenger*, which otherwise was not friendly to Japan, was "glad" that that nation "exposed [the] hypocrisy of America" by raising the question of "race" at Versailles.[9] But even while *The Messenger* criticized Japan for being a "hypocrite on the Korea Question," the thrust of its assault was directed at "Great Britain–Perfidious Albion." It called Britain the "hypocrite par excellence, on the Irish and Indian Questions," ably assisted by its transatlantic former colony, where "the Hindoos do not even find asylum as political refugees, because Britain follows them, maintains an espionage system over them, and dominates the American government's policy over respecting these persecuted and abused people. India should be free."[10]

Like the rabbit at a dog race, *The Crusader*—which was led for a good deal of its lifespan by West Indians such as Cyril Briggs, who were all too familiar with the depredations of the British Empire—set the rhetorical pace on India that was then followed by the UNIA, the NAACP, and others. Briggs and a number of his comrades were tied to the African Blood Brotherhood, which served as a bridge for some of them to enter the Communist Party, thereby signaling their ideological predilections. It was in the pages of *The Crusader* that the core idea of *Dark Princess*, an "Afro-Asiatic League" formed for the key purpose of "simultaneity [of] revolutionary activity," was touted. Why was such a group needed? *The Crusader* provided an answer: "The white tyrants are able to beat down the Egyptians and Hindus and others when these strike separately and at different times. But with coordination and simultaneity of revolution from the Straits Settlement to Agadir, not all the might of Europe or the League of Damnations will be able to stop the onslaught for Freedom."[11]

The linking of Africans with Asians was an important priority for these radicals. "Believing that any action of the Asiatics in 'booting' the European thieves will be reflected by similar action in Africa and other parts of the world," *The Crusader* said, "we have tried to keep our readers well informed on the Asiatic situation as much as on matters pertaining directly to Africa."[12] More specifically, it advocated a "'Pan-Colored' alliance against white domination" and the "elimination of white political control from Anatolia to the Philippines." London, understandably, was a primary target. "The British Empire was never in such peril of destruction," *The Crusader* proclaimed in July 1920, "since England embarked on her career of imperialism and world conquest three hundred years ago. And what is much more important, THE WHITE RACE ITSELF WAS NEVER IN SUCH PERIL OF SUBJUGATION BY THE CONQUERING MASSES OF ASIA AND AFRICA."[13]

Repeatedly, *The Crusader* urged Black America to adopt a more militant response to colonialism, asking exasperatedly at one point, "How long will we Negroes of America remain indifferent to the sufferings of our kindred under 'British' rule and blind to the vast power of the economic boycott to chastise our enemy and effect reprisals for the wrongs and insults heaped upon us by the supercilious Anglo-Saxons. A Negro boycott of British goods loyally carried out, would at any time be effective. But at this time, more than ever, since it would have the cooperation of the Irish whose boycott the British are already beginning to feel. And why not now? Should not two groups fighting the same enemy act in unison and move in co-operation"? Why not "hit them where it will hurt most—in their pocketbooks!"[14] India was seen as worthy of emulation, since it was there that "Soviets are now in formation in widely separated districts, and already the 'British' authorities are having their hands full in dealing with them. In the rioting in the Lucknow region, the police are reported to have been powerless and troops had to be summoned."[15]

Another son of the radical Caribbean, Hubert Harrison of the Virgin Islands, then Harlem, also was part of this ideological coterie. India, he said in 1920, was a "sort of seething, raging but suppressed volcano with a cover on which the Englishman sits, believing that if he but sits there the fires will no longer burn. But the Hindus believe that some day the wooden cover will [burn] through and something will get scorched."[16] There were parallels between Black America and the colonized world, he said, since "Jim Crow cars exist in Nigeria, India and Egypt"—not to mention the United States—and sharing solidarity and strategies thus made eminent good sense.[17]

The U.S. authorities were not indifferent to the thunderbolts hurled by *The Crusader* and its ally, the semi-secret African Blood Brotherhood. In early 1922, a Justice Department functionary attended a meeting at the Stuyvesant Casino, on Manhattan's Second Avenue between 8th and 9th streets, where it was reported that "about 200 persons were present. During the course of the meeting pictures were shown of the cities and buildings of India and there was dancing and singing. . . . [T]he meeting was attended by members of the African Blood Brotherhood, and . . . they were encouraged to attend same by Claude Mc Kay."[18] Before that, a military intelligence official, who had "been one of our agents for a long time," confided that "working, of course, on the Negro end [] in connection with this work, [he had] discovered some Hindu matters in New York."[19]

As Harrison saw it, India and Japan were driving global events, so for Black America to ignore Asia was worse than folly—irrespective of the surveillance and nay-saying of the U.S. authorities. "In America," he said in late 1921, "our white political experts have managed to dodge the real inner reason for England's Asiatic alliance with Japan. The reason is—India, which is the keystone of the British imperial system. The mere existence of a colored great power in Asia is a tremendous stimulant to Asiatic self-assertion." India itself could spark trouble, he noted, "if it should, in a spirit of unfriendliness assume the role of liberator or leader."[20]

Hence, although *Dark Princess* was the embodiment of the idea of an alliance between Black America and India, Du Bois was far from the only advocate of the notion. After reading one of Du Bois's perorations on this matter, A. K. Das wrote to him from London, asking plaintively, "Why could there not be an unity among what is called the colored races[?] I believe here is a big field which is yet undiscovered and there is work here for thousands."[21] Indians recognized that African Americans were sited strategically within the belly of a budding superpower and thus could be a potentially powerful ally. Perhaps that is why in 1927, A. R. Malik, writing from the Punjab, told Du Bois, "I have been trying to get as much information about you and your work as possible." Malik saw Du Bois's "sacred work of liberating the Negroes from the bondage of aristocrats and capitalists" as analogous to his own struggle in South Asia. "We ourselves suffer from the oppression of alien rulers," he declared, and "naturally view the struggle of Negroes with great sympathy."[22]

Thus, despite the heroic efforts of Hubert Harrison, A. Philip Randolph, Cyril Briggs, Marcus Garvey, and others, it was Du Bois and his NAACP who were at the center of the campaign to forge solidarity between Black America and India. "It was in 1914 that I had the privilege of personally meeting you in New York," K. D. Shastri of the India Home Rule League of America, a self-proclaimed "personal friend" of Rai's, wrote to Du Bois. "I want to avail myself of your company and consequently renew our friendship."[23] "I should be very glad to see you at any time," Du Bois replied promptly, suggesting where India stood on his list of priorities.[24]

The NAACP was becoming a fount of information for Indians who wished to undermine the idea that India's supposed "backwardness" ill prepared it for independence by pointing to the actual and atavistic racial backwardness of the supposedly advanced United States. N. A. Khan, secretary-general of the Bureau of Information in the Punjab, told Du Bois in the fall of 1927 that "so many students and other interested persons are asking us for *The Crisis* that once more we are compelled to request you earnestly for the gratis supply of your esteemed and valuable monthly."[25]

The Punjab was not the only place in India that relied on Du Bois for intellectual and political nourishment about the United States and Black America. Ahmedabad, the sprawling Gujarat metropolis traditionally associated with Gandhi, was also in this category. It was there—or, more precisely, at the ashram where he had been working side by side with the pre-eminent Indian patriot himself for the previous three years—that one "B. Chatuwedi" told Du Bois in the fall of 1924: "I entirely agree with you when you say that the different colored peoples and more especially the Indians and the American Negroes must get into touch and cooperation with each other. Your idea of visiting India, China and Japan is really excellent." He added wisely, no doubt aware of the fractiousness that often characterized African–Indian relations there, "I would suggest that East Africa should also be included in this list." India could play an "important part" in the "regeneration of the African races," and Du Bois, he wrote, was the man to speak with about such burdened matters. "As regards India," he offered generously, "your name is already known to a very large number of educated Indians," among whom he could be included, as he had been reading Du Bois's informative book, *The Negro.*[26]

Poona was not absent from the list of the sites in India where Du Bois was in contact. The journalist Shripad R. Tikekar told Du Bois in late 1927 that "the race problem, I mean the fight between the black race on the one hand & the white people on the other, is keen in India & as such all Indians have a feeling of sympathy towards the black Americans in their fight against the dominating people." We are "in the same boat," he said, and "can learn much by mutual exchange of thoughts."[27]

Such exchanges often unfolded in the pages of the NAACP's *Crisis*. A correspondent in Calcutta, referring to the horrific "Amritsar Riots and Massacre," added a piquant observation that no doubt resonated with Black America's experience when he averred that one "government official" had asserted, "We white folks must stick together, right or wrong!" The "incident illustrates the atmosphere in India," he said, and something similar could have been said about the United States. The writer also endorsed Albert Schweitzer, the "brilliant young professor who has gone out to Central Africa," saying, "When one realizes all the wrongs which the white races have inflicted on the dark races, it becomes, for a Christian White Man, a matter not of charity but of mere duty and atonement to give of the best he can in his own life to the service of the Colored Peoples."[28]

This uniting of the fates of Black America and India also embraced the question of the so-called mixed race, or "mulattos," and "Eurasians" and their respective roles. *The Crisis* brought attention to how people of "mixed race" were praised by a Calcutta journal; there, it was declared of *The Crisis*, "one would wish that more of our people supported and read it," not least because of the insight it might provide about the dilemma of miscegenation. For Du Bois said in July 1926 that "much of the anti-Negro hysteria in the United States is due to the fact that 'because so many white Americans have black blood which might come to light, they pounce and worry like wolves to prove their spotless family'—a psychologically only too probable explanation."[29] Apparently, Indians thought that they had something to learn from how Black America handled the progeny of miscegenation. "As members of the Eurasian community," one correspondent from India told *The Crisis*, "we are much interested in your affairs, [since] the progress of the Negro race provides an inspiring example for other races in a more or less similar condition."[30] In turn, *The Crisis* noted in June 1930 that "most American Negroes know nothing of Eurasians. . . . They have faced the same kind of problems as Negro–white mulattoes in America. Their physical and mental ability has been decried and lied about. They have been kicked down by the white folk and kicked out by brown people. They have had great difficulty in achieving any inner unity, and have continually faced the disintegration in their own ranks which made Eurasian men think of themselves as European rather than Asiatic, and let Eurasian women choose concubinage to cheap white men rather than marriage to Asiatics. With all this, we can sympathize only too well. We have been through it all, and we have conquered, and the Eurasians are going to conquer. . . . [T]hey are giving up lamentations over their Asiatic blood," just as many "mulattoes" had done. "At last the turning point has come," *The Crisis* announced.[31]

In reciprocation, Rai pointed specifically to Du Bois as a model for Eurasians to emulate. "Unlike the usage in India," Rai said, "where a Eurasian becomes a white man, claiming more or less the privileges of a white man, a Euro-African in the U.S.A. remains a coloured man for all generations and time. Dr. Du Bois claims a French descent. He is an accomplished man, a great scholar, writer, economist, psychologist and above all a master of the English language." Eurasians, said Rai, would be well advised to conduct themselves similarly.[32]

Likewise, Black America pointed to India as a model to emulate, on the premise that if Asians could be redeemed, then so could Africans. "At last Asia is rising again to that great and fateful moral leadership of the world which she exhibited so often in the past in the lives of Buddha, Mohammed and Jesus Christ, and now again in the life of Gandhi," stated *The Crisis*. "The black folk of America should look upon the present birth-pains of the Indian nation with reverence, hope and applause."[33]

A major vector for the transmission of ideas about India to Black America was the Christian missionary. Black missionaries had been streaming into South Asia for decades, but their presence increased as Indian independence approached. There they encountered not only a potential ally for their own struggles for equality in the United States but also, at times, a fierce critic of their religion and their homeland. African Americans were more upset by critiques of their religion than of their country. They also had to confront a British colonial power that also at times was displeased with their presence.

Max Yergan, an African American man on a circuitous journey from Christianity to communism to conservatism, was in Bangalore in 1916 on behalf of the Young Men's Christian Association (YMCA). Yergan was born in Raleigh, North Carolina, in 1892 and in 1914 graduated from that state's Shaw University, where he studied sociology and modern languages.[34] "The Christian element here . . . is too small almost to consider," he moaned, disappointedly, in a report to the YMCA. "Yet," he added guilelessly, "how easily one can tell simply by the expressions on their faces those who are Christians." Perhaps the harshness of conditions he encountered affected his point of view. "I haven't had a glass of water for a week," he wrote. "Indian food isn't after the ideal of good old 'southern' cooking." But one thing had survived his transatlantic passage: "It's funny to hear the same old color question," he declared. "It reacts on me in just a bit different manner from what I get in America. I have had some solid laughs on the missionaries here." However, he also asserted, curiously, "Much is due to the great liberal and wise policies of the British government. God grant that such principles might soon prevail in America."[35]

After two months in India, Yergan began to sober up, perhaps because he was recovering from a fever he had contracted in the interior of India. This, however, had not lessened the "growing grip of Christ upon me," he observed. "For the future I am more ready and willing to take up his cross whatever the consequences are. Thus I ask nothing for myself but prayer. It's the great need for Christ out here that puts me in this frame of mind perhaps. God knows he is needed badly." But after visiting "colleges, student camps and mission stations," he found that the "Indian student is questioning the Christianity of missionaries." The "war of course takes away the normal atmosphere," he said though the interrogation of his faith by Indians was probably constant.[36]

Yergan found no surcease in Bombay, where he was residing in December 1916. "The thermometer today has been kind to us," he said, paradoxically. "[It] stayed around ninety and ninety-five. That's good weather they say for this time of the year." The heat had not melted Yergan's boundless optimism, however: "God is opening up to us a most wonderful opportunity. When world maps are changing, Europeans becoming very familiar with all races (for I saw thousands of black troops in France) and the present war making men more cognizant of the conditions of other people and giving at the same time a sense of responsibility." The moment for a vast transformation of colonialism and the racial project was nigh. However, Yergan abruptly turned away from this point as he proclaimed with an excess of faith, "Should we not count these evidences of God's hand as warning to us [to] get ready for service?"[37]

The U.S. authorities sensed what had occurred to Yergan, but their policies were not driven by the idea that this was all part of "God's hand." Shortly after the Great War, which had caused so much upset to the racial and colonial status quo, the U.S. director of military intelligence was informed in a "Final Report on Negro Subversion" that "until about four years ago radical sentiment among Negroes was of a moderate character, [but then] their advent into the Socialist Party marked a new epoch in the political and social history of the Negro." Worriedly, the report said, "Unless there is some quick and radical departure . . . the time is not far distant when greater numbers of Negroes will be converted to Socialistic doctrines," a prospect that could mean increased scrutiny of the existing order.[38]

Inevitably, this atmosphere influenced Yergan, as he migrated from the role of the Christian missionary to that of the Communist missionary, this time in South Africa. By May 1918, his remit had extended from India to East Africa, which contained a sizeable South Asian population. By then the YMCA, long a vehicle through which African Americans obtained global experience, had dispatched "five Negro American secretaries" to the region, all "provided with portable cinemas, lantern slides, gramophones, [and] games," and their resultant influence. "These young men," a YMCA newsletter stated, "have touched the lives of thousands. One of them, within six months, gained a knowledge of the Swaheli [sic] language." Yergan, who had been one of the "secretaries," had recently returned to the United States. "He has been addressing large student audiences at Tuskegee, Talladega, Atlanta and other Negro institutions, presenting the claims of India and Africa," the newsletter reported.[39]

The service of Yergan and others was even more remarkable since, according to the attorney George Crawford of New Haven, Connecticut, the "overwhelming majority of Negroes" felt "downright hostility . . . toward the YMCA itself. This hostility is attributable to the treatment which Negro soldiers received from the 'Y' during the war." Fierce retribution was accorded to any who were so bold as to speak out, or so Crawford thought. "Ever and always," he lamented, "the Negro who speaks the ugly truth about these matters is either a seeker after 'social equality' or else is possessed of a 'bitter spirit.' . . . [T]he young Negro men of this country have next to no faith in white Christianity as exemplified in the conduct of the YMCA." Such reproaches of "white Christianity" also could pave the way for the flourishing of a "black Islam"—but this perception of a religion that was coded racially could impel the YMCA to seek to recruit aggressively African Americans for attractive postings abroad—for example, in India.[40]

It was also through the Christian church that Juliette A. Derricotte, secretary for colored student work at the Young Women's Christian Association

(YWCA), traveled to Mysore in December 1928 to attend the World Student Christian Conference. "Do you suppose you will have any trouble with the British?" she was asked before her departure. "How do you suppose the Indians will treat you, especially those who wear their turbans in the United States for fear of being taken for Negroes?" This question betrayed African Americans' unease about how some South Asians sought to distance themselves from the perceived and actual penalty of being denoted "colored." Derricotte, however, was distressed by what she witnessed in Mysore, where she stayed for seven weeks. "The wealth as well as the poverty of India haunts me," she wrote. "[H]ow can I tell of the control which oil and rubber and jute have in the relations of East and West."[41]

Du Bois, who knew Yergan and crossed swords with him later in his career, was near the center of the web of solidarity that connected Indian independence activists in Black America.[42] It was Du Bois who directed "my friend" Juliette A.Derricotte to Rai before she left India. "I shall be under great obligation," said Du Bois, "if you will give her and direct her to the best information concerning Indian conditions and see that she meets people of our way of thinking."[43] It was through such informed sources that Derricotte was able to garner keen insight into colonialism in India, information that she then transmitted to a larger audience. She visited several schools in the Southwest, including New Orleans and Straight Colleges, Prairie View College, Wiley and Bishop College, and Langston University. At Langston, she may have encountered Roy H. Akagi, secretary of the Japanese Student Movement in the United States, who was touring segregated African American colleges at the same time.[44] Also part of this network of African Americans were two future mentors of Martin Luther King Jr.: Benjamin Mays and Howard Thurman.[45] The burgeoning network also included such figures as C. F. Andrews, an "Englishman [who] spent of [his] life and energy in India" and who, after Derricotte's tour, traveled to Alabama, Georgia, and Florida to discuss British colonialism with students.[46]

As Derricotte's earlier comment about "oil and rubber and jute" suggests, these activists were struck by the crass exploitation of India. "India represents not only the largest body of subject people in the world today," said one commentator, "but the largest body of subject people the world has ever known."[47] Issues of white supremacy aside, there was fertile ground in the United States for the rise of a movement in solidarity with India, because "imperial preference" fundamentally handcuffed the efforts of U.S. business to penetrate that huge market. "There are only two American banks in India," said one observer in 1930. "There are too many instances of jute going to American buyers *via* London or Glasgow, of tea mainly going *via* London." There was "only one American bank to finance the growing amount of India's export trade with America! Can it be a matter for surprise that the British banks dictate everything and Americans play second fiddle."[48] Before an Indian sends money to America or Japan, it was reported, "the rupee . . . has first to go to England. . . . [W]hat actually governs the trade relations between America and India is first the exchange rate between England and America and not the direct relationship of trade between America and India." Such discriminatory linkages outraged Indians and U.S. nationals alike. "Instead of paying the freightage from India to America through the shortest cut," noted an exasperated South Asian analyst, "we pay the freightage from India to England first and thence to America. Thus, for every rupee we send anywhere outside India England gets ½₂ of a penny that is the charge for sending a rupee from India to England."[49]

Yet another Indian analyst stressed that "American manufacturers who deal in similar articles" as the British—for example, "military supplies, ships, soldier's clothing, rifles, bullets and a thousand other necessities"—had "little chance of selling their products in India." A "large part of our lucrative market is not open to America," the analyst reported, and "practically all the government offices with large salaries are the monopolies of the English."[50] The problem was whether any mass grouping in the United States—besides African Americans—would be sufficiently moved by this discrimination to speak out against it. Would the apparent "normalcy" of white supremacy compel acceptance of this reality?

Such base exploitation provided Derricotte and the other African Americans who streamed into India after World War I with much to ponder. It became easier to see that white supremacy was a global system and, therefore, that India and Black America might have commonalities. These commonalities did form the basis for a sturdy alliance.

Descriptions by South Asians of their own exploitation could only resonate with African Americans who faced similar circumstances. In early 1924, B. R. Dewan, an "eye doctor" from Lahore, asserted bluntly: "India is being ruled most autocratically. Englishmen live in this country like princes, they draw big salaries, live in fine bungalows, travel in first class carriages and motor cars and are keeping the people under subjection. And the people of this country are starving. Thousands die in this country by starvation only. Englishmen here set one class against another and are always planning to divide Hindus and Muslims."[51]

It was this state of affairs that Indian activists sought to bring to the doorstep of the United States, for they recognized that the postwar climate meant a rising United States and a wounded United Kingdom. Further, within the United States, African Americans, though despised and ostracized, were the constituency most likely to lend a willing ear to another oppressed grouping. Just as Derricotte was about to embark on her journey to South Asia, a prominent group of Indians in the United States informed the All India Congress Committee, the leading political force in the subcontinent, that "it is America and American opinion that will be the leading factor in future world politics. Since the Great War the leadership of the world is shifting from Europe to the United States of America. Not only as financiers and creditors," but in myriad other ways, the "balance of power [is] in her hands." Thus, there was "no wonder that the Britishers should . . . talk so much of the unity of [the] Anglo-Saxon race of America and England," a persuasive line that pointedly excluded African Americans. "British propagandists have shifted their center of activity from Europe to America," the group reported, and were "trying to overrun America from one end to the other."[52] This emphasis on the United States was accentuated when an important consensus emerged among a number of key pro-independence activists. As one put it in late 1930: "I am afraid that the Germans do not want to do anything which may be resented by the British." This served to underscore further the critical importance of the United States and the sector of the citizenry most predisposed to independence for India: African Americans.[53]

Thus, it may not have been a surprise when, in the late 1920s, an uproar smacked Howard University, a school with a predominantly African American student body. Mordecai Johnson, who was then a dean, had invited the British ambassador to speak at the university. A student of Trinidadian origin who was to attain notoriety subsequently under the name George Padmore knew that "what the Ambassador was saying [about colonialism was a] farce and that he was an apologist for British imperialism," as one observer tartly put it. "In the midst of the Ambassador's speech in the big auditorium, George interrupted and heckled him and questioned his statements about the British in Africa"—suggesting, in particular, that the diverse "black" population in the United States, which included a noticeable complement of the colonized from the empire, was hardly inclined to be favorable toward London, thereby providing another commonality with Indians.[54]

Padmore, who attended Howard and Fisk universities and became a prominent Pan-African revolutionary, also demonstrated a pro–India bias. For example, when the Indian nationalist Kamaladevi Chattopadhyayya visited Oslo in 1939, she immediately made contacts with like-minded people. "She had got our names from George," Ivor Holm reported much later in a letter to Padmore's widow. "We introduced her to other Norwegian Socialists," which was no minor matter, for when he was there "he got a great reception . . . everyone admired him. The papers presented him as 'the beautiful Negro' from the West Indies and London."[55]

Since Indians and African Americans were viewed widely as being part of the same group—the "colored," or those not of "pure European descent"—and because Indians could be easily mistaken for U.S. Negroes, it became easier for the two groups to bond. When the International Council of Women of the Darker Races, whose very name suggested a camaraderie between Black America and India, formed in 1920 and held its first public meeting at the Bethesda Baptist church in Chicago, "Two young women from India, students at the University of Chicago were present . . . and spoke in a most touching way of condition in their own country and of their hopes for India."[56]

The multilingual Mary Church Terrell, member of a prominent African American family, was at the center of the International Council of Women of the Darker Races. Her—and the Indian women's—elevated class status provided the group with broad influence. In 1925, Janie Porter Barrett, the superintendent of the Virginia Industrial School for Colored Girls, told the widow of Booker T. Washington, "In March we take up the women of China, in April the women of India. . . . [S]ome time later the women of Japan." The plan was to study and discuss issues relating to women of all three countries: "The plan is to have each one dress in native costume and carry out their customs and manners in refreshments as well as dress," Barrett wrote. This process was designed to reinforce ideas about the commonalities shared by the "colored"—that is, those not of "pure European descent."[57]

Typically, the women focused on "historical facts" concerning their native countries' governments, religious customs, international relations, and so on. Customarily, the council also recommended a reading list.[58] The council also contemplated hosting "several interesting meetings with interesting speakers, such as . . . Mrs. Hammachandra, who has recently returned from India."[59] This growing conflation of India and Black America was laden—potentially—with consequence for African American women in particular. One need look no further for evidence than journals of that era edited for that audience, which routinely carried advertisements for products such as "East India hair grower [that] will promote a full growth of hair." The idea, of course, is that there was something wrong with African American women's hair and that they could receive a new birth of freedom from the "East Indian" product.[60]

These varying ties were an emblem of a developing relationship between Black America and India—a relationship that was "integrating" the former not with its Euro-American counterparts (a supposed ideal of many in Du Bois's NAACP but certainly not that of the bulk of his nation) but with a sprawling subcontinent held in bondage by London. Such a relationship defied national boundaries and thus reflected a kind of "globalization from below" that anticipated and prefigured trends that would blossom in the twenty-first century. Certainly, the fictional child of the African American and South Asian protagonists in Du Bois's "favorite novel" anticipated this development.

6

Mission to India

The brown-skinned man with closely cropped black hair and sporting the orange jersey carrying the number "19" of Syracuse University faded back into the protective pocket to throw a pass. His football team was then losing the game by ten points to its archrival, the mighty and unbeaten Cornell, and another rout seemed in store. The man tossing the pigskin was a varsity basketball player better known for his pioneering feats on the hardwood, particularly his penchant for the "no-look" pass, but on this day he carved his name indelibly into the history of the game played on turf by completing six passes without an interception, good for 145 yards and three touchdowns, as the men in orange rallied.[1]

This was one more chapter in the developing legend of Wilmeth Sidat-Singh, whose passing and poise so impressed Grantland Rice that the hallowed sportswriter put him on a par with Hall of Fame giants such as Sammy Baugh and Sid Luckman. Sidat-Singh "could beat you with his arm and with his feet," said one commentator, who compared him to such early-twenty-first-century greats as Michael Vick and fellow "Orangeman" Donovan McNabb. As they would with latter-day "big men on campus," the "co-eds," according to one account, "would faint when he came by."

Sidat-Singh grew to maturity in Harlem: His home was 221 West 135th Street, near the YMCA headquarters in the heart of Black America's bastion. His father, Dr. Samuel Sidat-Singh, a physician of Indian origin, had studied at Howard University, the capstone of Negro education—again signifying how doors were opened in Black America for South Asians when they were

Figure 6.1 Wilmeth Sidat-Singh, a star African American athlete, was widely perceived to be of South Asian origin. (*Courtesy of Syracuse University. All rights reserved.*)

closed elsewhere. He had an office in the same block in Harlem, once more signifying how opening doors for South Asians was of benefit to African Americans. Dr. Sidat-Singh was well known uptown, as was his adopted son, a transplant from Washington, D.C., where he was born in 1917 to Pauline and Elias Webb, a pharmacist. Paula divorced her husband and moved to New York City, where she met Samuel Sidat-Singh, her second spouse—underscoring the ties of singular intimacy that often enveloped African Americans and Indians. Her son, an African-American like herself, was an excellent athlete in sports that ranged from baseball to tennis, basketball, and, yes, football. A shade under six feet and a bit over 190 pounds, Sidat-Singh was compactly constructed with explosive quickness and startling speed. His arm was equally powerful, and his talents complemented those of his roommate, Marty Glickman, the Brooklyn-born sprinter—and later, famous broadcaster—who was Jewish. Sidat-Singh had won a scholarship to Syracuse and starred in basketball for three years, leading the Orange to an undefeated season as a senior—a continuation of the success that had begun at New York's De Witt Clinton High School.[2]

Sidat-Singh was so valuable as a basketball player that his coach was reluctant to see him migrate to the turf, afraid that he would suffer a ruinous injury. He was an intense young man and craved to become a surgeon, like his father, for as the budding athletic star once said, "You can't eat footballs when you get out of college." A "sheepskin not a pigskin" was the object of his desire. He often accompanied his father on surgical missions to observe and learn. His stated destiny was not the nascent National Football League but the medical school at the University of Chicago; his excellence in zoology suggested that his aims were not misguided. Although he was no fan of poetry or English literature, he was versatile, a fan of his hometown, New York, and an avid driver who liked to tool along the Pulaski Skyway in New Jersey He was also a star in football, once beating Penn State by running thirty yards for the winning touchdown and intercepting a pass on defense. This was the "greatest thrill of his lifetime," he confessed,[3] although he could not have been unmoved by the many headlines that blared "Singh's Slings Sink" another hapless opponent.

But as sterling as Sidat-Singh appeared to be, he was not what he seemed. His alma mater listed him as "Hindu" or "Indian," but his name notwithstanding, he was neither. He was African American. And therein hangs a tale: Sidat-Singh had been asked by university officials to wear "Hindu garments" and a turban, but he refused.[4] Unlike other African Americans who chose to "pass" as South Asian to escape the harsher penalties imposed on those thought to be the descendants of those formerly enslaved in the U.S. South, he balked. "Passing" also revealed inferentially what African Americans had to gain from a relationship with South Asians.

When Sidat-Singh traveled to College Park to play a game against the University of Maryland, the sportswriter Sam Lacy, "outed" him by writing that he was not a "Hindu" but a "Negro." How did he know? As Lacy recalled later, "My sister was a classmate of Wil's mom."[5] The Maryland Terrapins, being staunch defenders of Jim Crow, threatened to cancel the game, and Syracuse ordered its star slinger to the sidelines. There he sat miserably, his head buried in his chest, embarrassed and humiliated. His roommate, Glickman, was faced with a dilemma of his own: Should he stand in solidarity with his friend? After all, on the eve of the 1936 Olympics in Berlin, U.S. officials had scratched his name from the four-hundred–meter relay team because he was Jewish. Glickman played against the Terps on that ominous day in October 1937.[6]

Sidat-Singh also was sidelined when the Orangemen played the U.S. Naval Academy in basketball.[7] Sidat-Singh, however, was allowed to play the Terps in 1938, and he led his team to a smashing 53–0 triumph, suggesting that opposition to his playing may have been doubly malevolent.[8] After leaving Syracuse, he played on the famed Harlem Renaissance basketball team, and after World War II commenced, he became a Tuskegee Airman. He crashed and perished on a training mission over Lake Huron in May 1943. He was twenty-five.[9]

The tragic story of Wilmeth Sidat-Singh also reflects the increasing engagement between Black America and India as the 1930s unfolded, an engagement that escalated as African Americans began flocking to India, often on religious missions and invariably conducting a pilgrimage to Gandhi's door. His mother's marriage to a South Asian man who had attended Howard, then adopted him, and his move to Harlem suggest the developing ties between India and Black America. That this talented athlete was in effect "passing" as Indian was a change from the historic pattern of "passing" as white,[10] suggested how the increasing migration of South Asians to the United States was creating more options for Black America. Sidat-Singh was not the only person who took advantage of this conjuncture. The famed jazz musician Dizzy Gillespie often told of similarly gifted Black artists who either converted to Islam or acted as if they had to gain perceived advantages that being a foreigner were thought to bring. Gillespie himself at times wore a turban so he would be taken for "an Arab or a Hindu."[11] As a critical mass of South Asians assembled in the United States, further opportunities for African Americans to escape bias were created.

The ties between Black America and India had been increasing for decades, propelled by persistent migration to the West Coast. Now, with the rise of the Communist Party and its assault on white supremacy, as driven by the titanic case of the Scottsboro Nine and the systemic and variegated crisis induced by the Great Depression, further space was opening for the growth of ties between the chief asset of the British Empire and the bête noire of its rising rival. However, as Sidat-Singh's banishing from sporting events demonstrated, much work remained to be consummated. As it turned out, the essence of this mission—which until then had been occurring on North American soil—was in the process of migrating to South Asia.

In the 1930s, the journeys of African Americans to India increased. One reason was an increase in the dispatching of Black missionaries. These were also journeys to understanding, as the often shocking reality of bias-inflected travel and coming face to face with bigotry abroad was an abject—and at times painful—experience with the global phenomenon of white supremacy. This bracing experience then drove the intensifying battle against the primary foes of Black America and India.

So it was with anticipation that the Christian philosopher Howard Thurman and his equally thoughtful spouse, Sue Bailey Thurman, arrived in the subcontinent in the mid-1930s. They sought to engage Gandhi but were challenged on religious grounds, another aspect of the encounter with India, as many there found it hard to understand how the oppressed and the oppressor could share the same religion. A graduate of Morehouse College, the alma mater of Martin Luther King Jr., and of the Colgate-Rochester Theological Seminary, Howard Thurman, eventually balding, perpetually with a fondness for crisply ironed white shirts and colorful ties, taught at Howard University. Gandhi called him a "dear friend" when he told him in June 1935, "I shall be delighted to have you and your three friends whenever you can come before the end of this year." With typical grace, Gandhi added, "If therefore we can not provide western amenities of life, we will be making up for the deficiency by the natural warmth of our affection." Thurman's "friends" included Edward G. Carroll, a bespectacled and bowtied dark-skinned man with shiny pomaded hair who was a graduate of Morgan College and Yale Divinity School; Grace Towns Hamilton, who was light-skinned and a graduate of Atlanta University and, like Sue Bailey Thurman, who was also a sojourner, a worker for the YWCA. After repeated and urgent invitations from the Council of Student Christian Associations of America—not to mention entreaties from Gandhi—this "Negro Delegation" decided to "visit the principal student centres of India, Burma and Ceylon during the cold weather of 1935–1936." On returning to America, they would "speak to students in all parts of the country."[12]

Thurman, then thirty-seven, was a prolific writer and influential Baptist orator and was not unfamiliar with India. He had invited Miriam Slade, an Englishwoman and friend of Gandhi's, to Howard, where, he discovered to his dismay, "There was little general knowledge of the vast subcontinent of India. Here and there were a few people who knew Indian students or lecturers who had come to this country, but that was all." However, he said, brightening, "There was keen interest in the struggle of freedom from colonialism between Gandhi and the British government. There was a stirring in the wind that we recognized." This was tapped by Miriam Slade during her campus visit. "Ultimately the effect of her address could not be measured," Thurman exclaimed, "but its impact that night was sure!" Her remarks on the theme of "He who has more than he needs for efficient work is a thief" struck a chord amid a student body with a deep historical memory of the theft that was slavery.

The far-sighted Thurman sensed earlier than most that engagement with India could be mutually beneficial, striking a blow against white supremacy globally, which would have a decided impact locally. Serendipitously, it was at that moment that the YMCA and YWCA asked him to chair a delegation to South Asia, a prospect that was not greeted with equanimity in London. "You do not know what you are asking," fumed one colonial bureaucrat. "If

Figure 6.2 Howard Thurman and his wife, Sue Bailey Thurman, were among a growing stream of African Americans who traveled to India in the 1930s. (*From the Howard Thurman Collection, Howard Gotlieb Archival Research Center, Boston University.*)

an American educated Negro just traveled through the country as a tourist, his presence would create many difficulties for our rule—now you are asking us to let four of them travel all over the country and make speeches!" Yet somehow, visas were issued, and plans were plotted.[13]

As others had been before him, Thurman in particular was struck by the predicament of the lower castes and intended to make that a focus of the delegation. He was "impressed" with the "discussion [of the] Harijan peoples," he wrote. "Due to my daily experience as an American Negro in American life, I think I can enter directly into informal understanding of the psychological climate in which these people live. While the details of our experiences differ, they do not differ in principle and in inner pain." To document this Harijan–Negro commonality more effectively, it was Thurman's "plan to take along a motion picture camera and to keep many notebooks."[14]

Despite their pleasurable surprise at obtaining visas, the intrepid delegation—aware of the unfortunately racist reputations of British and U.S. shipping lines took no chances and chose to sail on a French ship. They wound up spending more than four months in South Asia.[15] Thurman's wife, who was then thirty-three, had her own agenda. "I was very interested in representing American women," she recalled later, "above and beyond race." Thus, upon arrival, she quickly huddled with the All India Women's Congress but did not limit her encounters to this sphere. "I particularly enjoyed the time I spent with the poet Tagore," she wrote, while she "took classes at his international university, Visva-Bharati at Santiniketan, Bengal, and had in-depth conversations with him on a variety of subjects."[16] The Thurmans were invited to Tagore's "little house on campus" and "took seats in front of his chair. He sat looking at us, but also through and beyond us, and then he would make some statement, as he focused his mind, his eyes, on our faces; then he would take off again," said Howard Thurman. "I felt his mind was going through cycles as if we were not present." Later, he recalled, "three American Negro women students, Marian Martin Banfield, Betty McCree Price and Margaret Bush Wilson [future chair of the NAACP] spent a semester [there]."[17]

As it turned out, this emphasis on women's issues was one of the lasting contributions of the delegation's path-breaking journey. In addition to smoothing the path for the arrival of the three women students the delegation found, "Indian women" were "very keen" on issues concerning the "social developments of the Negro women." Just as African Americans were inspired by Indians, the Indian women were taken with the bright and assertive Negro women they encountered. "You folks are going to do India an accumulating amount of good," the Thurmans were told.[18]

The journey was so enlightening and enthralling that, at one juncture, it seemed as if the delegation's members had forgotten their homeland. "I am very anxious to hear from you," Sue Bailey Thurman's mother wrote during the sojourn. "I have sent two letters but have not had a line from since you arrived in India. How is your health? . . . [Do] the water and climate agree with both of you? I dream about you so often because I think of you night and day I suppose." Switching topics, she then queried intimately, "Baby, are you pregnant? If so, be careful with yourself," adding, in passing, "People are very concerned about that Ethiopian war."[19] But the delegation could hardly find time to write home. College students in South Asia were not alone in being "deeply interested in hearing about the American Negro," and they were inspired by the delegation's words.[20]

From the moment they set foot in the region, the delegation was caught up in an absorbing human drama. Besides, they had been briefed beforehand: They were instructed to keep their own counsel and to "remember that the Indians [think] of themselves as a superior race culturally. . . . [Y]ou and other members of the delegation should be cautious in talking too much about their being an underprivileged group." And—oh, yes—they "should have typhoid, paraphoid, and smallpox vaccinations."[21] Still, it did not take long for one delegation member to go "down with a temperature," while another was "worn out" and still another was simply "tired."[22]

On arriving in Ceylon, the delegation's "first encounter with the British government was the customs officer at the large table in the middle of the first-class saloon, who questioned us carefully," recalled Thurman. "He told us to step aside until our hosts arrived to take us off the ship. Then abruptly he changed his mind and gave us landing permits." It was a "totally new world to us," he said, still enchanted years later. "Suddenly I realized that the most subtle reaction was stirring in me. . . . [The] strangeness of the dress, the unfamiliar language, the aroma of spices [caused] this inner stirring that could not be defined. Suddenly what had been eluding my mind came to me. The dominant complexions all around us were shades of brown, from light to very dark; and more striking to me even [than] this were the many unmistakable signs that this was *their* country, their land. The Britishers, despite their authority, were outsiders. I had never had an experience like this," remarked this man who was a "minority" in his presumed homeland. "I did not know until that awareness came to me what a subtle difference this fact made in my reaction to my environment."

But this was only the beginning of an awakening whose tremors were later to reach the mighty edifice that was Jim Crow. One of Thurman's initial speaking engagements was at a law college. "At the end of the lecture there were two questions," Thurman observed, "one about an exhibit [on] the Scottsboro trial and the other about the lack of black Americans in jury service. Both questions were posed by young men who had never traveled beyond the borders of Ceylon." This suggests the reach of the anti–Jim Crow mission, the influence of the Communists who had made these Scottsboro defendants a global cause célèbre and the shrinking of the planet.

But Jim Crow was only part of the double-pronged inquiry that dogged the delegation during the course of its journey. The other was religion. The delegation had been in South Asia for only two days when a confrontation over Jim Crow occurred. The chairman of the Law Club, a "rather brilliant barrister," brusquely said to Thurman, "'I think that an intelligent young

Negro such as yourself, here in our country on behalf of a Christian enterprise, is a traitor to all of the darker peoples of the earth. How can you account for yourself being in this unfortunate and humiliating position?" That was not all: "What are you doing here?" the delegation was asked. "What do you mean?" Thurman asked in turn. The barrister countered, "More than four hundred years ago your African forbears were taken from the western coast of Africa by slave traders who were Christians; in fact, not only was the name of one of the English slave vessels *Jesus*, but one of your very celebrated Christian hymn writers was a dealer in the slave traffic." For three hours, they went back and forth on this matter. This query followed references to the role of Christianity—and Christians—in the slave trade, lynching, and so on. They were not easy questions to answer, although the delegation had a lot of practice in doing so. Although he had basically been sent to evangelize, and although he was often accused of being so, Thurman acknowledged, "I did not want to go as an apologist for a segregated American Christianity." Later he met Stanley Jones, author of *Christ the Alternative to Communism*; perhaps overburdened by the barrage of acerbic inquiries he had received about his own faith, Thurman told him bluntly that his tome's weakness was that the author found it hard to "document the teaching" of Christ by "living example, the best he could do was quote from the Bible."

Despite this remonstration, Thurman himself was interrogated relentlessly about religion during his lengthy stay in South Asia. "Everywhere we went, we were asked, 'Why are you here, if you are not the tools of the Europeans, the white people?'" The "central question was: is Christianity powerless before the color bar"—and the answer, sadly, was not self-evident.

Nonetheless, Thurman found Colombo "disturbing and depressing" in ways that harkened back to the bondage of his ancestors. There was an "irreverent disregard for the personality of the peoples of the country. Servants were everywhere and everywhere degraded. I recall how my soul was invaded with shock and anger," he said mournfully, "when during the meal in a teacher's home, he was making a crucial point to me and was frustrated because he had to pay attention to boning the fish on his plate. In disgust he put down his fork and fish knife and yelled, 'boy—come bone this fish!'" All Thurman could think at this disturbing moment was "shades of the United States." But this was not the end of the brutal recollections of his homeland engendered by his journey. "Another evening," he said, "I recoiled as we sat at dinner to see that the overhead fan was attached to a pole, the pole to a pulley, and the pulley to a rope that disappeared on the porch, where a man was seated, the rope attached to his foot, which he moved back and forth to make a little breeze and keep the flies away" from his supposed betters.

Thurman was overcome by the rush of such experiences. "At times, emotionally, I overreacted because there was much in the Europeans' attitude towards the Indians that I recognized as a part of my own American experience," he observed. But decidedly not part of his experience was being besieged by audiences and the press, both hanging on his every word, particularly when he commented about the obscenity that was Jim Crow. "Always there were reporters and other representatives of the media seeking interviews and attending the public meetings. We were quoted in all the papers and this itself was brand-new and [a] threatening experience for our delegation," since the authorities were not indifferent to their presence—or their words. "Naturally," he cautioned, "I found myself being extremely careful to choose terms because I knew that any statements of ours could easily be taken out of context, [as] our friends advised that our whole journey was under the watchful eyes of the British criminal investigation department. . . . [A]s long as I stuck to my interpretation of our own experience in America, referring to our struggle for civil rights and first-class citizenship, we would not offend . . . the British powers in control." Yet this stress on Jim Crow at once reinforced the Indians' idea that their being deprived of independence due to alleged backwardness was absurd in the face of the obvious social backwardness of the allegedly advanced United States. Moreover, this emphasis contributed to a gathering tide of global revulsion toward Jim Crow, thereby hastening the day when this system of oppression collapsed. In other words, the Negro delegation was instrumental in forging new links between the dual plights of Black America and India.

The surveillance was ubiquitous. In Calcutta, the group took a train to Bhojpur to visit Rabindranath Tagore. "There a man came up to say, 'where is your fourth member? Our information is that there are four of you in this party, . . . but only three are getting off the train.' Such was the constant surveillance! We suspected that our mail was opened and read." One night, Thurman was immersed in conversation with Indian Anglicans when one "beckoned and I went out to him. He said, 'I am sorry, I have failed you again. The man sitting to your left engaging you in conversation, even though he is an Indian,'" was a spy. "So," the disappointed Indian told Thurman, "let us Indians say anything we want to say, we are at home," but "you must not say anything critical of the government, because, if you do, they put you out at once."

Thurman heeded the advice but encountered difficulties nevertheless. "In my public lectures, the basic theme [was] 'The Faith of the American Negro,'" he said, but this seemingly anodyne topic "created the most uneasiness in the American colony." The father of the powerfully influential Henry Luce, publisher of *Time* magazine, wrote to Thurman from Lahore, criticizing him for allegedly leaving the impression that Euro-Americans had not been helpful to the Negroes' struggle. But Luce and his comrades should have rested easy, for it was London, not Washington, that was exercising those whom Thurman was addressing. Once he was asked, "Do you know why the sun never sets on the British Empire?" A stumped Thurman was then told acidly, "God cannot trust the Englishman in the dark."

But with all the skewering of the feckless English, Thurman understandably was taken by the presence of Euro-Americans. "It was our impression," he opined, "that [Euro-Americans] felt inferior to the British. . . . Americans tend to defer to the English—or did so until recently on the assumption that theirs is an old civilization and culture while ours is young and therefore uncertain and brash." He added, "Our national uneasiness in the presence of the English is rooted in a lingering collective guilt for rebelling against the mother country." This was coupled with a "contempt with which the colonials tended to regard the Americans."[23]

Despite the demonstrably horrendous experience endured daily by African Americans in the United States, the presence of this handsome, articulate, and thoughtful delegation could not help but leave a positive impression on South Asians. "The presence of the Negro delegation in Madras," said that city's *Guardian* newspaper in December 1935, "has been so sacred an experience that one is reluctant to record in print any impressions they have left. But so great a blessing cannot remain unnoticed." The journal was taken by the "renowned tragedy of Negro life," which served to undermine the British idea that India—and Indians—were uniquely retrograde. Madras, which contained the "largest . . . Indian Christian community . . . in the country," was not as susceptible to engaging in the religious critique of the delegation that followed its every step elsewhere. "Among the scholars, thinkers and students of world affairs that have visited this country," the *Guardian* proclaimed, "the members of this delegation must take high rank." So impressive was the foursome, the paper declared, that it would be a "tragedy if the contacts made with Negro life now are not kept open and widened as years go on." In fact, "Invite another Negro Delegation at an early date" was the insistent demand.[24]

This appeal was further confirmation of a developing relationship between Black America and India. From Tiruvalla emerged the idea of "securing a Negro doctor" for the hospital there.[25] There was an abiding affection between the two communities that a trans-oceanic chasm could not dilute. "I have loved your people ever since as a little girl I heard here in Calcutta the Fisk Jubilee Singers," Thurman was told. "The work of Booker T. Washington has been a source of inspiration also."[26] A correspondent in Colombo informed Thurman, "I should be very grateful if you would be so kind as to place me in touch with the means of acquiring some little knowledge of representative Negro poetry."[27] In nearby Travancore in southern India, a high-school principal told Thurman: "During my stay at the General Theological Seminary, New York and at the Chicago and New York universities, some of my closest friends have been coloured students and by my association with them I had access to some of your best homes and facilities to learn at close range the history of your race and your civilization."[28] P. V. Radhakrishnan, writing from Rangoon, was effusive: "I and several others have great admiration for you and your work and we shall be proud to be in touch with you even after your going back to America."[29]

In other words, the visit of Thurman and his delegation was both a heady confirmation of a mutually enriching decades-long relationship between Black America and India and further evidence that the relationship had reached a new plateau.

Of course, there were barriers that had to be hurdled. . "I had certain misgivings," confided Thurman, "that led me to believe that we would be considered as the spearhead of some kind of evangelistic movement from the West."[30] Thurman was not far wrong. Many in South Asia did see him as a Trojan horse on behalf of Christianity, which was not an ideal position in a region where Hinduism, Islam, and Buddhism reigned supreme. Inevitably, the suspicion washed over Black America itself. A newspaper in Colombo wondered "How it happened that he [Thurman,] an American Negro, was interested in Christianity." How was it that a "member of an underprivileged minority in America"—or "many of his fellow men," for that matter—could adopt the "religion of those who were their masters"? This was a "rather paradoxical picture" presented by those "brought from Africa [as] slaves."[31] Perhaps similarly motivated was the South Asian educator who was "disappointed" that the delegation "had no chance to meet with some of our Buddhist leaders," which actually was a reflection of the point that the journey was to no small degree a sectarian visit grounded in Christian bonding and recruiting.[32]

Thurman was "determined [not] to discuss or deal with questions of a political nature," which was wise, given the scrutiny he was under by the British colonialists, but this could hardly be avoided, since the matter of how certain religions became hegemonic was not purely personal. "I had for a long time been interested in the various dominant religions in Indian life," Thurman confessed. "I had talked with as many Indians in [the United States] as it had been my privilege to meet." Christianity "through the Syrian Church" had been in India since the first century, he noted, which made even more poignant the constant refrain that he and his Negro compatriots had somehow adopted the faith of their slave masters, although he did acknowledge that "slightly less than one Indian out of every one hundred is a Christian." So prompted, Thurman continued trying to make sense of this weighty matter. "The genius of Hinduism seems to be synthesis," he said. "It possesses amazing powers of adjustment and is profoundly elastic, [while] the genius of Christianity tends [otherwise]. It is an either–or genius." Signifying the value of his journey, he added, "I was not conscious of this until I went to India." Thurman was also concerned about the problem presented by missionaries, conversion, and the like—something he was accused of promoting during his visit. Thurman's view of Hinduism did not exude elation. It was a "very sad religion," he thought. "The devotees seemed heavily burdened," and, he said, there was "something grim about the worship that I frankly do not understand. Always Hindu temples tugged at my heartstrings, [while] the hold that their religion has on the masses of the people utterly amazed me."

However, Thurman noted, "the Mosques always inspired me," although Muslims were "apt to be less friendly than the Hindu. . . . Perhaps this was due to the fact that as Christians we seem to be greater traitors to Mohammedanism due to our African background than to Hinduism." Thurman visited Buddhist temples and found them "powerful but cold," though Buddhism was the "most relaxed of all the religions encountered. I was particularly impressed with what I saw at the Buddhist temple in Rangoon." Generally, he found South Asia "god-intoxicated," something he did not seem to be terribly upset about.

Yet South Asians were concerned about something else. While in the region, Thurman was queried relentlessly about his faith, including by one interrogator, who asked querulously, "I read one incident of a Christian Church service that was dismissed in order that the members may go to join a mob, and after the lynching came back to finish their worship of their Christian God." Then the interrogator challenged the stricken Thurman by concluding, "In my opinion you are a traitor to all the darker peoples of the earth."

Although it is hard to remember now, there was during Thurman's time a notion of the unity of "colored" people, with Japan leading the charge and India right behind. The outliers in this formation were thought to be Black Americans who, unlike the overwhelming majority of the others, not only professed Christianity but often prayed to a blond and blue-eyed deity. According to Thurman, such brisk exchanges made him "feel confident that the pilgrimage heightened the respect and regard that the Indian of culture and refinement has for the Negro peoples," but others were not so certain. Even Thurman had to concede, remarkably, "It was but natural that we would have some misgivings about the possible treatment we would receive from American missionaries."

Something else caught his attention that reified the old bromide that those who point the finger of accusation have three of their digits pointing at themselves. "Coming out of the West where all my life I had been victimized by racial separateness and segregation within the Christian Church, I was acutely aware of every sign of it that I saw in India," Thurman said. And so, as South Asians raised rather bluntly the question of religion, Thurman in turn raised the similarly heavy matter of race. "It had been our experience," he said, "that Indians who came to America to study soon found it to their advantage to have as little to do with Negroes as possible," for "if they associated too intimately with Negroes, or if they were thought to be Negroes by the American white man, they would be subject to the same disabilities, civic and what not, to which the American Negro is subjected." As a result, he said, many African Americans "regarded the Indian as someone who would not wish to associate with him, but who rather wanted to be white. There was a general impression also that the Indian considered himself so very superior to the Negro."

Moreover, Thurman "noticed certain forms of discrimination as between Indian and European, discrimination based upon race and not religion." He was fascinated by the distinction made between the Indian and the Anglo-Indian because it had "significance for the problem that exists between the American white man and the Negro" and the "mulatto." Like so many others, he was captivated by "untouchability," which he called a "very terrible thing. . . ." Once, "I was introduced in a public meeting by an Indian who had been to America. He told me how a white man had refused to shake hands with [a] Negro American and as he observed the spectacle he thought of the great throngs of untouchables." During his 133 day visit in 1935–1936, Thurman stayed in "the Malabar district. . . . [O]ne evening after retiring I heard someone knocking gently at my door. I turned the light on and went to the door and there I saw the head of a little boy peering up at me—he must have been twelve or fourteen. He said with his head down, 'I have listened to your words and I have come in the night to ask if there is hope for me. I am a nobody, a less than nothing, but your words give me hope. Tell me, can I be anything, ever?'" Thurman, understandably, was devastated and thought once more of his homeland as he concluded, "Because they have been despised over so many decades, they have at last come to despise themselves."[33]

But the sad plaint from this distressed tyke was not the only question posed to Thurman. "Will [you] sing Negro spirituals?" asked one educator. This, noted, Thurman's interlocutor, Edward Nolting, was a "question the students and others [were] continually asking."[34] A "great deal of expectation has been raised here in your visit to our country," said the delegation's host in Rangoon, but there was a dampening factor. "We have been told you are not eager to sing the Negro spirituals," he said sadly, "but I wonder if you cannot be persuaded to sing some at a few special meetings. Our people here have been greatly helped by the spirituals."[35] Previous visits by the Fisk Jubilee Singers had at once created enormous goodwill while creating the expectation that Negroes would warble automatically those exceedingly beautiful, emotional, and uplifting tunes called "Negro spirituals." For this reason, the delegation and other pilgrims who journeyed to South Asia were likely to be greeted warmly.

But a particularly salient result of Thurman's delegation—and that of others—was the abject challenge to their Christian faith that they were compelled to confront. This experience also suggests the impact of South Asian migration to the United States over the years and the resultant effective proselytizing of Muslims of various stripes. For Thurman, these repetitive episodes deepened his commitment to Christianity, but it also opened a door to an enlightening vista of philosophical nonviolence that, in the long run, was to be even more important. Yet Thurman and the other pilgrims recognized— much more so than their Euro-American counterparts—that it would be extremely difficult for Christianity to make inroads in South Asia, not least since the faith had "made its peace with color and race prejudice in the West."[36] Simultaneously arising—and inextricably bound to the gathering idea about the viability of nonviolence—was the notion that Black America and India faced a similar foe in white supremacy, which deepened and enriched their relationship. Later Thurman observed:

> I remember one night traveling through en route to Calcutta from the Musilapatam and being compelled to spend most of the night at the Bezwada Junction; an Indian student secretary was traveling with us part of the way. In the railway station at the Junction there are rooms in which one may spend the night that are divided one-half for Europeans and one-half for Indians; because the Indian was a part of our party we wanted him to spend the night with us. The Indian attendant refused to permit this saying to the Indian, "you know you have no business in the European section."

A dumbfounded Thurman, confronted with this reminder of home, could only respond, "It reminded me a great deal of the 'land of the free and the home of the brave.'"[37] A pilgrimage to India became a pilgrimage home. A mission to India was transmogrified into a mission to the United States.

More than four decades after this journey, Thurman remained enthralled with his visit. "Heavy clouds crowded the North Indian sky all through the Christmas holiday. From Darjeeling, 7000 feet above sea level, Howard and

Sue Thurman could see Mount Everest poke its head through this aerial cover," he told a fellow writer in 1981. "Early one morning Howard Thurman joined a group of Indian students who were walking up Tiger Hill to watch the sun rise over Kinchinjunga. The darkness was total; no Christmas star blinked its light to lead the way. Soon a delicate touch of pink brushed the sable sky. Sunlight exploded over Kinchinjunga. In an instant the whole landscape shimmered in luminous detail. The solitary mass of Everest glowed with radiant energy. Jut as abruptly the clouds closed. Darkness returned." This was a "transcendent moment of sheer glory and beatitude," said Thurman. He had been allowed to gaze "into the depths of what is forbidden for anyone to see," he said, and he "would never be the same." Nor would Black America, for Thurman, a man of robust humor who was generally to be found in ill-fitting tweeds and flannels; a man who never owned a car or a house and never flew in an airplane but was an excellent cook fond of exquisite desserts—went on to become one of the most effective preachers in the land and laid the conceptual foundation for the civil-rights struggles of the 1960s. Appropriately, Thurman was fond of penguins, for like them he defied categorization.[38] His encounter with the land of Gandhi was transmitted to Black America, and the knowledge gained about nonviolence transformed the site of his birth.

However, Thurman was not altogether singular, for among his comrades was Benjamin Mays, a future mentor of Martin Luther King Jr. at Morehouse College. "When Mays later gave his famous Tuesday morning Morehouse talks," according to Orville Burton, "he drew upon his [1930s] discussion with Gandhi to encourage young black men who had to live in a prejudicial society."[39] When Mays sat down years later to recollect his memories in his autobiography, his sharp impressions of that voyage to India had not deserted him: "The poverty I saw in Egypt was surpassed only by what I saw in India. It gave me no comfort to realize that the plight of the poor in Egypt and India was even worse than that of poor Negroes in the United States." With such ideas in mind, he made his way to Bombay (before arriving in Mysore) for the All-India Congress, where he "talked briefly with Nehru [and] at greater length with Nehru's sister, Mrs. Vijaya Lakshmi Pandit." Mays wrote that he had an "appointment [to] see Mahatma Gandhi on December 31, 1936. Later, when I told the Mahatma that I had preferred talking with him to seeing the Taj Mahal, he responded, 'you chose wisely. When you come to India again, the Taj Mahal will be there, I may not be here.'" His "ninety minutes with Gandhi were spent mainly in his replying to two of my questions," said Mays. "I asked him: 1) to tell me in his own way what 'nonviolence' meant to him; and 2) why he didn't declare war on the caste system as well as make an attack on untouchability. . . . Gandhi's response was that the nonviolent man is law-abiding in that he is willing to pay the price when he disobeys unjust laws. Later, this part of my experience was to give me a deeper understanding than most persons of the program of Martin Luther King Jr." As for the latter query, Mays came to realize that, "as bad as untouchability was in 1937, I predicted that it would be legally abolished before segregation was legally abolished in the United States. I was right. Untouchability was abolished [*sic*] when India became independent in 1947." What made this more remarkable for Mays was that he deemed untouchability to be "worse than segregation in the United States."[40]

So it was that in early 1937, Mays, too, was able to encounter Mohandas K. Gandhi. African Americans were coming to view India as a fount of knowledge about how to dismantle oppression, and this topic was certainly high on the agenda when Mays was given the opportunity to confer with Gandhi. "Passive resistance is a misnomer for non-violent resistance," Mays was told. "It is much more active than violent resistance. It is direct, ceaseless, but three fourths invisible and only one-fourth visible." Mays replied, "I have no doubt in my mind about the superiority of non-violence but the thing that bothers me is its exercise on a large scale, the difficulty of so disciplining the mass mind on the point of love. It is easier to discipline individuals. What should be the strategy when they break out? Do we retreat or do we go on?" That was not Mays's only pointed query. "Is it possible," he asked, "to administer violence in a spirit of love?" And, he asked, "How is a minority to act against an overwhelming majority?"[41]

In January 1937, Mays made his way to Mysore, following in the footsteps of Juliette Derricotte, for a YMCA confab. There were "more than two hundred official delegates" at the conference he attended, "representing thirty-five nations," all "assembled to study the complex problems which confront the youth of the world." He and Channing Tobias, a future chairman of the NAACP, were two of the thirteen official delegates representing the United States. As ever for a dark-skinned person seeking to traverse the planet, all manner of obstacles were strewn in his path. "I was advised by friends, both Negroes and whites," Mays said, "not to travel on an English boat across the Atlantic, but to take instead an Italian or French steamer because on these liners race prejudice is less pronounced than it is on English or American vessels." While traveling from Marseilles to Egypt, he sensed bias:

> I remarked about this to an English friend also en route to Mysore. He commented that I probably sensed correctly, [since] when the average Britisher leaves Marseilles . . . he is a different individual. He is moving toward India and there he must maintain the 'British prestige.' Young Indians returning home from study in England told me

that many Britishers who are perfectly cordial and kindly disposed toward them in London cease to be that way when they board the ship for India.

Inevitably, the dark-skinned Mays was grouped with South Asians—literally. "I thought at first it was merely an accident," he recalled later, "that the dining room steward seated me at the table with Indians. (I did not mind, for the Indians were delightful companions)." Moreover, this seating patterns had a positive byproduct, as Mays declared, "It is testimony to the Indian people's lack of prejudice . . . that the Indians will not object to the presence of American Negro," though he acknowledged that "some Indians have queer notions about Negroes and all of them do not desire to abandon English rule; especially is this true of some who happen to fare well economically." Mays was also stunned by "possibly the most theologically correct people [at] the Conference"—that is, the "representatives from Germany"—who "in private conversations . . . justified what Germany is doing to the Jews." He was similarly struck by the chauvinism he witnessed in India, which he viewed through the lens of his own experience as an African American. "It is my firm conviction," he said, "that the British–Indian situation, though greatly aggravated and complicated on account of caste, is further complicated because the Indians are colored people and do not belong to the so-called 'white race.'" It was, he stressed, "imperialism built on racism," a phenomenon that his experience in the United States disposed him to comprehend.

The conclusions he left with were far-reaching: "I discovered no prejudice based on color among the Indians; none among the Chinese, and none among the Japanese," he asserted, although he concluded, with equal profundity, that "the problem of race is world-wide."[42] These conclusions were driven by Mays's experience at the Mysore conference, where "members of different races and nations met on a plane of absolute equality. The Conference leadership was distributed without regard to race. . . . Channing Tobias, an American Negro [and future chairman of the NAACP], headed one of the commissions. . . . [H]ousing was assigned irrespective of race and nationality." Without exaggerating, he added: "There were few places in the United States where a conference like this could have been held in [the] thirties, and nowhere in the South. While at Mysore I was invited by the headmaster of an 'untouchable' school in a neighboring village to speak to his students." Mays reported that he was "introduced as an untouchable who had achieved distinction." The headmaster told the assembly that he had "suffered at the hands of the white men in the United States every indignity that they suffered from the various castes in India and that I was proof that they, too, could be 'somebody worthwhile' despite the stigma of being members of a depressed class." Initially, Mays said, he was "horrified, puzzled, angry to be called an untouchable," but his indignation was short-lived, for it was then that he realized "as never before" that he "was truly an untouchable [in his] native land"—especially in the U.S. South. "I had been slapped almost blind because I was black and had been driven out of a Pullman car with pistols at my back," he confessed. "I—just as they—through the mere accident of birth, was indeed an untouchable!" He called his participation in the Mysore conference a "great experience": It took a journey of thousands of miles to propel him toward insight into his homeland. It was in India, "speaking to college students," that he saw that his experience was not terribly peculiar: "They, too, were groping for a better life and needed motivation and inspiration. They responded warmly to my speeches, expressing their appreciation by long applause."

Yet the hero's welcome Mays received in India was an ironic and paradoxical confirmation of the fact that his "untouchability" was not universal. To his surprise, "The press and photographers [in India and Ceylon] were more interested in having a press conference with me than they were in having one with my white comrades. Their interest was not so much because I was a Negro, but because as a Negro I had experienced discrimination in the United States, and they were eager to hear what I had to say about the race problem [in the United States]." In fact, said Mays with wonder, "They wished to talk about nothing else. They were sometimes reluctant to talk about caste and the depressed classes right on their doorsteps." As Mays discovered, this was a reality that was to transfix U.S. travelers to India for decades: Talking about the plight of Negroes was in some ways an evasion, a way to avoid discussing "untouchables."

Still, Mays reveled in his temporary celebrity. "As the train arrived in Madras, Madura, Trivandrum and Colombo, the photographers were invariably there to take my picture," he said, "and the reporters to interview me. Never before had I experienced such preferential treatment over white people." Such a startling experience for a U.S. Negro was hard to contain in the confines of India. Inevitably, it would have spillover effect in the United States itself, as it did when Mays became a spearhead against the "racial" inferiority embedded in Jim Crow and an inspiration for its ultimate vanquisher, Martin Luther King Jr.[43]

At the same time, Channing Tobias, a Negro leader of the YMCA, also had an opportunity to question Gandhi. Decades later, as chairman of the NAACP's Board of Directors, Tobias was to preside over a historic press conference hailing the 1954 U.S. Supreme Court decision that marked the formal end of de jure segregation. But it was in the 1930s that he bumped into Gandhi "riding third class, with a spinning wheel and basket [of] oranges beside him. At

Figure 6.3 Mohandas K. Gandhi, a key leader of colonized India, was critical of the maltreatment of African Americans. (*Courtesy Library of Congress; artist unknown.*)

first, questions and answers were written, for it was Gandhi's day of silence, but later he spoke."[44] Tobias mentioned that some 12 million African Americans in the United States were "struggling to obtain such fundamental rights as freedom from mob violence, unrestricted use of the ballot, [and] freedom from segregation," to which Gandhi responded, "I had to contend against some such thing." But, added Gandhi, it was "on a much smaller scale in South Africa." The struggle was hard and bitter, he continued, but "there is no other way than the way of non-violence, a way, however, not of the weak and ignorant but of the strong and wise." Gandhi's words and India's example were to be exemplified in years to come by Black America. But as this new year of 1937 was dawning, Tobias had one last question for Gandhi: "What word shall I give my Negro brothers as to the outlook for the future?" Gandhi replied, "With right which is on their side and the choice of non-violence as their only weapon . . . a bright future is assured."[45]

Like other African Americans, Tobias had been inspired not only by his historic encounter with Gandhi, but also simply with being in India. "The moment I set foot on Indian soil at Bombay," he said, "I felt a sense of satisfaction in seeing people who were not white running affairs." Yet "on the boat Indian [labor] was confined to menial work while white men directed everything. On shore the customs officials as well as the coolies who carried our luggage were Indians." Tobias was "pleased to note there is no color prejudice among Indians themselves. They vary in color from the almost white population of Kashmir to the pure blacks of Southern India."[46] Farther south in Ceylon, he found "Europeans doing the same kind of work as that being done by high grade Ceylonese," yet they were "paid twice as much." Perhaps as a result of such transnational Jim Crow, he observed, the "natives [were] very definitely lined up in their world sympathies with the darker races." Indeed, he discovered, "Of the speakers who have visited Ceylon in recent years, none has made a more profound impression than our own Howard Thurman."[47]

By the time the famous Harlem Renaissance writer Jean Toomer arrived in India during the late summer of 1939, the connection between Black America and India was sufficiently resonant that he was asked repeatedly upon returning home "Did you meet Gandhi?" This, he said, "is the one question, and the first question, asked by almost everyone who knows that I went to India. Even school girls ask it." Although by late 1939, Toomer was disclaiming the popular idea that he was a Negro, Gandhi's importance had grown to the point where any connection with the great man was viewed with astonishment.[48]

Two decades later, Mays, then reaching the twilight of his distinguished career, gave a commencement address at the University of Minnesota. Drawing on his experience in India, he asked, "How long would Mahatma Gandhi have had to wait for Britain to free India voluntarily and for the upper caste men to give up untouchability?"[49] To him the answer was self-evident, and the lesson to be drawn—and that was being drawn as he spoke—was that the praxis of nonviolent resistance that had rescued India could likewise rescue Black America.

This was the primary importance of this Black American mission to India in the 1930s. The "missionaries" came home imbued with the fire of nonviolence, which then began to immolate the kind of bias that had ensnared the young Syracuse University athlete who had sought to escape exclusion by posing as a South Asian.

7

INDIA AND BLACK AMERICA

I t was a typically warm day in South Asia when the delegation led by Howard Thurman approached a small bungalow over which flew the flag of the Indian National Congress. It was 21 February 1936, and Thurman's Washington, D.C., home was enduring wintry weather, but the warmth he was about to experience seemed to be emerging from a blast furnace. For coming toward the group was a small, brown-skinned man whose visage was becoming the global face of India: Mohandas K. Gandhi. As he walked toward his visitors, his secretary turned to Thurman and commented, " 'This is the first time in all the years that we have been working together that I've ever seen him come out to greet a visitor so warmly.' "[1] Perhaps the Indian leader was aware of London's conclusion that winning public opinion in the United States was essential to maintaining colonial rule in India and that African Americans were the constituency most likely to disagree with this domination.

Certainly, Gandhi was no stranger to Black America. He had said at one point that he "hoped Harijans would study the life and work of Booker T. Washington, whom he looked upon as one of the great men of the world, and draw their inspirations from it."[2] He was familiar with both the Hampton Institute and the Tuskegee Institute, he had said a few years before the delegation arrived at his bungalow. "There is no doubt," he said, that these schools are "worth studying by all Harijan workers and Harijans." He also felt, however, that since India had made " "the artificial and assumed superiority of the so-called high castes over Harijans a matter of religion, . . . the work of the Hindu reformer in India is more urgent than that of the white reformer in America, as it also becomes more difficult." Nevertheless, he insisted, "Tuskegee Institute is a model for Harijans. Booker T. Washington has [shown] to the world what a man of a despised race can do in the teeth of enormous odds."[3] In mid-1935, he remarked: "Look at Booker T. Washington. . . . Have any of us suffered as much as he did?"[4]

For Gandhi, the abuse of Washington was emblematic of the hypocrisy of the United States itself. "Even in the United States of America," he said in the mid-1920s, "where the principle of statutory equality has been established, a man like Booker T. Washington who has received the best Western education, is a Christian of high character and has fully assimilated Western civilization, was not considered fit for admission to the court of President Roosevelt and probably would not be so considered even today!" But it was not just Washington who was ill treated, he opined. "The Negroes of the United States have accepted Western civilization: They have embraced Christianity. But the black pigment of their skin constitutes their crime, and if in the northern states they are socially despised, they are lynched in the southern states on the slightest suspicion of wrongdoing."[5]

But it was not just the Wizard of Tuskegee who captured Gandhi's attention. Like those visiting him from Black America, he was drawn to comparisons between "Harijans" and African Americans and, in contemplating the latter, was drawn to slavery more generally, including within the British Empire. Britain's "abolition of slavery was a legislative act," Gandhi stated in the early 1930s, but "[t]he slavery of the heart was not abolished then, [and] the lapse of a century has hardly abolished it altogether. This is written, not to belittle the great act of 1833, but to clear our minds and to understand the limitations of the effort of 1833."[6] American "'untouchability' towards the Negroes," he was told in 1936, "is rooted in the land-greed of the white man who first traveled to America in the 'Mayflower.'"[7]

In turn, Gandhi was not exactly an alien to Black America. He was the "greatest colored man in the world," crowed the NAACP's *Crisis*. He had "toiled in South Africa to remove race prejudice," while in India his "watchword [was] agitation, non-violence, refusal to cooperate with the oppressor." Most impressive, said the journal in July 1929, was that Gandhi "stretche[d] out his hand in fellowship to his colored friends of the West." Continuing the love fest, Gandhi responded in the pages of *The Crisis* with words that have yet to be fully digested in a nation whose landscape continues to be marked by monuments to a treasonous government that sought to perpetuate human bondage: "Let not the 12 million Negroes be ashamed of the fact that they are the grand children of the slaves. There is no dishonour in being slaves. There is dishonour in being slave-owners."[8]

Gandhi's interest in Booker T. Washington and Black America mirrored developments in his homeland. When Washington died, the Depressed Classes Mission Society in India, along with other groups, sent notes of sympathy. Further, as one scholar has noted, "During the 1920s, the South Asian press went into great detail describing American lynchings. . . . [The] annual Tuskegee Institute lynch statistics used to be studied in great detail in South Asia. When there was a decline in the lynching rate or when a lynching was prevented, there was some publicity of these trends." Even more publicity was given to the Scottsboro case. The Indian Trade Union Congress and other groups sent appeals to the President for release of these Alabama Negroes who had been accused wrongly of rape of two white women. As Gandhi was to do with Thurman, it was typical in the region to juxtapose the promise of Christianity with the dire reality of African Americans. This was stressed over and over again by these South Asian nationals because of the gulf in theory and practice among Christians in the United States. As one Indian intellectual put it, "The Negro problem was the sin of Christianity."[9] And as one Bombay journal put it in 1935, lynching was a "reminder that no nation is so perfect that it can point the finger of scorn at another as wanting in humanity." Referring to a particularly grisly episode in that year, the *Indian Social Reformer* said disdainfully, "The state of mind of practically the whole population of the district in which the lynching took place is indistinguishable from that of savage cannibals. . . . [E]ven a member of a persecuted race like the Jews approved of the lynching. This is nothing strange. The oppressed are always the worst oppressors. They enjoy inflicting on others the tortures they had to endure." The attitude of educated Euro-American women toward the lynching also shocked the writer. This, he said, undermined any attempt to suggest that the supposed "backwardness" of India barred independence, for until the United States eradicated this "dark blot on her fair name, she must suffer the mortification of being regarded by human men and women in every land as tolerant of savagery lurking behind her mighty material achievements."[10] The targeting of lynching was also a priority for Bombay's *Independent India*, edited by the premier Marxist M. N. Roy, which demanded "energetic measures" in light of the "racial war against Negroes in the Southern States."[11]

This firm solidarity between India and Black America did not emerge magically. Du Bois recalled that, when the NAACP was founded, the "'Colored People' referred to in our name [were] not originally confined to America." After all, as this premier civil-rights organization was being founded, the South Asian population in the United States was increasing, and seeking allies against white supremacy in India had crossed Du Bois's mind. Similarly, Du Bois recalled with a tinge of sadness "the discussion we had on inviting Gandhi to visit America and how we were forced to conclude that this land was not civilized enough to receive a colored man as an honored guest."[12]

Thus, as Thurman and the others ambled toward Gandhi, they were approaching a man who was ignorant neither of Black America nor of Black Americans' concerns. Gandhi had in his possession *The Philosophy and Opinions of Marcus Garvey*, which would have provided further insight into Black America—and, indeed, into Africa and its diaspora.[13] Yet with all that, after they had settled down for a face-to-face encounter beneath a lovely mango tree, Thurman's first question to the saintly leader was: "Did the South African Negro take any part any in your movement?" Though this mutual concern held by Gandhi, who had lived and campaigned in South Africa, and Thurman might to the untutored have seemed a diversion from their mutual concerns, it was actually the kind of issue that could further bind them.[14] It is also possible that Thurman wanted clarification of the percolating stories suggesting that Gandhi was less than friendly to Africans in the region stretching from Durban to Nairobi, who had frequent interactions with South Asians in their midst.

Naturally, Gandhi had his own questions, which occupied a good deal of the three-hour session. "Never in my life have I been a part of that kind of examination," recalled Thurman. Gandhi posed "persistent [and] pragmatic questions about American Negroes, about the course of slavery, and how we had survived it," he said. "One of the things that puzzled him was why the slaves did not become Muslims. 'Because,' said he, 'the Moslems' religion is the only religion in the world in which no lines are drawn from within the religious fellowship. Once you are in, you are all the way in. This is not true in Christianity, [and] it is not true in Buddhism or Hinduism.'" Gandhi "wanted to know about voting rights, lynching, discrimination, public school education, the churches and how they functioned. His questions covered the entire sweep of our experience in American society."[15]

That it did. The Indian version of this epochal discussion, this summit between Black America and India that led to a deepening engagement between two of the most important—albeit oppressed—groupings on the planet, differed only slightly from Thurman's recollection. Gandhi wanted to know if the "prejudice against colour" was "growing or dying out." Thurman could only offer in response, "It is difficult to say." Gandhi wanted to know whether the "union," or marriage, "between Negroes and the whites [is] recognized by law." The discussion on South Africa veered toward a "very interesting discussion of the state of Christianity among the South African Negroes."[16]

But all of this discussion about South Africa, Black America, and India and how they could cast off the iron grip of their respective oppressors inexorably led to a discussion of the role of violence. Sue Bailey Thurman recalled asking Gandhi, "If you are using non-violence against prejudice and hatred, how do you apply this to places where prejudice runs very deep? Where there are guns and lynching at the end of every trial, and there are no real trials anyway, and no courts to protect people?"[17] Is nonviolence a "form of direct action[?] . . . How are we to train individuals or communities in this difficult art?" asked Howard Thurman, anticipating an inquiry that was to wrack Martin Luther King's brain decades later. And, recounted Sue Bailey Thurman, "[I] could not go away without asking the question with which [I knew I] would be confronted any day. 'How am I to act, supposing my own brother was lynched before my very eyes?' 'There is such a thing as self-immolation,' said Gandhiji. 'Supposing I was a Negro, and my sister was ravished by a white or lynched by a whole community, what would be my duty?—I ask myself. And the answer comes to me: I must not wish ill to these, but neither must I cooperate with them . . . refuse even to touch food that comes from them, and I refuse to cooperate with even my brother Negroes who tolerate the wrong. That is the self-immolation I mean.'"[18]

Gandhi told the delegation, whose members were hanging on his every word, that nonviolence was not "one form" of direct action but "the only form," for "without a direct active expression of it, non-violence to my mind is meaningless. It is the greatest and active force in the world. One cannot be passively non-violent." The delegation was suitably impressed. "We want you to come to America," they said. Sue Bailey Thurman added, "We want you not for white America, but for the Negroes; we have many a problem that cries for solution, and we need you badly." Modestly, Gandhi replied, "I must make good the message here before I bring it to you." But then he offered a response that was to echo through the ages: "It may be through the Negroes that the unadulterated message of non-violence will be delivered to the world."[19]

After spending hours with Gandhi, the delegation was about to leave. Then Gandhi asked, "Will you do me a favor? Will you sing one of your songs for me? Will you sing 'Were You There When They Crucified My Lord?'" He added, "I feel that this song gets to the root of the experience of the entire human race under the spread of the healing wings of suffering." The request was to Sue Bailey Thurman, but it was her husband who recalled that "under the tent in Bardoli in a strange land we three joined in music as one heartbeat. Gandhiji and his friends bowed their heads in prayer. When it was over there was a long silence and there may have been a few words that Gandhi used in prayer; then we got up to leave." Thankful for the beauty of what had transpired, Gandhi gave Sue Bailey Thurman a basket of tropical fruit"[20] after the stirring "We Are Climbing Jacob's Ladder" was concluded.[21]

As word of the delegation's uplifting session with Gandhi trickled back across the Atlantic, an invitation to commune with the "world's greatest colored man" became a highly prized ticket for African Americans. Months after the meeting, Benjamin Mays and Channing Tobias had an opportunity to share ideas with Gandhi.[22] The focus was primarily nonviolent resistance, a preoccupation of Black America in decades to come.

The question of "untouchables" was the hallmark in relations between Black America and India, as Gandhi's remarks to the Thurman-led delegation suggested. As it turned out, a leading member of that group spent considerable time in the United States, on the outskirts of Harlem. B. R. Ambedkar emerged from a so-called lower caste to study in 1913 at Columbia University. He was merely one of a number of Indians who flocked to Manhattan at that time, a migration that included L. L. Rai. As Ambedkar recalled later, "An unusual number of students from my College [in Bombay were] coming to Columbia rather than going to some English university."[23] In addition to residing cheek by jowl with Negroes in Harlem, Ambedkar was able to accumulate three thousand books destined for India, but, he recalled, "As ill luck would have it, the steamer carrying [the load was] torpedoed and [the] whole of them went to the bottom of the sea." For Ambedkar, it was a "very grave loss" that even insights gained from living in New York could not replace.[24]

Like Gandhi, Ambedkar believed that Black America offered lessons for South Asia to heed. Renowned as the chief architect of the post-independence Indian Constitution, Ambedkar was "impressed by two important things" in the United States, writes Mohan Dass Namishray. The first was the Fourteenth Amendment to the U.S. Constitution, which sought to guarantee newly freed slaves equal protection under the law, and the second was the life of Booker T. Washington. These two steeled him as he absorbed the "insults, inhuman treatment, indignities, discrimination and humiliation inflicted upon him by an unjust, ruthless and caste-ridden society—the Hindus, Muslims, Parsis and the Christians. . . . [It] gave him such a shock such as he had never experienced before it and it forced him to think about untouchability, [which] left an indelible impression on his mind." Namishray, in comparing the basis for discrimination in India and the United States, has argued: "It was in the interests of the Brahmins to keep another group—the Sudras—suppressed in society in order to ensure their social and economic superiority," he writes. "So also, Europeans in the early Middle Ages formed no conclusions about their racial superiority . . . but later with increasing political domination and prospects for greater commerce and economic wealth, the nationalistic powers of Europe started justifying their political and economic designs upon the colonized with subtle theories of racial masterhood."[25]

Ambedkar regarded Washington as "one of the remarkable men America has produced, a man born in slavery but lifted by his own vision and perseverance to a position of leadership and power," and thus believed that the untouchables should not "forget the fate of the Negroes."[26]

Surely Ambedkar's experiences as a person of lower caste resonated in Black America, for, notes D. R. Jatava, "this was the man to whom his staff did not hand over office papers but threw them on his table. This was the man who was not considered fit for the principalship of a college, not because he lacked the required qualifications, but because of his low caste." And as they did for some in Black America, Ambedkar's dire experiences impelled him toward radical remedies. Thus, he advocated a "separate Muslim state," and, says Jatava, "the most consistent note in Ambedkar's life was his almost continuous onslaught on Hinduism and the caste system." The secular left did not escape his wrath, either, as he was "very critical both of Indian Socialists and the Communists."[27]

Ambedkar was uniquely positioned to empathize with the Negroes he encountered in Harlem, not least due to their shared experiences. His caste status meant that, when he was a child, barbers refused to cut his hair, and wayside cafes routinely denied him entrance. Unsurprisingly, in the museum devoted to his life in contemporary India, half of the books in the library are about figures such as Harlem's Malcolm X and the Black Panthers, who once trod the concrete canyons of Manhattan. Inspired by these Harlemites, a group of "untouchables" in India subsequently founded a group that emulated the Panthers.[28]

Yet, as Ambedkar also found, while Black Americans were engaging India, South Asians were being compelled to endure what had been constructed on the backs of those of African descent: white supremacy. In 1938, Majoor Dad Khan returned to India from California, and what he had to tell his fellow Communists in Bombay was not pretty. There are "two thousand Indians in California," he reported, and the "humiliations our countrymen have to suffer in this land of Democracy and Freedom [are awful]. . . . Indians are made to feel every minute of their existence that they belong to a slave nation." In other words, they were being treated as if they were part of Black America. It is "no wonder," said Khan in an analysis that escaped many who examined similar trends in Black America, that "every Indian becomes an ardent nationalist in America. . . . [The] Ghadr Party . . . formed in 1912 was the first organized expression of this nationalism. Its members played a heroic role during 1914–1917 when attempts were made in Punjab to bring about an armed insurrection by the Indian troops." It was no accident that this ideology was born—and borne—in the land that exalted white supremacy, Khan continued. Ghadar had a current membership of six hundred and published a regular journal in San Francisco. "Every party member pays 5% of his income," an earnest sign of intense commitment", Khan reported, and "Puran Singh, the President of the party, is one of the most respected Indians in America."[29]

As the clouds of war loomed ominously and Japan was seeking in jujitsu fashion to turn white supremacy into a deadly weapon against Washington and London, the concomitant flourishing of anti–Indian bigotry and Ghadar should have been a dire storm signal. But it was not. Instead, 1938 found the Indian writer K. A. Abbas in the United States, and he was as displeased as Khan with what he witnessed. Like Khan and most Indian intellectuals, Abbas leaned to the left, which made it easier for him to bond with a Black America that, unlike Euro-America, tipped in the same direction. "Like most young men in India," Abbas told the similarly inclined writer Upton Sinclair, "the practical socialism of Nehru appealed to me more than the mystical idealism of the Mahatma." But, it seems, Abbas's tête-à-tête in Pasadena with Sinclair was the only uncontroversial moment he encountered. For instance, when he traveled to Beverly Hills to appear on the radio station KMPC, Abbas said, he "took advantage of this opportunity to give a bit of my mind to Hollywood producers about . . . anti-Indian pictures." Just as Negroes were complaining about their cinematic depictions, Abbas tossed down the gauntlet, declaring, "You ought to be ashamed of yourself, Hollywood, for slandering a friendly people through your films." He had read the script of *Gunga Din* and was not amused, calling it a "most objectionable film and a libel on India" and saying that he planned to "warn [his] countrymen against it."

This was only the beginning of Abbas's travails. While taking a train from Seattle to Los Angeles, he spoke to a little boy who, like many he met, "possessed [an] amazing wealth of misinformation about India. . . . [The child] thought we all rode elephants, and kept snakes as pets, that all Indians above the age of twelve had seven wives each and legions of children. He was representative . . . of the great American public." It was during his trip from Los Angeles to New York City that Abbas "first became conscious of the Negro problem in America." On his first day on the train, he recalled, he went to the dining car for lunch and found it crowded:

> There was only one seat vacant on a table occupied by a buxom woman and her two children. The little boy, finding me looking about for a seat, pleasantly beckoned me to come and take my seat on their table. But the mother stopped him with an audible whisper. "No, not him. He is a nigger." The boy looked at me suspiciously, the occupants of other tables stopped eating to find what was the matter, a

suppressed bitterness was visible on the countenance of the Negro waiters and the manager of the dining car, obviously perturbed, hastened to whisper to the woman that I was not a Negro at all but a "Hindu." This seemed to have a soothing effect on the woman and she said, "Oh, that is different. You can sit here, young man."

But Abbas was displeased. "[I was] not going to take this lying down. I replied, 'But it is not different. Now I refuse to sit [at] the same table as you.'" He then stormed away. "The incident," said Abbas, sounding not altogether unhappy, "created quite a sensation. . . . [The] dining car manager came running [and said that] even if I was a Negro, I had [a] perfect legal right [to] sit [at] the same table whether the woman liked it or not. He was obviously afraid that I would report him to the higher authorities" (though it is not clear why and how those authorities would reprove him). The "race-conscious woman came from a southern state," Abbas discovered, and had "higher authorities" of her own to consult, which very well could trump any Abbas could muster.

For his part, Abbas "rarely found" African Americans to be "petty" or "over-sensitive," which was amazing, he said, in light of the routine abuse they were compelled to endure. Yet "some of them harbour a soul-searching bitterness," he reported. Moreover, "Like some of the Indian capitalists who saw in nationalism a means of their economic gains, this coloured bourgeois seeks to gain the Negro market by raising such slogans as 'boycott non-Negro shops.'" It was with that thought in mind that Abbas attended a "huge" gathering in Harlem of the pro–Tokyo Ethiopian World Federation. The speaker "invited us to join a coloured world front against all white people and said in so many words that when we gained ascendancy we should do [to] the white races exactly what they had done to us," he said. "This remark was greeted with tremendous applause." However, Abbas inferentially revealed the value of having pro-socialists among the "colored"—and suggested what would occur when their numbers diminished—when his turn to speak arrived and he dismissed such race-tinged talk. "At least a few voices" replied affirmatively to his provocative words, but this response was far from being unanimous in 1930s Harlem.

As had other South Asians before him, Abbas compared the status of "mulattos" in the United States to that of their counterparts in his homeland. "Again and again," he said with awe, "I would meet some boy or girl of pure white complexion, who would surprise me with the statement that he or she was a Negro. . . . [Y]et in our country there are thousands who would do anything to be called Europeans, Eurasians or, at least, Anglo-Indians!" Such episodes "taught me self-respect," said Abbas.[30]

The evident sympathy for African Americans expressed by Abbas suggests that Black Americans' solidarity with Gandhi and India was being reciprocated. Yet he was not alone. Krishnalal Shridharani was also in the United States in the 1930s. Born in 1912, Shridharani was roundish and well fed and favored cigars and three-piece suits from Brooks Brothers.[31] He was a graduate student at Columbia University who had accompanied Gandhi on the famed March to the Sea in 1930, a potent protest against the British salt tax. His presence in northern Manhattan, just a few blocks away from the office of the Fellowship of Reconciliation, a pioneer of the Civil Rights Movement that brought such leaders as James Farmer and Bayard Rustin to the fore, was to have a dynamic impact on the relationship between India and Black America. By the time Shridharani arrived in Morningside Heights, "Gandhi's work was rousing the imagination not only of white pacifists but also of some within the black community," says John D'Emilio. "For more than two decades the African American press had paid attention to Gandhi, [and] by the 1930s as the Indian independence struggle escalated, Gandhi's way was a regular topic of commentary in black newspapers." Du Bois was "directing the attention of his readers toward India, telling them: 'we are all one—we the Despised and Oppressed, the 'niggers' of England and America.'"[32]

Thus, it was no great surprise when Shridharani turned up in the late 1930s at the World Youth Congress at Vassar College in Poughkeepsie, New York. There, he recounted, a

> pious resolution was contrived which condemned the Nazi ferocity [in Europe. All of] the delegates, including the Indians, were agreed on that proposal, so far as it went, but the Hindus wanted to go further, [since] to the Hindu delegate the afflicted Jew was important because he was a part of a larger category of the persecuted minorities all over the world. Efforts were therefore made unofficially to include in that resolution cases of Negroes in the United States, untouchables in India, Indians in South Africa and minorities all over the world. One of the Indian delegates even suggested that there should be common cause among all persecuted minorities irrespective of creed or color, race or religion.

But then a delegate touched on a sore point that went to the core of the "whiteness" construction so critical to the social reality of the United States. He "went on to point out that it was a pity that the Jewish minority in the United States behaved no better than the Gentile majority when it came to dealing with the minority Negroes. He also added that the Jewish minority in South Africa had made common cause with the majority to exploit the Indian minority there."[33]

These comments should be read as an indictment of "whiteness" more than anything else and as an expression of delicate sensitivity to the plight of Negroes and how their degradation was of consequence for the Indian minority in places such as South Africa—and the United States. This sensitivity did not emerge via legerdemain but was a product of patient tending by far-sighted people in India and Black America. Near the same time that Indian delegates were engaged in intense negotiations in Poughkeepsie, their future prime minister Jawaharlal Nehru was being informed that he should "spare 5 minutes to read the enclosed article: it says simply what Negroamericans [are] saying 'all over the place. And when you have finished with it please have your secretary send it to some Indian papers for reprinting, it deserves publicity." In turn, plans were afoot to publish Nehru's autobiography in "the Negro Press."

What Nehru, the formidable intellectual, was being asked to peruse was a lengthy article by Du Bois, with Nehru's intermediary, the writer Cedric Dover, seeking to bring the two great thinkers together. Despite the delegations, despite the missions sent in both directions—Ahmadiyya and Christian alike—Du Bois expressed concern in the article that the "great difficulty of bringing about understanding, sympathy and co-operation between the Negroes of America and the peoples of India lies [in] the almost utter lack of knowledge which these two groups of people have of each other." Black Americans, most notably, had "almost no conception of the history of India," while the "knowledge which educated Indians have of the American Negro is chiefly confined to the conventional story spread by most white American and English writers"—that is, that "ignorant black savages were enslaved." Then there was the issue that dare not speak its name: "Negroes have long been enmeshed in a veil of sectarian Christianity," Du Bois observed, which bent any outreach toward South Asians in the direction of off-putting evangelizing. However, and perhaps more understandably, he said, "The Indian, also, finds it difficult to conceive of intelligent men who have no real knowledge of either Buddha or Mohammed." The two communities were "at opposite ends of the earth," which in itself hindered mutual solidarity and knowledge.

But that was not the only barrier. Du Bois pointed out that it was "difficult for an American Negro to get the English Government to visa his passport for a visit to India, and if the visa is obtained, usually it is under pledge to limit his words and activities. The accommodations offered by steamships often involve racial discrimination, while the cost of such trips is of course prohibitive to the mass of Indians and Negroes." When South Asians did make it to the United States, they met a "peculiar variation of the Colour Line. An Indian may be dark in colour, [but if he] dons his turban and travels in the South, he does not have to be subjected to the separate-car laws and other discriminations against Negroes." Such "public recognition of the fact that he is not a Negro may and often does flatter [the Indian's] vanity," said Du Bois with restraint, "so that he rather rejoices in this country at least he is not as other dark men are, but is classified with the whites." But, Du Bois also pointed out, "While an African Negro can become a citizen of the United States, an Indian of the highest caste cannot." Yet, he continued, "American Negroes have long considered that their destiny lay with the American people, [though this was] erroneous [in that this group] exists as representative of two hundred or more million Negroes in Africa, the West Indies and South America. . . . [Thus,] no matter what its destiny in America, its problems will never be settled until the problem of the relation of the white and coloured races is settled throughout the world." India has also had "temptation to stand apart from the darker peoples and seek her affinities among whites. She has long wished to regard herself as 'Aryan'," said Du Bois, no doubt recalling Bhagat Singh Thind's case in the U.S. Supreme Court, "rather than 'coloured.'"

Despite these formidable barriers, it would be naïve, thought Du Bois, to ignore the other side of the ledger—for example, the case of Rai, who, "during his enforced exile from his native land . . . gained wide acquaintance with American Negroes," or that of "Indians [who] appeared in the four or five Pan-African Congresses." Hence, although "American Negroes" had "in their own internal colour lines the plain shadow of a caste system," Du Bois concluded, this meant that learning from India was a must and that "the problem of the Negroes . . . remains a part of the world-wide clash of colour."[34]

After scanning Du Bois's article, the exceedingly busy Nehru, then seeking to hold an organization—and a nation—together, wrote from Allahabad in the spring of 1936 expressing hearty gratitude for the article. "I should like to write something about the Negroes if I have the time," Nehru wrote, but, alas, "time is lacking."[35] Later, the head of the Indian National Congress's Foreign Department pledged to "pay particular attention to the Negro movements for freedom. . . . Pandit Jawaharlal Nehru has kindly drawn my attention to an article by Du Bois."[36]

It was not just Du Bois who was reaching out to Nehru's organization. In 1936, Robert O. Jordan of the Ethiopian Pacific Movement in Harlem told Nehru: "We, the coloured peoples in the West Indies and the United States, highly appreciate the wonderful spirit of the Indian people." Seeking solidarity, he added: "We, the coloured people in the Western Hemisphere, are suffering the same as our brothers in India and we hope it won't be long before the dark people of the world will get away from the [yoke] of the white man."[37] Breathing rhetorical fire, Jordan then forwarded a letter he had sent to U.S. Secretary of State Cordell Hull complaining about Italy's invasion of Ethiopia and warning, "The hand writing is on the wall. There is still a little time left to save the white man's civilization. No doubt you are aware that it will be very unpleasant for the entire universe if you compel the dark race to step in and prepare a new civilization. The dark race has been driven to the extremities."[38] The League of Nations was informed that it should do something about this aggression, or "We will be compelled to call every dark man, woman and child in the entire universe into *united action*." The international community was thereby notified that, "if we are compelled to this extreme movement, no one can foretell the disaster that will occur."[39]

An ambitious Black Nationalist, Jordan was seeking a strategic entente with the Indian National Congress, praying that "the relationship between our organization and the Great Nationalist movement of India will grow 100%."[40] To that end, Jordan strained to indict Washington, so as to win the Indian National Congress over to this view. A typical missive in the fall of 1936 informed Swaraj Bhawan of the Indian National Congress about the persecution of the Scottsboro defendants, then appended the idea that "the condition of the United States of America in regard [to] the colored people [is] worse than in India, China or any other part of the world." The "feeling of Nationalism has arisen since [Italy's] Ethiopian quest," he wrote, because it has been "discovered that the entire white world is out to destroy the darker people." Although this was a Pan-African phenomenon, in the United States, "sentiment" along this line was so profound, Jordan declared, that an "extra police force is placed into every colored district." He referred to a recent revolt in Harlem, then said, "The colored people are thirsty for freedom. I'm afraid that our so-called white master will not be able to hold us any longer. . . . White people receive relief [during this Great Depression and] colored have to work ten hours a day to receive just one meal." One response Jordan suggested was a "commercial treaty" between his forces and those of the Indian National Congress.[41]

Jordan's intervention did not go unanswered. Rammanchar Lohia of Congress proclaimed, "From the correspondence that we are carrying on with the coloured peoples and their representatives in different parts of the world one supreme fact arrests our attention. . . . Ethiopian heroism in resisting Italian invasion seems to have produced remarkable changes in the outlook of the coloured peoples, [for they are] no longer prepared to play the second fiddle to white [folks]." Lohia enclosed a clipping from the Indian press that, he noted, "deal[s] with your movement. This news item was given wide publicity."[42]

Expressing a similar vein of solidarity, George Padmore, writing on behalf of the Pan-African Federation in London, told Lohia that "national sections" of his transatlantic organization chose to "pledge our whole-hearted support," not least since "our enemy is a common foe." The "united front of the colonial peoples [has] long been our dream," he said, although we are "so engrossed . . . with the immediate day-to-day struggle of our people that we have not had the opportunity" to express this sentiment concretely.[43] In his own hand, Nehru made it clear that Congress "heartily reciprocate[s] your sentiments. . . . [W]e have the warmest feelings for the African peoples in Africa and elsewhere and follow their efforts to emancipate themselves with every sympathy."[44] Apparently, so much correspondence from Africa and its diaspora was reaching Congress that its ranks were instructed to "remember always to write Negro with a capital letter," a touchy point particularly for those in North America.[45]

The relationship was bearing fruit, as shown in August 1936, when the influential Claude Barnett of the Associated Negro Press declared, "We will be glad to serve as a distributive agency for news items from India or elsewhere."[46] Cedric Dover, the recipient of this good news was so "childishly excited" by the letter that he told Lohia, "I am sending it to you by air mail instead of including it—more economically—with my weekly sending."[47] At this juncture, Congress was also in close touch with such opinion molders among Negroes as Charles Johnson of Fisk University,[48] James Ford of the Communist Party,[49] and Max Yergan of the YMCA, who by that time was residing in Johannesburg and representing the All African Convention.[50] Subsequently, the peripatetic Yergan wrote to Lohia from New York City on behalf of the Council on African Affairs, whose members included Channing Tobias, Ralph Bunche, Paul Robeson, and Mordecai Johnson. He reminded Nehru that he had "had the privilege and pleasure of meeting" him in India in 1929 and again offered solidarity and mutual support.[51] Yergan, who wore many hats, including that of the communist-oriented National Negro Congress, also briefed his Indian comrades on the brutal killings of Haitians in the Dominican Republic in 1937.[52]

In turn, Lohia informed Yergan that "some of our newspapers are vitally interested in the Negro race, its problem and its awakening. One of our important journals is bringing out an international number and has selected 'Negro Awakening' as one of the topics with which it intends to deal."[53] Dover, as the broker in the relationship between India and Black America, was pressing for "Coloured Unity" of the broadest sort. "I suggested to an Indian friend that we should try to organize a meeting of the coloured delegates [to a global peace conference to] discuss the prospects of an united front," he said, "but I found that he had already been busy arranging such a discussion.

So had a Negro and other comrades. [The] same idea had occurred to most of us." Soon, he reported, "[we were] sitting around a table drafting a joint memorandum which was submitted to the [Indian National] Congress after signature by Indians, Chinese, Indonesians, American Negroes, West Indians, South Africans . . . and a Tunisian." This was a "partial answer to those who believe that 'local loyalties' will prevent the progress of coloured amalgamation," he noted. It also showed that "we would not divorce ourselves from the Left Wing ideologies and the international proletariat in so doing. In fact, the growth of socialist elements [is] implicit [in our activity]."[54]

Dover informed Nehru that he would forward "some source materials derived from my travels and contacts during the last three months in the States for developing relations with American Negroes. I have found among them a tremendous interest in India."[55] This interest was bilateral, as shown when Lohia contacted Roger Baldwin of the American Civil Liberties Union on "lynching and the law," as reflected in the Scottsboro case.[56] Du Bois captured the essence of this relationship when he told Gandhi, "We are fighting a battle in some respects similar to that which the people of India are carrying on."[57]

Lohia was simply expressing a deepening interest within Congress about the pressing matter of racist discrimination, a phenomenon that did not afflict African Americans solely but had assumed global reach. Nehru's own "activism against racial discrimination dated back to the early 1920s," according to Dennis Kux. "Serving in his first public office, as chairman of the local government in the home city of Allahabad, Nehru in 1923 sponsored a resolution deploring the treatment of Indians in [British] colonies and the United States."[58]

In the United States itself, Dover concluded in 1937, "The Negroes are sensing their affinity with other coloured peoples. In Paul Robeson, for example, the feeling of cultural affinity is so strong that he [is] convinced that a Negro could get more out of Moscow or Peking University than from Oxford or Cambridge. And because of this feeling he has been able to learn Russian, like other Negroes I know, with comparative ease, and prefers it to the English or German language for artistic expression." After World War II, the affinity between Moscow and New Delhi became a staple of the emergent Cold War, and radicals such as Robeson sought to solidify the tie, a process that was made difficult by the persecution they faced from the U.S. authorities. Dover, one of the few who was conversant with the situations in both India and Black America, was among these radicals. He also held Du Bois in high esteem, asserting that "the idea of a coloured alliance dominates Afroamerican literature, how strongly Du Bois' *Dark Princess* alone will show." Further, Dover argued, "Du Bois did not exaggerate when he wrote in his

Darkwater that wild and awful as this shameless war was, it is nothing to compare with that fight for freedom which black and brown and yellow men must and will make unless their oppression and humiliation and insult at the hands of the White World cease. The Dark World is going to submit to its present treatment just as long as it must and not one moment longer." Dover highlighted the "ebullient Marcus Garvey" and his remark that "was not merely oratorical"—that is, when "he shouted at a colossal gathering of Negroes the conviction that the 'bloodiest of all wars is yet to come, when Europe will match its strength against Asia, and that will be the Negroes' opportunity to draw the sword for Africa's redemption.'"[59] This idea was not unique to Garvey. In fact, it was becoming a consensus in Black America. "Once there is unification and reasonable oneness of purpose between Japan and China," then between those nations with India, and finally between "Yellow Asia and Black Africa," said *The Crisis* in 1933, a "new era will open in the world and the impossible domination of one mad race will end."[60]

But it was not only Du Bois and Garvey—as influential as they were among Black Americans—who looked to India for inspiration. Others also saw themselves as part of this vast and densely inhabited land in Asia that contained an indivisible "colored" population. In the run-up to World War II, Gandhi and India were attracting ever increasing interest among a broad range of commentators within Black America. This was notably true of the *Pittsburgh Courier*, the newspaper of record in Black America,[61] though it was far from being alone in maintaining this almost obsessive interest.[62] Robert Vann, publisher of the *Courier*, summarized the sentiments of many when he announced in 1930: "The eyes of the entire world are on India. . . . [If the] Indians do succeed in spite of their myriad conflicting castes and prejudices in launching a great revolution, it will sound the death knell of the British Empire, the foremost exploiter of black labor in the world. . . . [A]ltogether, the work of Gandhi tends to make the future look rather bright for the dark peoples of the world."[63]

8

THE UNITED STATES VERSUS INDIA

I write," said the Indian writer Kanhaya Lal Gauba, "that the truth about American life may be made known as fearlessly and as fully as Miss Mayo has made known what she only believed to be true about India."[1] Gauba was referring to Katherine Mayo and her infamous 1927 tome, *Mother India*, which painted a devastating portrait of India and, perhaps not accidentally, presented a rationale for British colonialism. For as solidarity between India and Black America was surging, challenging the very bases on which Jim Crow and the British Empire were predicated, advocates of white supremacy and the empire were not resting supine. Mayo's book was a gauntlet tossed down at the feet of the India of Gandhi and Nehru and was meant to disrupt their ties in the United States—ties that were becoming ever more important as world war again loomed.

As Mayo put it, "The British Administration of India, be it good, bad or indifferent, has nothing whatever to do with the conditions [afflicting a land] nearly half as large [in land mass] as the United States." No, she argued passionately, "inertia, helplessness, lack of initiative and originality, lack of staying power and of sustained loyalties, sterility of enthusiasm, weakness of life-vigour itself—all are traits that truly characterize the Indian not only today, but of long-past history." The "huge population" was not only "illiterate" but was "loving its illiteracy," she said. Moreover, Mayo threaded repeated references to U.S. colonialism in the Philippines into the text and did not often refer to this island chain positively, which tended to suggest that colonialism should be the way of the world for those of a darker hue. Because of the possibility of Indians' migration to North America, she believed, India represented a vector of disease for the United States, not least since "Hindus, anywhere, dispense with latrines." This alleged propensity toward disease, "added to infant marriage, sexual recklessness and venereal infections, further lets down the bars to physical and mental miseries."[2] Mayo's words were all the more potent for as she acknowledged, "What does the average American actually know about India? That Mr. Gandhi lives there; also tigers."[3]

Mayo's book was wildly popular in the United States, and in many ways it was the portrait of India recognized by all too many on this side of the Atlantic. She followed the book with another popular work of questionable analysis, *The Face of Mother India*, which also was designed to appeal to U.S. audiences with its recitation of little-known points such as that Elihu Yale, a native of Boston and governor of Madras from 1687 to 1691, had his name given to the university in New Haven, Connecticut, not least "because of his gift of funds, earned as an officer in the East India Company's service, making possible the completion of the University's first building."[4] In some ways, this second book, published as Thurman and Mays were traveling to India to confer with Gandhi and Nehru, was more damaging than the first. Its publication signaled that solidarity between India and Black America—which was gaining in strength and intensity in the Depression decade—would not be allowed to proceed unimpeded. If Mayo did not exist, she would have had to be invented to meet the formidable challenge she sought to face down.

The publication—and popularity—of Mayo's books was symptomatic of the heightened profile of India in the United States. Similarly, the sharp riposte to Mayo by Gauba similarly suggested contrary trends. In her tellingly titled *Uncle Sham*, Gauba incisively identified the flaws of the United States, which was already beginning to be seen as an epicenter of modernity and "civilization." The inference was that if the United States had demonstrable weaknesses, then certainly India could be allowed to have them, too, and this liability should no more serve as a bar to independence than it should bar the sovereignty exercised by Washington.

The flaw on which Gauba focused insistently was that involving "The Negro," the subject of an entire chapter. She termed the treatment of Black Americans the "most grave and perplexing of domestic issues" and "the largest blot on the institutions of the American democracy." The so-called Negro problem was "not of the Negro's making," she noted. "No group in the United States is less responsible for its existence than the Negroes." Yet the plight of this despised minority was indeed horrendous, she pointed out, as Black Americans were "much more liable to arrest than whites," although their "crime rate [was] exaggerated," a function of the fact that "fewer Negroes than whites escape arrest and conviction." Indeed, the "list of the atrocities perpetrated in the domains of Uncle Sam's civilized government, or even a partial list as revealed in various courts, would take more space than is available here," Gauba wrote, because "barbarism and mob violence are promoted [in the United States]." This slashing indictment—made all the more riveting by Gauba's decision to target the United States rather than the colonial power Great Britain—was capped off by a book cover featuring an ugly, menacing, hunched-over Uncle Sam holding a mask with a friendly face.[5]

Gauba was not alone. To discredit Mayo, the *Bombay Chronicle* repeatedly referred to the depredations of the Ku Klux Klan and its assault on Negroes and to "other sensitive issues in America."[6] And these were just a few of the many responses to Mayo's work,[7] although none raised as sharply as Gauba's the issue of African Americans. L. L. Rai, for example, vividly described the lynching and burning of blacks as a way to express scorn for the idea that India's flaws somehow prevented it from deserving independence.[8] Further, Rai argued, "Belgian atrocities in the Congo 'depict white civilization in its true colors.'"[9] Mayo, he said, was an "agent of the British government."[10] (Actually, she was treasurer of the British Apprentice Club, based at the Hotel Chelsea on 23rd Street in Manhattan, an Anglophile group founded in 1921.[11])

Writing in the left-wing *New Masses*, Agnes Smedley referred to Mayo as the author of the "Bootlickers' handbook of India" before turning her attention to "lynching [and the] miserable social conditions of the Negroes." Until "two centuries ago," Smedley argued, "India was the richest and most prosperous land on earth, [but] today [it is the] poorest land on earth." This certainly was London's fault, she stated. After all, what if Japan were to "conquer and establish its rule in America?" she asked in a jab that must have hit close to home, given the prevailing global tensions. Something similar to the fate of India would unfold, she suggested.[12] Continuing this transatlantic analogy, another reviewer suggested that Mayo was depicting the "whole nation [of India] as a community of thieves"—in other words, that she was painting Indians the way African Americans were portrayed in the United States.[13]

To have their predicament emblazoned in print by relative strangers was heartening to African Americans; it was a harbinger of the glare of the global spotlight that was to do so much to alter the trajectory of white supremacy in the wake of World War II and the rise of the Cold War. At the time, however, Mayo's démarche received considerably more attention. It was a runaway bestseller and received huge publicity around the world.[14] The somewhat undistinguished and frumpy Mayo became something of a public figure as a result.[15] Participants in a discussion at Manhattan's Town Hall referred to her work as the "Uncle Tom's Cabin" of India,[16] although instead of being the woman who helped to start a war and end an oppressive social system, à la

Harriet Beecher Stowe, Mayo helped to perpetuate colonialism. As the *Houston Chronicle* put it, Mayo was "noted for throwing the searchlight on conditions among the darker races of the world with a seeming intent to demonstrate just why they should have no objections to the white race ruling over them."[17] This approach was not helpful as the Atlantic powers skidded inexorably toward war and needed the backing of the formally colonized (India) and the formerly enslaved (Black America).

The sardonic assessments of Mayo were not far from the mark. Writing about the Philippines, an early interest, Mayo observed that the "first known inhabitants [there] were a race of woolly-headed pygmies—little black flitting creatures close to the bottom of the human scale."[18] She also wrote a story about a "bad nigger" about to be lynched by "the good old Pennsylvania Dutch" in a chilling, detailed, and explicit fashion that suggested a verisimilitude difficult to obtain from studying dusty court records.[19]

This may help to explain why African Americans, among others in the United States, sought earnestly to transform nascent anticolonial sentiment into progressivism. After all, the United States itself was born as the result of such a rebellion. Du Bois, for example, was a member of the National Council of Friends of Freedom for India, which, contrary to Mayo's warnings about Indians' admission, sought to "demand the right of asylum for political refugees from India" and "to present the case for the independence of India."[20] It was Du Bois, in his capacity as a representative of the International Committee for Political Prisoners, who argued passionately in the fall of 1931 that the "trial for treason now taking place at Cawnpore, India [and, more specifically, the] charges against M. N. Roy" should be resisted. Roy was "well-known in circles friendly to the Indian cause in the United States," and it would be unfortunate if he were to be convicted, since the punishment "carries with it the death penalty."[21] Again, this solidarity was not limited to Du Bois and his NAACP. *Negro World*, the journal of his erstwhile sparring partner Marcus Garvey, staunchly pleaded for "U.S. citizenship" for a number of Indian patriots, since "deportation means death because of [their] fight for India's freedom."[22]

One of the most potent lobbies on behalf of India was the YMCA, the association that had dispatched Benjamin Mays, Channing Tobias, and others to the subcontinent. In remarks on CBS radio in 1938, one speaker touted the "Y" by noting that "such nationally known athletes as [William] DeHart Hubbard, Eddie Tolan, Edward Gordon and Jesse Owens grew up as members of the Boys Department of the YMCA," not to mention the influential publisher Robert Vann. "In fact," listeners heard, "to call the name of prominent Negroes who have been served by the YMCA or are at present in the directorship of its services would be to include a large part of the Negro Who's Who in America."[23] This was not far wrong. As Channing Tobias put it 1932, in a peroration broadcast by NBC radio on the "contribution of the YMCA to the progress of the American Negro," the YMCA "ministers to the spiritual life of the rising leadership of the Negro in 140 schools and colleges through student associations and in 275 public high schools." Moreover, "Four college presidents once served as 'Y' Secretaries," he remarked, including Mordecai Johnson of Howard University.[24]

For a long time, the YMCA had been sending African Americans far and wide. One of them was Max Yergan. Yergan's multiple skills were put to good use during his travels in India.[25] It was well that he did, for beyond the confines of Black America, the U.S. movement in solidarity with India was not as energetic and well organized as it should have been. "I regret that not more work is being done here in New York for the cause of India," the activist J. T. Sunderland confided to Rai in 1925. "[W]e have been compelled to largely give up organized propaganda for lack of funds." Further, he noted, the Hindustan Association of America, a student group, had to retrench because of lack of funds.[26]

Sunderland himself provides some indication of why the pro-independence movement was encountering such difficulties in the United States. Despite the clear prominence of pro-independence sentiment in Black America, in 1935 he did not include one Negro in his long list of "Eminent Americans Whom India Should Know." To his credit, though, he did acknowledge that London "claims she is ruling the people of India for their benefit." It is "interesting to recall," he added drolly, "that in the days of American slavery slave-owners made exactly the same claim regarding those they held in bondage."[27]

Despite his evident inability to galvanize a powerful pro-independence movement, Sunderland was an articulate advocate for the cause. Certainly, he could not ignore the key strategic question: how the cause of Black America intersected with that of India. "If and when any of us in America protest against British tyranny," he said, "the reply is sometimes made by Englishmen and not without reason: 'physician heal thyself.' . . . Would you Americans like it if we Englishmen protested against your Negro lynchings[?]" Sunderland did not flinch and thereby revealed inferentially why these two noble causes were attracted to each other. "If such questions were asked Americans oftener than they are," he argued (suggesting, perhaps, that he saw "Americans" and white as interchangeable), "they would set us wondering whether it would not be wise for us to substitute for our glass-houses other houses less fragile. . . . [The] truth is [that] the world is one in all its deeper and real interests. Every nation is related to every other, and all are related to the whole." As Sunderland saw it, "The possession and forcible rule of India by Great

Britain has probably been the most powerful single influence in the modern world, against democracy, against just government based on the will of the peoples governed and in support of autocracy, imperialism, government by force." This meant that freedom for India perforce would be a boon for Black America.[28]

Later, as Japan moved toward waging war on the British Empire and the United States, the *New Age* of Madras, the organ of India's Communist Party, received a letter from the famed writer Theodore Draper on behalf of the left-wing Manhattan based journal *New Masses*. In it, Draper noted that *New Masses* had "republished most of Pandit Jawaharlal Nehru's speech at the Faizpur meeting of the Indian National Congress. To my knowledge," he said stunningly, "this is the first voice from India in the American press in years."[29]

The Indian national Taraknath Das was similarly disenchanted. "I must tell you we feel much disappointed," he told Sunderland in 1925, "about our former 'friends' (?) in America; many of them have seen fit even not to answer letters written by us."[30] It was true that Sunderland was an exception. The "snowy-haired upstanding Poughkeepsie clergyman," as *Time* magazine described Sunderland, had "sold in thousands" a book about India intended as a refutation of Mayo's broadside.[31] And although in 1925 Sunderland was lamenting the decline of the movement in solidarity with India in the United States, the liberal icon Oswald Garrison Villard was being monitored by London as he addressed a banquet in Manhattan on behalf of the Hindustan Association of America and the India Society. Villard, according to an official report, "spoke slowly from notes, saying British rule in India was a terrible crime but that Americans treated the Negroes just as badly!" The "faces of cultured Indians [were] a study during these remarks," said the London representative who made the report. He was obviously unimpressed: "It is now half past ten and no one has said anything interesting, except perhaps Villard, who was obviously a crank."[32]

But one man, even one as talented as Sunderland or, apparently, as interesting as Villard, could not do the work that a community could—an African American community, for example. Although he was disappointed about pro-independence activism generally, Das recognized that there was a segment of the United States that merited attention and care. His spouse, he informed Sunderland, had written "a long article for [a journal in] Madras on the subject of the Negroes in America and untouchability in India."[33] Why this concern captured the attention of Das and his wife was exposed when they traveled to Manhattan in 1926 and were "refused at many hotels . . . because [the hotels] would not take Hindus. Also," added Mary Das angrily, "when I went out to look for an apartment, we were told they 'would not rent to Orientals.'" This was rancid "race prejudice" of a sort that any Negro could well understand.[34] Thus, largely scorned by the Euro-American majority and seeing the similarity of circumstance, Indians turned to Black America.

The Indian literary giant Tagore, for example, read *The Crisis* and, he said, found himself "deeply [in] sympathy with the broad human outlook which animates and illustrates its pages."[35] Similarly, in 1937 *Independent India*, edited in Bombay by the renowned left-winger M. N. Roy, happily published a "message [from the] world famous Negro singer" Paul Robeson, who informed readers there why "artists cannot be neutral."[36]

Yet perhaps because of his unfortunate encounters in Manhattan, it was Taraknath Das who repeatedly took up the cudgels on behalf of Black America, instructing his Indian audience about U.S. Negroes' plight and positing their example as worthy of study in India. "Lincoln once said," he asserted in 1927, "that a nation cannot and should not remain half-slave and half-free." Well, he continued, "If India is to become a nation and not a slave-holding nation, economic and social slavery imposed upon the 65 millions of the so-called 'Untouchables' by the upper class and landed aristocracy of the Hindus must be removed, [since] the lot of the 'Untouchable' Hindus is no better than that of the 'Negro slaves' of America."[37] Likewise, the Madras-based *Indian Social Reformer* deployed the stirring words of the abolitionist William Lloyd Garrison as its motto.[38] This was a trend. For example, according to J. N. Uppal, Gandhi "took considerable pains to acquaint [his] readers . . . with [Henry David] Thoreau's life and work, bringing into focus his role in the movement for abolition of slavery in the United States."[39] The U.S. diplomat Chester Bowles was struck by the fact that, when Gandhi was jailed in 1902 in South Africa, he "chose to wear the same prison garb as the Negro inmates. This is said to have included a plain white cap, which later became famous in India as the 'Gandhi Cap', the badge of the independence movement."[40] Such touches were endearing to African Americans.

It was such confluence and compatibility of interest between India and Black America that compelled two South Asian scholars to conclude, with wonder, that "no case appears to have been recorded of an American black of any standing in the community having defended British rule in India or attacked the attitude of the Indian National Congress." Taking this a step further, it would be equally difficult to find an "American black [with no] standing" who backed London's position.[41] In return, Indian intellectuals continuously reproached the United States for its racist practices and, arguably, contributed to a tidal wave of global public opinion that caused Washington to retreat. Writing for Rai's Lahore-based *The People*, one journalist told his audience that a "great opportunity lies before the United States. To her has been given the task of unifying into one nation, a great brotherhood, people from all ends of the earth." Yet during a "recent visit to America, which lasted over three months," he wrote in 1926, he was not pleased by what he had witnessed. "This discrimination against the Asiatics raises a vital issue, [but] it is difficult to get at its underlying causes for Americans are rather reticent about the subject."[42]

As war with Japan approached, many informed Indians had less than warm feelings about the United States. Washington's man in India, Thomas Murray Wilson, noted in his diary months before the Japanese attack on Pearl Harbor that "Sir Girja [Shankar Bajpai] asked me if he should take his cook with him to the United States—also if I thought they would have trouble because of any prejudice as to color." Wilson, taken aback, replied: "I tried to quiet his fears. [as Sir Girja and his wife were] light in color [and] would never be taken [as having] African blood, and that I believe is where the trouble if any would arise."[43]

There were other reasons beyond similarity of circumstance for the solidarity between India and Black America that often set both apart from dominant elites in the United States. In 1940, the prominent U.S.-based pro-independence activist and clergyman John Haynes Holmes, leader of the American League for India's Freedom, found it "incredible that there should be any discussion pro and con about our [organization's] joining in a public meeting in protest against Nehru's imprisonment. What are we in existence for if not for things of this kind?" But other issues were involved that pointed to why India often looked to Black America. "We have Communist influence at work among us," Holmes commented suspiciously. "I regard this as an intolerable thing, and, if my suspicion is justified, I shall have to withdraw [from the coalition because these] Communist activities among us [are] utterly disreputable and wicked." Holmes's American League for India's Freedom was not without African American influence: Du Bois, Tobias, William Pickens of the NAACP were among those affiliated with the organization. But Holmes was the chairman, and he wielded more influence. Because the African American community generally was not as bothered as other constituencies were about Communist influence, it was more in tune with Nehru, who likewise was not opposed to aligning with Communists, be they of the Indian variety or otherwise.[44] Holmes, a dedicated anti–Communist—and an enthusiastic supporter of the eugenics movement, which tended to believe that population growth among those of a darker hue was problematic[45]—was not necessarily reassured when the moderate NAACP leader (a frequent foil to Du Bois) Walter White "hasten[ed]" to tell "Dear John" that, "on behalf of Mr. [Thurgood] Marshall and the Association, . . . neither he nor the Association 'gave support to the Communist locals.'"[46]

White had to tread carefully in dealing with Holmes, because he was influential within the NAACP, too. In his memoir, Holmes noted, a bit modestly, that the NAACP was a "movement in which I had a part." Waxing nostalgic, he wrote, "I can seen now the dingy little office—a table, a few chairs, a feeble electric light—in which we met for our deliberations." Indeed, he asserted, "My part in the founding of the NAACP and in close affiliation with its work, constitutes one of the chief prides and joys of my life." The problem was that Holmes's influence—notably, his hawkish monitoring of relations with "Reds"—was not necessarily helpful to the NAACP ties to Nehru's Indian National Congress, which was not similarly inclined.[47]

Moreover, as leaders of the India League of America announced just before the United States embarked on war with Japan, "Rigid war censorship has once more banished India from the American press." In the United States, they warned, "powerful forces [are] at work today . . . to misrepresent the situation in India and to discredit the India National Congress."[48] It was only in 1938, in any case, that the India League of America was founded, and, according to the British leader Sir Alfred Watson, it had "become the most articulate and widely known organization" on this front. Watson was concerned that "the American people take a closer interest in Indian affairs than do [British] citizens, [but] that interest has been perverted, [as] the average American believes he is sympathizing with a downtrodden people." But, he countered, "We are trying to deal with India as America has dealt with the Philippines"—not an attitude likely to curry favor with African Americans, the sector most likely to "take a closer interest in Indian affairs."[49]

If Sir Alfred had been paying closer attention as war beckoned, he might have noticed that relations between India and Black America were deepening to the point that cultural and political exports from the former were being implanted in the latter. At the end of the Depression decade, the Fellowship of Reconciliation (FOR), a group of activists and students with ties to the University of Chicago, began studying nonviolent direct action. "All of us were afire with the idea of Gandhian non-violence," recalled Bernice Fisher, a member OF FOR. "The cell's members studied and debated, chapter by chapter, Shridharani's *War without Violence*, a description of Gandhi's philosophy and methods, and they discussed ways of adapting Gandhism to the struggle against American racism." Subsequently, Bayard Rustin, another African American activist who was to play a leading role in the following decades, "called for whites to imitate Gandhi's attitudes toward the untouchables and to identify with oppressed blacks by becoming an integral part of the Negro community."[50]

Thus, at the moment that Sir Alfred was expressing concern about U.S. attitudes toward the "downtrodden" of India, FOR—which was to go on to play a huge role in the battle against Jim Crow—was contemplating the establishment of a "Harlem Ashram." FOR was "seriously considering as a special service project the creation of a cooperative living center for the dozen or so boys of sixteen to eighteen who 'graduate' each year from the 'Colored Orphanage' in Riverdale and are then usually set adrift with appalling human wastage. Some of these boys have joined the army, quite against their will, as the only visible open door." Strikingly, FOR noted in early 1941, "Our present group of about a dozen prospective members includes three Negroes and a Hindu."[51] From this tiny acorn of an ashram was to grow a mighty oak of opposition to Jim Crow that would be manifested most dramatically during the rise to prominence of Martin Luther King Jr.

Eventually, the Harlem Ashram was established as an experiment in cooperative living at 2013 Fifth Avenue. By the summer of 1941, it was already leaving its imprint on a community that was reeling from the withering effects of poverty, racism, and disease. "We represent a group of Negroes and whites," the ashram's leaders told the YMCA, "some of them religious and social workers, who have been studying weekly, for the past few months, such social evils as discrimination. Ours has not been an academic interest. . . . Some of us, having lived since December in this cooperative fellowship in Harlem, have come into close contact with the raw wounds made by race discrimination in the spirits of our Negro brothers, and have been moved, somewhat as Lincoln was when he first saw a slave auction to say, 'by the grace of God, this evil must go!" The ashram's leaders confronted the YMCA because some of their supporters had been "told of the practice of the downtown YCMA's in excluding Negroes from their dormitories and facilities in general." Specifically, "Mr. Homer Nicholas, recent President of the Abyssinian Baptist Church and a member of our group was refused a room in Sloane House YMCA and was told in a matter-of-fact way, 'we send *you fellows* up the Harlem Y.'" Such a policy "bristles with inconsistencies," they said. "Here is a *Christian* association violating the basic tenet of Christian brotherhood."[52]

This was embarrassing to the YMCA, which had its own pretensions when it came to antiracism, and it was denunciations such as the ashram's that eventually drove it to reform. The YMCA knew full well that it had real problems in the realm of racism. The 1937 YMCA conference in Mysore that featured Tobias and Mays acknowledged that, in the United States, there was a real question whether

men and boys [should] be admitted to full membership privilege regardless of race[.] The answer to many American associations is no. The exceptions are generally in towns having a small non-Caucasian population. . . . [In] some Pacific Coast associations, Negroes [are] more welcome than Orientals, the former being few in number and the latter many. The colour bar is drawn against Mexicans and Filipinos in the South and on the Pacific Coast, almost as strictly as against Negroes. Even in the northern states, a British Indian who is a stranger is likely to be denied full membership privileges, on the assumption that he is a Negro. Hence, Indians sometimes wear a turban to signify their race.[53]

This sheds light on one more reason that the ashram's leaders chose to question the YMCA: If they could erode bias there, it would be beneficial not only for Black America but for India, as well.

Such initiatives, according to the ashram's leaders, "providentially" attracted a new member to Harlem: Bayard Rustin, who, as FOR Youth Secretary for New York state, spent a most profitable summer with Friends Work Camp in Puerto Rico, gleaning valuable information about "Yankee imperialism." This was critically important, they noted in October 1941, "since the [Roosevelt] Administration seems to be [bent] upon a 'union now' of British and American imperialism, and even speaks of policing the world for the next century." Moreover, "as a Negro, [Rustin had] entrée to the people of the islands as whites have not." His arrival was hopeful news, along with the ashram's relocation to a new home at 179th Street and Boston Road, only a block from Bronx Park.[54]

At this point, James Farmer, a burly black activist with a booming and stentorian voice, penned an important memo to A. J. Muste of FOR outlining an ambitious "Brotherhood Mobilization" plan. "Ironically enough," he wrote, "the present unfortunate circumstances brought on by the war afford an excellent setting for immediate spade-work in this direction." It was true that the attack by Japan, until then viewed in influential circles in India and Black America as leading a V-shaped assault formation on white supremacy, created enormous strains in London and Washington. Both powers had reason to fear that, unless timely concessions were made, they would face incipient revolts that could handicap the war effort. So Farmer was on to something when he set out what may have seemed to be the overly ambitious goal of seeking to "abolish Jim Crow." Such an approach, Farmer asserted, led "naturally into a study of the Gandhian movement," and, he added, "This quest has been served mightily by the clear analysis in Shridharani's *War without Violence*." Ironically, Farmer mused, the coming of war meant that "new vistas have been opened, new horizons revealed."[55]

So moved, the Harlem Ashram launched a major direct-action project in 1942: a two-week Interracial Pilgrimage from New York to Washington in which fourteen persons walked 240 miles to dramatize the anti-lynching and anti–poll-tax bills that were then before Congress.[56] As the South Asian activist and intellectual Haridas T. Muzumdar recalled later, it was the Reverend Jay Holmes Smith who, "in association with me and other friends, founded the interracial Ashram in Harlem" that pioneered in bringing the tactics and strategy of nonviolent direct action to the highways and byways of the United States.[57] What was driving the ashram—and, ultimately, FOR— was clear. "The urgency of the problem of race discrimination in our country is beyond question," said the FOR in 1942. "Some of us who live close to racial cross-currents cannot escape the sense of being near the edge of a volcano." As war with Japan accelerated, the United States ran the risk of an eruption of racism that, like molten lava, would burn to ashes the nobility of the war effort.[58]

Pauli Murray recognized this more than most. Born in Baltimore in 1910 "within the same 24-hour period in which Leo Tolstoy . . . died," as she once put it, she had grievously direct experience with U.S. racism: Around 1923, her father was "murdered by a guard in [a] hospital who was a Polish immigrant. . . . [H]e beat him to death. Struck him from behind. It was a very gruesome murder." That experience, however, had a different effect than one might suspect. "The total impact it had on my life," Murray insisted, "was to seek an alternative to violence." This led her inexorably to India. "I was probably one of the earlier students of the Gandhi technique," she asserted, along with Bayard Rustin, James Farmer, and a handful of others.[59] "I was a young socialist at that time," she said years later, and ideologically there was "no place for me to go except Norman Thomas," the perennial Socialist Party presidential hopeful. "I was a creative non-violent activist and had begun reading Gandhi as early as 1938 or 1939, not so much Gandhi, but one of his young followers, Krishna Shridharani."[60]

In 1940, Murray said, she "commuted back and forth between New York, where I was living and working, and Durham [North Carolina] where my older relatives lived. And I was going home for my Easter vacation in 1940 when my friend and I were arrested on a Greyhound bus at Petersburg . . . for refusing to move back to a broken [racially segregated] seat . . . over the wheel of the bus. . . . [A]t that time, I was reading Gandhi; so we proceeded to try non-violent action in the jail. Our fellow prisoners were prostitutes and Negroes who'd been picked for drinking and getting into fights." Murray was acquainted with Eleanor Roosevelt, who heard about the incident and communicated with the state's governor about it. "[T]hey sent us soap and towels. Everything we asked for," she recalled. Reflecting later, she observed, "What some of were trying to do was to combine the ideas of [Gandhi] with essentially American techniques." This was nothing new, she discovered. "In 1871 the Negroes of Louisville, Kentucky were carrying out exactly the same type of direct action techniques, when they sat on the Louisville buses and refused to be segregated. . . . [B]ecause of the disturbances that arose as a result of their confrontations then, they finally got, that is the country finally got, the Civil Rights Act of 1875."[61]

Actually, had Murray gone back to the era of slavery, she could have ascertained—as did the scholar Joseph Kip Kosek—that "in the American context, black slaves in particular used various kinds of sabotage and subterfuge short of open revolt in order to assert their autonomy and improve their material conditions." This made U.S. Negroes practical precursors of Gandhi-style methods and excellently predisposed pupils when these methods attracted a new wave of publicity.[62]

As a result of such experiences, Murray became an early stalwart of the Harlem Ashram. By early 1941 she was making pledges to causes: "$5 to FDR," a similar amount to the NAACP, and "7.50 to $10.00—wkly—New York Ashram." But this was not just a matter of donating funds. The Ashram had a decided impact on the way Murray lived her life. On 5 January 1941, she noted in her diary: "5:30 A.M. Monday. An Ashram problem faces me, involving the matter of self-discipline"—that is, relinquishing the habit of smoking cigarettes.[63]

Meanwhile, in India the U.S. emissary was having a grand time, enjoying a whirl of lavish dinner parties, with alcohol sloshing about. "At 8:30 I dined with the Chief Justice, Sir Maurice Gwyer," Thomas Murray Wilson wrote in his diary on 25 November 1941. "It was a man's party and I think there is a good deal to be said for men's parties these days." But his androcentric passions were disrupted: He wrote on 8 December, "The news of the Japanese war action came after all as a complete surprise." But, supremely confident in the predicates of white supremacy, he also wrote, "We always refuse to believe that a Jap [*sic*], a Wop . . . can be as damnable and ruthless as they are." Wilson's abrasive insensitivity was not so different from that of Katherine Mayo, whose wildly popular books had hardly prepared the nation for a challenge from those not of "pure European descent." But as it turned out, the harsh approach to India favored by Mayo backfired, for in response, Gandhi himself had dispatched an emissary to the United States, who found a willing audience in "Negro churches [and] colored women's clubs."[64] When the *New York Amsterdam News*, the leading black weekly in Harlem, blared the headline, "Negro Should Create His Own God, Says Hindu,"[65] it was indicative of the subversive message that Gandhi was imparting—a message conducive to neither wartime unity nor domestic race relations. Thus, Wilson could not entirely suppress the nervousness that gripped his otherwise racially determined consciousness: The Japanese attack, he concluded was, literally and figuratively, a "complete bombshell."[66]

9

RACE WAR!

Both London and Washington had distinct disadvantages when war with Japan erupted in December 1941. London was trying to keep the lid on a restive empire in Asia that Japan was appealing to by adroitly playing on feelings rubbed raw by white supremacy. Washington contained a similarly disillusioned African American community whose favor Tokyo had been currying for decades.[1] As it turned out, neither the British Empire nor the "empire of Jim Crow" could survive this brutal encounter in the Pacific.

The problem London and Washington faced was that, for years, Japan had been seen by many in India and in Black America as their beau ideal, a nation to be emulated, a country that had exploded the lineaments and innards of white supremacy. Part of the glue that bound India and Black America was mutual admiration of Tokyo. This was particularly noticeable after Japan's defeat of Russia in 1905 and came clear a few years later, when the *African Times and Orient Review* began publishing. The head of the publication's New York office was John Bruce, who became a comrade of Marcus Garvey.[2]

Initiated by Duse Mohammed Ali, one of the founding fathers of Pan-Africanism, the self-proclaimed "Pan-Oriental" and "Pan-African journal" was produced at the "seat of the British Empire" in London. "The Black race, the Brown race, the Yellow race, this is *your very own Journal*," the *African Times and Orient Review* announced. "We want to hear from you, the young and budding Sun Yat Sens, the Mustapha Kamils, the Blydens, the Conrad

Reeveses, the embryo Frederick Douglasses." The journal was inspired by the Universal Races Congress that recently had convened in London, the "Metropolis of the Anglo-Saxon World," and thus had a ringside seat as the machinations of white supremacy and colonialism were played out. "Herein will be found the view of the colored man, whether African or Oriental," said this journal that deeply influenced Marcus Garvey. Expansive in view, it planned to engage the region "from the Pillars of Hercules to the Golden Horn, from the Ganges to the Euphrates, from the Nile to the Potomac and from the Mississippi to the Amazon."[3] In "a word to advertisers," the journal announced in early 1913 that its coverage would include "India, Egypt, Japan, South America, Ceylon, East and West Africa, South Africa, the Gold Coast, Brazil, Argentina, San Salvador, the West Indies, Peru, Mexico, and in fact that vast section of the world in which the colored races predominate."[4]

"I wish your enterprise every success," Sir Krishna G. Gupta of India told the rapidly expanding journal,[5] while a "Dr. Ichimura," who taught at Kyoto Imperial University, took to its pages to proclaim that "white men consider that they alone are human beings and that all colored people are on a lower scale of creation."[6] When Ananda T. M. Satchit declaimed about "Social Life in India," he framed the issue by noting that "slave hunters have gone to an African village, and have, by means of their weapons, reduced the inhabitants to bondage [and] through a similar artifice, cunning men have contrived to enslave the entire Hindu population of India."[7] The "unification of the colored races of the world [is] no more fanciful or dreamy than were the ideas of the steam engine," the journal's readers were instructed, and this coalition decidedly included Asia and, specifically, Japan.[8]

Naturally, Garvey's *Negro World* continued this pro–Tokyo line. In limning how "Asia for the Asiatics has Europe quaking," this popular periodical noted how Japan was contesting "control of China and India" by the major powers.[9] In July 1927, a front-page banner headline blared, "Japanese journalist's message to U.S. Negroes." In the accompanying article, Haruji Tawara argued that "we have five great men in the racial movement today." Marcus Garvey "for the Africans" and Mohandas K. Gandhi "for the Hindus" seemed to be foremost among them. "While Japan is one of the colored races, we have none of these great men," he added modestly, "so every Japanese watches the work of these men." Tawara reminded "Negroes": "You must work hard. You must not depend on any white nation. You must see that Mr. Garvey comes out from his . . . prison in Atlanta" He added, "I read every line of the *Negro World*."[10]

Garvey's journal provided ample coverage of the "recent meeting of the . . . Opprest [sic] Nationalities at Brussels," which, along with "the Pan-Asiatic

Conference at Nagasaki a year ago, the Pan-African Congress of Paris, the annual meetings of the Indian National Congress and a host of other gatherings of protest," according to one analyst, reflected the "revolt of the colored against the white dominance of the world."[11] This embrace of Tokyo was accompanied by repeated darts tossed at London,[12] accompanied by a warm embrace of Indians.[13] "The British Empire is disintegrating before our eyes," the journal claimed in the fall of 1925,[14] not least since the "color line" was growing.[15] Continually, complained the journal, "the black and off-color people, subjects of Great Britain, in the West Indies, Africa, East India and Australia are told bluntly that there is no equality of citizenship for them in the British Commonwealth of nations, and that if they want it, they must fight for it." Well, *Negro World* stated with conviction, "They will fight. They are now protesting."[16]

This approach, which combined scalding denunciations of the British Empire and hosannas of praise for Japan, was echoed in the otherwise pro-socialist *The Messenger*, controlled by A. Philip Randolph. When Japan raised the matter of racism at Versailles, this journal proclaimed, "We are glad . . . that Japan exposed this hypocrisy of America."[17] Although its class politics prevented a wholehearted embrace of Japan—unlike Garvey's Black Nationalism—Randolph's organ still detected an advantage to be gained in Tokyo's rise. After Japan condemned lynching, *The Messenger* conceded that

> under normal conditions the international thieves maintain a code of honor (or dishonor) whereby no official criticism of the other is permitted. Especially rigid is this rule with respect to the treatment of colonies, classes or races by the ruling capitalist government or empire. For instance, the United States will not criticize Great Britain's oppression of Ireland, her rape of India. . . . [W]ho does not remember how quickly Rustem Bey, the Turkish Ambassador, was forced to be recalled a few years ago because he compared the Negro lynchings here with the Turkish massacres of the Armenian?

This, *The Messenger* concluded, made Tokyo's harsh words all the more welcome.[18]

That even the Black left—predisposed to be hostile to an increasingly militarist Tokyo—could see some value in Japan's hectoring about the pestilence that was racism was suggestive of how the rise of Japan was upsetting comfortable racial nostrums. Even Langston Hughes, the bard of Harlem, who was certainly no friend of Japan's policies in China, turned up at the Pan-Pacific Club of Tokyo in mid-1933 claiming that the "American Negroes are proud of and have a feeling of sympathy and friendship for Japan. We feel it is the only large group of dark people in the world who are free and independent and that means a lot to us psychologically."[19]

This attention to Tokyo was reflected within organizations, although solidarity with Japan was not necessarily the motive. Such was the case with J. T. Sunderland, who seemed to be motivated by a concern with the idea that the vision of Japan leading a coalition of the colored was all too real. Thus, he posed the intriguing question, "Rising Japan: Is She a Menace?" The query itself exposed the answer he had in mind.[20]

Black America was not as nervous about Japan's rise. In March 1928, Dr. Roy Akagi, secretary of the Japanese Student Movement in the United States, "spoke to the Atlanta Students in a special meeting that was held recently at Spelman [College]."[21] This engagement with Asia was nothing new for African American students, for just before that meeting, Frank T. Wilson, a Negro, had been chosen as "one of the ten American delegates chosen to represent the students of the United States in the Pan-Pacific Student Conference [in China]."[22]

This approach in Black America was mirrored in India. *The Independent*, published in Allahabad, claimed to have "the largest circulation of any daily paper in Northern India."[23] Its extensive coverage of Japan—particularly in the wake of that country's demands for racial equality at Versailles—is even more striking to contemplate. This widely read newspaper published a lengthy missive from Tkiichi Sugita, member of the House of Peers and chairman of the Japanese Conference for Race Equality, who announced: "We, representatives of thirty-seven Societies in Japan—political, religious, press, army and navy veterans' associations, held a meeting in Tokio on the 5th of February 1919, concerning the question of racial discriminatory treatment."[24] L. L. Rai was not a stranger in Japan. He was featured in his authoritative journal *The People* in authentic Japanese-style dress, which was more than an affectation.[25] Like the *Negro World*, *The People* seemed to take heart from the difficulties encountered by the British Empire. Rai noted in his memoir that, while he was in London at the outbreak of World War I, "Everywhere you met the Indians you found them giggling over the difficulties in which England found itself . . . talking of the war as if it were an occasion for jubilation. This group included some of the highest placed Indians, Hindus as well [as Muslims]."[26]

The People covered the activities of the Pan-Asian Union, which included R. B. Bose, who was of Indian origin but by 1926 had become a Japanese citizen and had adopted wholeheartedly the line on race then rising in Tokyo. As he saw it, "The League of Nations is working for the vested interests of the white races and not for the coloured races."[27] *The People* also spoke of "Japan's debt to India," which included Buddhism.[28] The very existence of white supremacy was a gift to Japan's foreign policy in that it convinced the world's Asian and African majority that they should perhaps give serious consideration to joining Tokyo's V-shaped formation. Arriving in the United States from Canada, the fabled writer, Rabindranath Tagore was asked "whether he could read and write and whether he would not be a burden on American finances." Tagore "left the 'silly asses,'" *The* People noted approvingly, "and started immediately for Japan."[29]

A fter December 1941, London and Washington were wary of the presumed affection of Black America and India for Japan—and their concomitant hostility toward the British Empire.[30] Simultaneously, powerful forces in the United States and United Kingdom thought that the best way to defuse this potentially explosive problem was to grant more rights to Black America and independence to India. But there were also powerful lobbies in both nations who were entrenched in their opposition to such measures.

At the same time, there were some in the United States—even those who were hostile to Japan—who had become fed up with the British Empire and were angered that the colonial pretensions of the tiny island kingdom had started the massive bonfire of war. "Nearly all the wars of Great Britain for a hundred years or more, in all parts of the world (and she has fought more than any other nation)," argued Sunderland, "have been caused directly or indirectly by her possession of India." In fact, he asserted, "The greatest danger now threatening the future of mankind is a conflict between Asia and Europe—the yellow and brown races with the white. . . . [A]bove all, [it was] Britain's possession of India" that hastened this eventuality. Moreover, this colonial tyranny had noxious byproducts: The British Empire had become the "greatest producer of opium in the world," which had facilitated India's becoming the "political slave of Great Britain." Sunderland even went as far as to blame London for the rise of U.S. imperialism itself, since "except for Britain's India career, the United States would never have gone away to the coast of distant Asia and seized the Philippines." More than this, Sunderland stressed that India could become a global power if only its sovereignty could be restored.[31]

Sunderland, as noted, was no friend of Tokyo, and he was furious that the white supremacy embedded in British colonialism was providing opportunities for Japan to win friends and influence people—of color. Black America also was not embracing London unreservedly. The South Asian scholars M. S. Venkataramani and B. K. Shrivastava put it even more starkly:

The relevance of the Indian issue to the wider problem of colonial exploitation and racial discrimination was clearly and poignantly understood by the leading personalities of the Black community in the United States. "Free India—and free the Negroes", tersely declared one of the most respected American Negroes, A. Philip Randolph, head of the International Brotherhood of Sleeping Car Porters. In an address at the convention of the American Federation of Labor, Randolph proclaimed that the struggle of the Indian people against British rule was just as that of the Czech, Norwegian and Greek people against their fascist masters.

That was not all. "It was hypocrisy to speak of the war as one of democracy while democracy was denied to India, [Randolph] said. India was the key to the entire colonial issue, declared singer Paul Robeson." And, Venkataramani and Shrivastava added, "The tendency of some Black leaders to identify their own problem with that of India was not viewed with equanimity by the Administration."[32]

A problem for London and Washington was that a socialist (Randolph) and a presumed Communist (Robeson)—both of whom were uncompromising in their backing of Indian independence—were widely viewed as being part of the mainstream in Black America. A larger problem was the pro–Tokyo sentiment that abounded in both Black America and India. A message to the All India Trade Union Congress in 1943 stressed that the war is "purely a WHITE PEOPLE'S WAR. The colonial people are involved in it only to ensure domination for the whites. So long as China or Russia is unable to alter this unfortunate context, her presence in no way modifies the imperialist and race arrogant character of the war. Whoever loses this war, Finance Capital will be on top and not all the Russian and Chinese blood can alter this stern fatality."[33] Then there were those beyond the mainstream who were not only pro–India but sympathetic to the more radical factions in Tokyo who sought to overturn the existing racial order. The Federal Bureau of Investigation (FBI) in Washington, D.C., was keeping close tabs on the Moorish Science Temple of America (MSTA), for example, which was an early religious influence, and something of a precursor, of the group that became the Nation of Islam. In a "confidential" report in May 1942—just after Britain was ousted from Singapore—the FBI observed that MSTA was "said to have evinced much sympathy with Japan, even going so far as to make loudly favorable comments when Japanese victories are reported in newspapers."[34] In another "confidential" report, the authorities reported that the MSTA had been founded in 1913 in Newark by Noble Drew Ali, who "proclaimed himself prophet of Islam. . . . [A] great number responded wholeheartedly, so that in a comparatively few years 30,000 members were enrolled."[35] Ali, it was reported later, originally was named "Timothy Drew," and he "went to Asia at one time and brought back information to the effect that the people commonly known as 'Negroes' were in truth Moors."[36]

The FBI thought it had reason to believe that the MSTA was involved in more than debating nomenclature. A letter in its possession from the MSTA religionist William Briggs-Bey of Brooklyn asserted boldly, "I, myself, . . . will leave for Tokyo, Japan as soon as I can raise $1000 to help cover my expenses. I will try to investigate and try to find out what attitude do the Japanese people have toward the Black People of the Great United States and the world as a whole."[37] Noble Drew Ali embodied what the British Empire and the empire of Jim Crow feared not only because of his influence on nascent Black Muslims and his sympathy for Japan, but also because he had a connection to India: He was influenced by "Hindu fakir[s] in circus shows [whom he] accompanied."[38]

It was not just the FBI who thought that Black Nationalists of various stripes had seized the opportunity provided by the Pacific War to proclaim their undying allegiance to Tokyo's "Race War." In a lengthy article that the FBI chose to retain, the left-leaning Harlem newspaper *People's Voice* wrote ominously about the "BB Plan," which involved "Buddhist lamas in Tibet, Mongolia, Thailand, the Nepal states of India and other parts, Java and Ceylon . . . continuously telling the populace secretly that the success of Japan as a world power is due to the fact that Japan is Buddhist and that Japan will deliver and liberate all the Buddhists." What was the heart of this plot that also implicated Black America? An "invasion" of India, a plan that had revealed a "connection between the world BB Plan and the activities of Duse Mohammed Ali who operated the Moorish Science Temples."[39] The MSTA was being taken seriously because it was "pro–Japanese. Members are instructed that they are Asiatics and not Negroes. . . . [They hold] secret meetings [and are] identical with the Islam Temple and closely identified with the Development of Our Own and the Pacific Movement of the Eastern World." All of these were exemplars of Black Nationalism.[40]

Even more worrisome for the U.S. authorities was their own investigation, which revealed that the MSTA's leader C. Kirkman-Bey, who "took the title of 'Sultan,' . . . was born at Mobridge, South Dakota on September 7, 1898 and . . . his father was a full-blooded Sioux Indian, while his mother was a 'Moroccan' who came to the United States at the age of fourteen." More striking, according to the confidential report, was that Kirkman-Bey claimed "to have attended the Delhi 'University' in India for six and a half years. . . . [and] with the aid of Japan, . . . was to be set up as ruler of the United States. When this occurs, the position of the white man and the Negro will be reversed"—a fate worse than death in the eyes of the ideologically hardened. This diabolical scheme was part and parcel of the "agitation of the Mohammedan races," the report said, that "was instituted by Japan as early as 1904."[41]

Kirkman-Bey was not singular. Yet another "confidential" report concerned "Doughty Williams," a forty-two-year-old man described as "colored" who was five feet, four inches tall; weighed 174 pounds; and was "employed as a butcher" in Detroit. But, intriguingly, in 1932, according to the report, "The subject stated that he was planning to [go] to India to live. . . . [Then] he had a dream and in it was told not to go [to] India," so he stayed in the United States. Williams was said to have declared that "Hitler will be defeated" but that "the Japanese will fight on. . . . [T]hree informants contacted by this office stated that the subject has been a member of the pro-Japanese organization believed to be the [MSTA]."[42] As the FBI saw it, the MSTA was a domestic version of its nightmare of a united coalition of the colored. One invitation the MSTA was said to have issued in the summer of 1942 was directed to "only genuine Moors, East Indians, Syrians, Turks, Arabs, and other children of Allah."[43]

The MSTA was viewed as conspiratorial, as if it had something to hide. Its members were "unusually quiet and very little is heard or seen of their activity," stated an FBI report. "They always talk in whispers or very low voices. Occasionally they are heard to sing as a group." For some reason, "They receive a very large volume of mail, [and] one of the members was overheard to make the remark in a grocery store nearby that the group was in full accord with the principles of Mahatma Ghandi [*sic*] and in fact followed principles set forth by Ghandi." Yet despite a supposed membership in the thousands a few years earlier, by the summer of 1944, the report noted, "The total membership of the group living in the vicinity totals approximately 50 members."[44]

But its depleted numbers aside, the MSTA had to be taken seriously. In Flint, Michigan, the authorities encountered Walter J. Jones-Bey, who "denied any talk in his temple about Japanese." But then, his home was searched, and a "large picture of Tojo in uniform" was found, along with a "news clipping about the 'untouchables' of India" and an "unregistered revolver." In fact, the U.S. War Department reported, "Leaders of his Temple told members (as late as November 1942) that the Japs would win; that the Japs would save the dark-skinned people." Perhaps equally alarming was the fact that Jones-Bey had a "son in the United States Army."[45]

The MSTA and those of that ilk could be isolated and crushed—which they were. Harder to grapple with were the leaders that were seeking to have the powerful gusts created by the movement toward Indian sovereignty pull their own anti–Jim Crow struggle along to fruition. This was particularly so for the NAACP. In 1934, W. E. B. Du Bois had left the organization he had founded, but he returned in 1944, eager to capitalize on the progressive breezes. Yet even during that interregnum, the patterns he had set were difficult to erode. So it was that his nemesis, Walter White, found himself in London during the war, to the consternation of the British Empire.

White was no Walter-come-lately to the Indian struggle, though admittedly he was not as engaged as Du Bois. In the spring of 1942, on behalf of the NAACP, he forwarded "fraternal greetings in this hour of decision and peril" to the "All India Nationalist Congress"—that is, Nehru's Indian National Congress. In it, he exhorted, "Problems arising from prejudice based on skin color face peoples throughout the world and must be solved to end permanently greed of all exploiters."[46]

White was cultivating ties in India because he was seeking to travel there, particularly because of the presence in that country of thousands of African and African American soldiers fighting on behalf of two nations—the United States and the United Kingdom—who had white supremacy etched deeply in their respective escutcheons. He had reason to be concerned. In July 1942, Franklin D. Roosevelt's aide Harry Hopkins was told by London that the "Foreign Secretary raised the question of the proportion of coloured people included in the USA troops being sent to this country. . . . [H]e thought there was a danger that this might give rise to trouble between our people and the American troops, more particularly, perhaps, through certain sections of our people showing more effusiveness to the coloured troops than the Americans would readily understand."[47]

To that end, a crisp spring morning in 1942 found White in the regal abode of Thomas Lamont—possessor of a major fortune—at 107 East 70th Street in Manhattan., There he conversed with Lord Halifax, a man of some influence in London. "The interview began at 10:50 and lasted until 11:40," a confidential memorandum reported. Lord Halifax "stated that he and his government were concerned about the attitude of colored people in the United States and elsewhere towards the war. [He] cited the attitude of the Burmese and of the Indians as part of this attitude of colored peoples throughout the world." Included in this congeries were African Americans. Continuing a trend that had become evident once the war commenced, Lord Halifax sought to deflect attention away from London's weaknesses in the sensitive area of racism and toward those of Washington. He "stated that he found it difficult to comprehend the American attitude towards colored people. He cited criticism or amazement on the part of some distinguished white Americans who, visiting India at the time that [he] was Viceroy of India, had been astonished when at formal dinners [he] conducted an Indian woman in to dinner, she [was] thus outranking many white women. Lord Halifax stated that some of the American whites had expressed bewilderment and even some resentment that any Indian woman, however, high born or important, should outrank a white person." Now, whether Lord Halifax was being tactically sly, cruelly untruthful, or something in between, it augured well for both Black America and India that London's man was seeking to portray himself and his government as antiracist. This was an indication of how the press of war had concentrated wonderfully the minds of certain ruling elites.[48]

But London was desperate, particularly after Britain's smashing loss at Singapore, which had occurred weeks before Lord Halifax spoke these shocking words. For as the increasingly confident White instructed Du Bois (whose opinion of White was not high), it was at Lord Halifax's "invitation" that they had their "long talk," and it was Lord Halifax who "asked me a number of questions regarding the race problem in the United States and regarding the effect on Negro morale of the situation in the Far East, Africa and the West Indies." Further, added White—a man who was addicted dangerously to the fumes emitted from the corridors of power—he was demanding that "President Roosevelt be asked to appoint immediately a commission of from three to five persons who would go to India . . . [and] this commission would talk with Nehru, Gandhi and other Indian leaders. . . . As a preliminary to their departure and as proof of the sincerity of the United States on the matter of color, President Roosevelt would take a sweeping and unequivocal stand against discrimination on the basis of color in the United States."[49] No further evidence was required of how the destinies of Black America and India had become inextricably intertwined. For near the same time, in a meeting with the State Department official Sumner Welles, White had "urged that Roosevelt call a Pacific conference to be attended by the President, Indian leaders and Chiang Kai-shek. The United States was then to mediate the Indian problem through a commission which would include one prominent American Negro." At the recommendation of Welles and other State Department officials, White "was ignored." But White's ideas could not be easily quelled, particularly since he not only led the powerful NAACP, but also because he served with Albert Einstein, Henry Luce, and other power brokers on the advisory board of the India League of America.[50]

Sensing the momentum generated by the war, White then contacted the White House, speaking in ever more assertive tones. He instructed Roosevelt to be alert to the "seriousness of the situation of the United Nations should India be taken by the Japanese government," for it was "conceivable that it may be too late to do anything about the Indian situation." Anticipating the nay-saying, White declared, "You will doubtless ask why an American Negro [is so concerned about India and traveling there]. . . . I am informed by those who know India well and also by those who have very recently been in India

that the treatment of Negroes in the United States is among the most frequently publicized and mentioned topics of discussion in India regarding the
United States. While the people of India do not think of themselves as Negroes, they are keenly aware of the inequality of races based on skin color
from which they have suffered." The "Japanese," White reminded the president pointedly, "are industriously broadcasting to the people of India such
episodes as the recent lynching at Sikeston, Missouri."[51]

Somehow the controversial columnist Drew Pearson got wind of the "full
story of Lord Halifax's visit" with White—a story, he reported breathlessly,
that has "never been told. It was probably the first time a British Ambassador
conferred with a Negro leader," which was suggestive of the radically altered
climate. London's man, said Pearson, "opened with some remarks about
Negro war morale" and the like, and White responded, "Your Excellency, do
you want to confine this to the U.S., or may we talk about other places which
affect it?'" Lord Halifax was not amused, Pearson reported. He "looked surprised," particularly when White "pointed out that the Indian question had
great effect on Negroes."[52]

This surprise of Lord Halifax was minor compared to that of Whitehall
and 10 Downing Street when the determined White showed up in London.
"Mr. Cruikshank telephoned to say that he had heard that Walter White,
president of the Coloured Men's Association in the United States, was actually in this country," reported one British bureaucrat. "He thought it strange
that Mr. White should have arrived without intimation from the Embassy; he
suggested that a gentle reproach be sent to the Embassy for not having kept
him informed."[53]

"White as you know is a person of some importance and his tour may
clearly cause us embarrassment," said another report. "For instance in a Negro newspaper . . . he launched an attack . . . and he is quoted as saying, 'it
appears that Negroes are not the only [ones] who are cursed with Uncle
Toms'" (a scathing reference to one of London's allies in India). "At the same
time, he is said to be a person of some personal charm," the report noted,
which bolstered the predisposition to engage him, not least since "he pro-
poses to write a good many newspaper articles, to report to the President on
return and to write a book on the promising theme, 'this global war is seen in
terms of race.'"[54]

The aforementioned R. J. Cruikshank, though well aware of White's connections to the White House and his desire to push for the conjoined interests of Black America and India, thought the situation could be manipulated
on London's behalf. "White's two preoccupations are 'the resentment of the
coloured troops at race discrimination' and the position of India. He has
some interesting stories to tell of the way in which Berlin and Tokio radio

play on the race theme," Cruikshank said, damning White with faint praise. Brightening, he added, "I think there is a key to the solving of the White problem here: he is an imaginative and impressionable character, and if our people can show him stirring and remarkable things when he goes about the Empire, it will do much more good than arguing over his race theories. We have a hard nut to crack, but he is well worth taking a lot of trouble over." The British were in a sense flummoxed by White, because he was "as white as his name, and does not appear to possess a chemical trace of colored blood. His accent is only very faintly Southern American," although, Cruikshank also noted, he was a "cultured and intelligent man; has great charm of manner; and it is difficult to believe that he is as inflexible in his outlook as he really is."[55]

London was in a bind. To prevail over Tokyo, it had to inspire the downtrodden and those it had colonized with the vision of a bright new future. However, liquidating the empire was viewed as beyond the pale. Speaking convincingly to these diametrically opposed priorities required considerable finesse, particularly in the face of White's constant hammering. He took his complaint directly to the doorstep of the Washington agency that regulated the increasingly important radio airwaves: He protested to James Fly of the Federal Communications Commission "regarding the reported refusal of the three chief broadcasting systems to a broadcast by Pandit Nehru to the United States to have Nehru tell the Indian side of the negotiations conducted with Sir Stafford Cripps recently."[56]

White agreed to broadcast propaganda messages to Japan targeting the sensitive matter of racism but then had a change of heart, as he told Alan R. Murray of the U.S. Office of War Information. "I regret [that] the action of [the] British government in imprisoning Messrs. Gandhi, Nehru . . . and other Indian leaders makes it impossible for me to broadcast tomorrow to peoples of India and Japan." Then in brusque words reflecting how the war had placed London at a disadvantage as it had empowered Black America, White laid down a marker: "If and when Britain frees leaders and indicates her willingness to grant freedom to others it demands for itself I will be glad to make broadcasts should they still be desired."[57]

Exuding confidence, White then proceeded to lecture President Roosevelt. "Anglo-Indian relations are no longer exclusively a matter of British concern," he said. "One billion brown and yellow peoples in the Pacific will without question consider ruthless treatment of Indian leaders and people typical of what white peoples will do to colored peoples if United Nations win. You can be sure Japanese broadcasts out of Tokyo to Pacific peoples and German broadcasts to Latin America are today industriously and gloatingly pointing this out."[58] He demanded that Roosevelt pressure his British ally to free the then imprisoned Indian leadership so that war could be waged more effectively. The war had emboldened the often timorous White to such a point that he informed the President rather bluntly of how "deeply disturbed [he was] to hear from several persons that you have expressed irritation or resentment at suggestions which I have made regarding India. I deeply regret this." These strains were a reflection of the fact that Anglo-American elites were seeking to maintain either the British Empire—or the empire of Jim Crow—yet the press of war had doomed both, irreversibly and irrevocably.[59] In turn, White "heard from several reliable sources that the President had expressed irritation or resentment over some of his suggestions on the Indian issue."[60]

By this point, India was beginning to recognize that one of its most strategically sited allies was Black America, which was being appealed to blatantly by Japan, yet was essential to the war effort against that nation. Characteristically, the philanthropist and activist Anson Phelps Stokes told White during this pivotal spring of 1942, "I happen to know that when an American friend of mine met Gandhi he asked him particularly about Dr. Du Bois."[61] Such passing and seemingly quotidian remarks had no small resonance in the face of the attempt by Anglo-America to foment discord between Black America and India. In a discussion with Pearl Buck, the intellectual who had expressed the most dire concern about the potential impact of Japan's racial appeals, White remarked, "I understand that one of the political advisers of the State Department—Wallace Murray, Chief of the Division of Near Eastern Affairs—opposed the proposal I made on the ground that the people of India consider American Negroes to be in the same class with India's untouchables, and that they for this reason would resent the presence of an American Negro, however distinguished, [on a Roosevelt-appointed] commission." White was not pleased. "Is this true? Or is [it] the typical white bureaucratic interpretation? I strongly suspect it is the latter," he added with justifiable confidence.[62]

Divide and conquer was a tactic that had served the British Empire well over the centuries, but the onrush of war had overcome its effectiveness in splitting Black America from India. Instead, H. W. Sewing of the Atlanta Insurance Company, speaking "as a member of the NAACP" and "assuming that the cause of Indian freedom is identified with the cause of our freedom," suggested to White that "Negroes of the United States should take some kind of group action to emphasize the identity of interest between the Indian people and the Negroes of the United States." What if a "week of meaning and sympathy for India [were proclaimed] for the collective participation of Negroes in the United States?" he asked. What if "arm bands or badges for India [were] worn for an entire week[?] During this particular week of meaning, telegrams and letters, wholesale, might be sent to our President to intervene for immediate Indian freedom; cablegrams might be sent to our President to intervene for immediate Indian freedom; cablegrams might be sent to Mr. Churchill." The beauty of India, Sewing noted, was that such a protest would "at the same time emphasize our own American problem upon the conscience of American white folk."[63]

The bloodlust of world war often has the perverse effect of spawning clarity, forcing to the fore ideas and formulations that can go unmentioned when peace reigns. Chester Himes, who was on the verge of being touted as one of the most talented novelists—certainly, black writers—the United States has produced took Sewing's bold words to heart. Speaking to the readers of a Communist Party journal while the Indian leaders were imprisoned, he demanded "immediate independence" for India, then went further. Anticipating the time that Moscow would replace Tokyo as a capital of contention, he also called for the opening of a "second front" in Europe, thereby lessening pressure on the Soviet Union, which had been bearing the brunt of the war in Europe. But unlike some within leftist and Communist ranks, Himes asserted that the "independence of India is of equal political and military importance to the opening of a second front, for only by the [advocacy] of both can the political power of the proletariat be strengthened."[64] Recognition of this was, perhaps, one reason that London and Washington were eager to avoid both of Himes's objectives.

Still, as the war plodded on, mercilessly and bloodily, the realization was solidifying that something was fatally wrong with a world in which those with darker skin were automatically deprived of human rights. That Japan was drumming on this point gave it further resonance. Pauli Murray argued in the summer of 1942, "Perhaps of all Americans the Negro is best qualified to express what he believes to be the desires of the Indian people." Murray also found it "not difficult to understand the bitterness of Nehru and other Indian Nationalist leaders at the patronizing attitude of the British government toward the whole problem. The Negro gets it here at home in the paternalistic attitude of many southern white people (and some not from the south) who scotch the wheels of progress with the claim that the Negro is not yet ready for equality." In fact, she noted, Nehru might easily have been taken for A. Philip Randolph when he spoke of London's increasingly strained pro-colonial rationales. "Change the word 'Asia' to 'Negro' and the word 'independence' to 'equality' and the comparison is complete," she said. Black America had hitched its wagon to the star of India, said Murray, and she joined with legions of others in asserting that "the eyes of the colored peoples of the world, including our own national minority of Negroes, are fixed upon India today."[65]

This message was ratified when R. Lal Singh, a prominent leader of Nehru's Indian National Congress, spoke at the NAACP convention in the pivotal year of 1942.[66] His presence was an aspect of a deepening relationship between Black America and India driven by the exigencies of war, a relationship reflected in the bustling activities of the NAACP's Coordinating Committee on Indian Freedom, which included James Farmer of FOR.[67]

Homer Jack, who became a prominent cleric, was ideologically similar to Farmer and Murray. After the war was launched, he, with a few other students at the University of Chicago," began "attempting to apply Gandhian techniques of non-violent direct action to lessening racial discrimination in the University neighborhood. Out of these experiments came the establishment of the Congress of Racial Equality. CORE was one of the most important groups involved in the civil-rights upsurge of the 1960s, thus confirming once again the significance of the confluence of India and the war for Black America.[68]

In retrospect, the perception that Japan was waging "Race War" and the threat this was thought to pose to the British Empire and to the empire of Jim Crow created favorable conditions for "equality" concessions to Black America and sovereignty for India. Tacticians such as Walter White were sensible enough to detect that conflating these two causes could only assist both, though this perception originated not with White but decades earlier. Yet at the time, there was understandable concern that Japan's appeal was being listened to much too attentively, especially in Black America, and that this could have consequences too ghastly to contemplate—minimally—for the theory and praxis of white supremacy. "The Fifth Column which hopes to conquer America by fragmentation has pounded steadily on the Negro minority," warned a liberal group that was a precursor of Americans for Democratic Action. "In the guise of 'nationalism' or 'racism' the agents and two-by-four operators have been working tirelessly for a long time to convince American Negroes that their hopes lies in some dark nationalism and not in the 'unfruitful' promise of democracy." Referring obliquely to the wave of Black Nationalism that had washed across Black America in the form of the MSTA, the Nation of Islam, and like-minded organizations, the Americans for Democratic Action precursor launched harpoons of anger at "the doubts implanted by the crack-pot fraternity in Harlem [which] fit into the larger world Axis pattern." The committee raised concern about Ethiopia—the fixed star in Black America's constellation—and Addis Ababa's historical ties to Tokyo before reaching its major point: "A dozen Harlems throughout the United States have their eyes fixed on India, [and] American Negroes for the first time feel a unity with the 400,000,000 other colored peoples in the world." Therefore, it was announced soberly, "Unless

India and Britain find a democratic solution to the problem [and] unless segregation and discrimination against Negroes cease [and] unless the colored citizens of America and their brothers in India are given more than a few vague words about the Four Freedoms, the effect on the war effort will be disastrous."[69]

10

AFRICAN AMERICANS WAGING WAR
IN INDIA

Private Herman Perry was on the run in Burma. The war with Japan had heated up, and he was among the thousands of the traditionally despised African American minority who had been dispatched to— supposedly—fight for freedom. His flight to freedom illustrated the difficulty the British Empire and the empire of Jim Crow would face while fighting a purported "Race War" in South Asia against a foe—Japan—that for decades had pursued a strategy of making special appeals to those with dark skin.

Private Perry was not happy. He was considered the "escaped murderer of Lt. Harold A. Cady, white, of Woodhull, New York," and had been a "chased [and] hunted man in a jungle [for] nearly a year." He was slated to be hanged. But in a "series of exciting and almost fantastic events," reported the *New York Amsterdam-Star News*, which catered to an African American readership, he had evaded his captors. Almost giddily, the paper recounted how "the cunning Perry, like a hunted, wounded and crazed beast, consistently eluded his pursuers in the perilous depths of the Burma jungle (escaping twice after capture and once from the clutches of a well planned ambush . . .)." Once his potential captors "approached a shack located in the Naga hills where Perry was supposed to be sleeping," but again he avoided their grasp.

Perry was the "most hunted man in the India–Burma theatre, the man with a 1000 rupee price upon his head." He was described as "a 'fast-talker,'" "well educated," and "dangerous." For his part, Perry was resolute. "I'll die and go to hell before I go the guardhouse and I'm going to keep my rifle!'" he had insisted. The crafty Perry, fed up with fate in the steamy jungle that destiny had handed him, had "commandeered a truck and told the driver to take him down the road [while] the unarmed Cady advanced upon [him] holding his rifle, exclaiming as he did so, 'I'll put you in this jeep with my fists!'"

"'Don't come up on me,' warned Perry, at the same time throwing the safety off his rifle. As Lt. Cady advanced to within a few feet of him, Perry fired twice and both bullets plowed into the officer's body." One of the well-placed projectiles "damaged blood vessels around [Cady's] heart and pierced his spinal column," leaving him dead. Perry fled and traveled deeper and deeper into the wooded jungle hills, where he found refuge among some of the "Naga tribesmen in the remote village of Tgum-Ga. At first the natives were unfriendly. Their attitude soon changed when Perry began to cure malaria among them with quinine and atabrine. These drugs had been stolen for him by natives [*sic*] when he had been ill with the fever soon after he had fled from the scene of the crime. Perry learned the Naga language and became quite a favorite among his newly-found friends. He married the high chieftain's daughter and her family set them up in good fashion for heavy housekeeping. Perry hired natives to farm for him and raised rice, marijuana and opium." Perry himself, it was said, "was a user of dope and the 'ganja.'"

When not partaking of the intoxicating weed, Perry "hunted tigers in the nearby hills [while] his wife and the rest of the natives kept a constant lookout for the persistent searching parties." As he became more familiar with the region, Perry "took a sojourn up among the Chindit tribes and learned their language and customs also." Dark-skinned like his new comrades, Perry "joined them and the British and fought for a while against the Japanese."

But his adventure was not to last. Once while trying to escape captors, Perry was shot "twice through the chest" and was taken prisoner by the U.S. authorities, who had never relinquished the idea of bringing him to justice— or bringing justice to him. Perry confessed that he had "never intended to return to the Army or the United States but meant to remain in the jungle with his wife, whom he loved, for the rest of his life." Instead, he was tried, found guilty of murder and desertion, and sentenced to hang. But somehow, during a "heavy fog" on the night of his scheduled execution, Perry escaped "by cutting through the wire surrounding the stockade, using a blanket to muffle the sound." He disappeared. Presumably he made his way back to his Naga wife, whom he loved.[1]

The thousands of African Americans who were dispatched to the battlefields of South Asia were generally not so eager to flee their posts as the peripatetic Perry, but their conditions of service were similarly difficult. That Washington felt compelled to dispatch thousands of Black Americans to South Asia, just as London had to dispatch thousands of Africans from its colonies, suggests how desperate both were in the face of Tokyo's challenge. The North Atlantic powers had reason to know that these soldiers would be disaffected, given the bias to which they constantly and torturously had been subjected. They also had reason to know that this alienation would not dissipate in South Asia, where some independence leaders had been imprisoned, souring the mood of the indigenes, and others, such as the influential S. C. Bose, had chosen to fight shoulder to shoulder with Tokyo. The concatenation of these tightly linked events ultimately spelled doom for both Jim Crow and colonialism in India. Neither Washington nor London could afford to risk the distinct possibility that a future Private Perry might not only flee but be embraced by indigenes.

In the meantime, though, how could the Allies expect to prevail against a wily foe such as Japan when their own prejudices were fueling the effectiveness of Tokyo's racial propaganda? Would this mean the loss of India? Would the Black Nationalist dream of lording it over the hated whites be realized, with a boost from a victorious Japan? Would the future be determined on the plains on South Asia?

There was reason for such anxiety. A secret 1945 report from the India–Burma Theater revealed there were "approximately 22, 400" Negro troops there, with about 6 percent serving in combat units and the rest in service units. "Would you rate the overall manner of performance of Negro troops as above average?" commanders were asked. Their response was terse: "below average." One anecdote that had shades of Perry's experience was seen as being symptomatic: "After having bivouacked in close proximity to combat lines for more than sixty days, a Negro sentry shot and wounded, without having properly challenged, both the corporal of the guard and the relief sentry as they moved along a jungle trail between the company area and the company motor pool." Lest anyone see this incident as atypical, it was added, "Individual Negroes almost without exception display little pride of self or organization and they are particularly irresponsible in the handling of equipment and the care of clothing. They often are lazy, and dislike manual labor." Moreover, the report said, "Racial sensitivity is noticeable among all Negro officers and easily leads to agitation, non-cooperation and charges of racial discrimination."

Of course, even the ordinarily racially obtuse U.S. military could detect complexity. "Senior white officers," it was reported, "often develop the conviction that they are not being supported by Negro officers, and junior white officers usually consider themselves the superior of Negro officers, regardless of relative rank." It was not easy for Washington to wage a war for freedom with a Jim Crow army against a foe, Japan, that had made a specialty of appealing to the bruised sentiments of those manhandled by white supremacy.

The task was not made easier on the battlefields of South Asia, which also had been seeded with Tokyo's inflammatory propaganda. According to a secret report, there were "two Red Cross Clubs in Calcutta for all American personnel. One was for white troops and was staffed by white Red Cross personnel and the other was for Negro troops and was staffed by Negro Red Cross personnel. . . . .[A] single communal swimming pool for all U.S. personnel [was] restricted to the use of Negro troops 2½ days per week, and used only by white personnel the remaining 4½ days per week." So much for equality. In fact, "The Headquarters believes that segregation at all levels is desirable," the report declared. "Headquarters" also evidently viewed as acceptable collateral damage the fact that "tension between Negro and white troops . . . resulted from the publication of a schedule of attendance for the Special Service swimming pool in Calcutta." African Americans also brought nonviolent resistance to India in "complaining of segregation. . . . Negroes have boycotted the pool." The report also resorted to racial cliché when it said, with solemnity, that "Negro troops are able to operate in a tropical climate with less adverse physical effect than whites and that they are not as susceptible to skin diseases."

But even the morally blind can occasionally see. The military brass did notice that "Negroes get along with civilians (predominantly dark-skinned) in [the] India–Burma Theater as well or better than do white troops. . . . [It is the] Negroes [who] frequently are invited to attend native civilian parties to which white troops are not invited. Many Negro soldiers attempt to adopt native civilian children as 'mascots.' "[2] In a public confirmation of this general perception, U.S. General Joseph Stilwell "lauded Negro trucking units . . . especially for their ability to get along well with the various racial groups they came in contact with. The Negroes, he said, made friends at once with the Chinese and Burmese."[3] Stilwell could have included Indians, too. One Negro newspaper, Baltimore's *Afro-American*, featured a picture of a Black baseball catcher behind the plate as an "Indian policeman" with a bat received "some pointers on how to swat a baseball."[4]

When a nation premised on white supremacy plopped dark-skinned U.S. troops in a region teeming with dark-skinned people in the midst of a war for "freedom," it was bound to inspire contradictory impulses. Another secret report filed from the headquarters of the India–Burma Theater observed quizzically that "the care of equipment by Negro units is far below that of white units." For some reason, the report noted, "Negro privates seem to lack an understanding of their part in the war. . . . Morale of colored troops is slightly below average. . . . The cause for this may be attributed to the fact that morale is quite often largely dependent upon an individual being able to understand his part in the fulfillment of the overall mission." In other words, the brass seemed unable to see why Negro troops were having a hard time comprehending a war that purportedly was being fought for a freedom that they themselves did not enjoy. Thus, the report suggested that "assignment of Negro military police among white troops would be highly unsatisfactory, as the average white person resents the exercise of authority over him by any colored person." However, in a presentiment of why the United States felt compelled a few years later to move away from juridical Jim Crow, the report observed keenly that "segregation creates the persecution complex and the [colored] officer is forced to turn to the colored enlisted men for companionship, thereby lowering his efficiency and ability to handle the men under his command." That is, Jim Crow was undermining unit cohesion and jeopardizing national security. "Special care should be exercised when commissioning colored personnel, to insure that they do not possess strong racial tendencies," the report stated, because, among other reasons, "those with strong racial tendencies have been observed as being agitators." In addition, Washington recognized that, going forward, U.S. troops might have to be dispatched to the colored zones of the world, and sending Negro troops to such areas presented a unique set of issues. "Native persons here," the report said of South Asia, "are of a dark race and the Negro fails to respect their rights and privacy."[5]

To hear the authorities tell it, having Negro troops was hardly worthwhile. "They are far from dependable," yet another secret report revealed. "They take the attitude that [they] are serving in the Army only because they have to and therefore do as little as they can get by with." The Black soldiers were moral reprobates, the report said. "Truth means nothing to them. . . . [M]any Negro troops smoke mari-juana [and they are] very easily influenced to misbehave." Yet there was an upside, it was thought, to having Negro troops. Although an earlier report had said that Negro troops did not respect the indigenes, this report asserted, "[They] get along excellently with civilian women, both Indian and Anglo-Indian. They rarely have trouble getting a sufficient number of civilian girls to attend their dances." The issue of social interaction was a nettlesome one. "On one occasion a Negro soldier, uninvited, tried to attend a house-party given by a civilian for some white troops," the report recounted. "After being expelled from the party he returned to his organization recruited a load of Negro soldiers who waited near the location of the party and when the white soldiers departed the Negroes beat them up."[6]

The practice of Jim Crow was compromising the exalted principles on which the United States was said to have been built, the First Amendment to the U.S. Constitution being chief among them. In the India–Burma Theater, an official report noted, "The person suspected of being most responsible for the dissension that exists among Negro troops of this command is Mr. D. J. Brookes, a Negro war correspondent representing the *Chicago Defender.*" The report also said that, although it was "immaterial whether the attached medical officer [was] white or Negro, [the] chaplain should be Negro."[7] Plus, Chinese allies had taken notice of the despicable manner in which Negro troops were treated and decided they wanted nothing to do with them, either. "The Generalissimo does not favor the use of colored troops in China," Lieutenant-Colonel Edwin O. Shaw said of Chiang Kai-shek, "and the Commanding General (China Theater) does not wish to ask for dispensation from the Gimo [Chiang] in that regard. . . . [T]hus colored drivers should be used the shortest possible distance into China, it being preferable to stop them at the China–Burma border." The mandate, therefore, was to "provide white drivers" and "supplement that activity with Chinese drivers . . . ."[8] How could South Asians credibly accept the stated war aims of the United States when it treated its own citizenry so atrociously? Perhaps worse, how could one begin to prevail against the crafty foe from Tokyo while fighting with a sable arm tied behind one's back? The "war may be decided in India, professor from there says," reported the Negro-owned *Oklahoma Black Dispatch* in September 1942, speaking of a college in neighboring Arkansas.[9] If so, things were not looking bright for the Allies then, and Jim Crow was no petty reason.

Black and white alike were well aware of this dilemma. A group of Negro troops in India reported that, "First off . . . the ship a lecture was given by Dr. Paul D. Lindbergh and he asked the Negro troops not to mention racial prejudice in the States." Presumably, hearing about this reality would overly excite the indigenes. As if this forbidding forbearance were not sufficient, "Right on the ship," a Black soldier noted sourly, "we weren't allowed to drink from the cool water fountains. Then the first thing we encountered in India is segregation. American, British, Chinese and Negro troops, all attend the same show and Negroes are piled in a huddle right in the rear."[10] Keeping these troops in good humor was no trivial matter, since many would be compelled to make the ultimate sacrifice. The *Chicago Defender* was not in error when it informed its readers, "It has been said that for every mile of [the] Ledo–Burma Road a Negro lad lost his life," and this supply line was critical for the defense of India and China against Japanese incursions.[11] As the official military history of World War II put it, "In large measure, the Stilwell Road was a monument to the strength, skill and endurance the Negro soldier. About 60 percent of the U.S. troops who worked on the road were Negro engineers. Their superiors considered that their morale was higher than that of the white soldiers working on the road."[12] Interestingly, another Negro newspaper, the *Afro-American*, reported that, in "building a New Burma Road . . .

white and colored soldiers are working together, braving dangers, fighting stubborn forces of nature." There "'is no color line [here]," one chaplain claimed.[13]

If there are no atheists in foxholes, as so often has been claimed, perhaps it is fair to say that white supremacy also has difficulty surviving as bullets and other projectiles fly overhead. Certainly, the presence of U.S. troops—and Negro troops—in South Asia had consequences that may not have been intended. Reporting from a "key town in India fortified by thousands of American troops," Herbert Matthews of the *New York Times* observed that "the Americans get three times the pay of the British and nine times what the Indian troops get. Imagine the effect on a town that suddenly finds thousands of American Negro troops as well as white troops gaily spending far more than the British can possibly afford. It is revolutionizing the psychology of the poorest Indian here." In other words, how could Indians continue to believe in the magic of white supremacy when African Americans often had more money than the British?[14]

The question of how poor treatment of Negro troops by their own nation affected Asians' perceptions was not a minor one. This may, in fact, have colored concerns in India about "murders and murderous assaults committed by Americans and American Negroes"—note that a distinction is made between the two—on Indians." It did seem that alleged transgressions by Negroes were accorded more attention and concern. A September 1944 report was typical: "Subjects had been stabbed by three unidentified Negro assailants." The "driver of the taxi cab was Mr. Kapur Singh who told these agents that he had been engaged by three American Negro soldiers in front of the Continental Hotel [in Calcutta] at about 8:00 P.M.; [and that the] boys were under the influence of liquor but not drunk, [that] it had been drizzling and the boys had asked him to go faster and he refused. The passengers appeared to object to that and talked among themselves." One of the "Negro passengers reached out and grabbed [the driver's] brother Chenan Singh by the queue, pulling his back across the seat." An "exhaustive inquiry" was promised. Meanwhile, the report noted, "550 Negro soldiers [remain] on rest leave at the transient Rest Camp at Howrah."[15]

Yet even such cloudy episodes revealed, perhaps, a rainbow of possibilities. For as the official history of the India–Burma Theater put it, "One troubled area was in relations between Negro troops and the local peoples. Incidents between Negroes and Indians were out of proportion to the number of Negro troops. The explanation may be a simple one—that the Negro troops mingled more freely with the Indians than did their white comrades, and that if the number of contacts could be correlated, the incidents would fall into a truer proportion."[16]

A confidential report filed during the war's early stages suggested why seeking to fight Japan in South Asia with a Jim Crow military was tempting fate. "The Negro soldier [in] World War II is . . . a different type of man from the Negro soldier in World War I or in the peace-time Regular Army," it said. "Nearly 1 in 3 Negro enlisted men have come from the North. This change is due to the great Northward migrations. . . . [T]he most significant change is in the educational levels of Northern Negroes, [which has] created new problems for the Army." As an example, the report cited "the problem said to arise when well-educated Northern Negro privates are placed under less educated Southern Negro noncoms. . . . [F]requently the Negro graduate from Columbia or Northwestern [university] finds himself commanded by a less educated Negro from a Southern plantation." It also cited the closely related "problem of a Negro high school graduate or college man who might be assigned to a pick and shovel."[17]

"I have been hearing so many tragic things about racial tensions and racial violence on the home front," said President Roosevelt in July 1943.[18] He need look no farther than Mississippi to receive confirmation of his deepest anxieties. In the same year, the attorney J. C. Ross of Gulfport, noted with concern, "I am advised that there [are] Negro civilians, both male and female, now teaching different groups of white soldiers in the military camps in this locality." Worse, Ross wrote, "The military men [are] required, so I am also advised to address these Negro instructors, as Mr. and Mrs. and to pay all deference to them as they would white women and gentlemen occupying the same positions." This was beyond outrageous, Ross thought, and to indicate that action would follow outrage, he concluded with rising anger: "There are graves in the central and northern part of Mississippi and in the other southern states occupied by white men, Negroes and carpetbaggers as a result of the same idea that [is] mention[ed] above and the same condition is bound to result from the matter here discussed." A copy of his inflammatory message was forwarded promptly to President Roosevelt.[19] How could a nonracial army be constructed that could appeal to South Asians when such odious sentiments persisted, particularly when Roosevelt's own party was dependent on the Jim Crow South?

Such raw sentiments were not peculiar to the United States. From the United Kingdom came a disturbing report from what should have been a gala event: "The management wishes white American soldiers attending the dance to leave." The reason? "American Negro soldiers at the dance had been ordered by white American soldiers to leave. Laughing couples fell silent, then applauded."[20]

What this incendiary rhetoric and action could lead to was exposed in the midst of war when the 100th Regiment of Coast Artillery, a "colored unit, had as much segregation as it could stand last week and went berserk." The Baltimore-based *Afro-American* reported that the men "fired 5000 rounds of ammunition, an amazing quantity considering 24 rounds are regarded as sufficient for one soldier to carry into battle. Firing lasted from 10 P.M. to 1 A.M. before ammunition was exhausted." Though "only one person was killed and five wounded," the *Afro-American* said, the "intolerable segregation and Jim Crow" were bound to foment further discord.[21] A further warning of what was bound to come can be found in a report that stated, "Negro Harry Carpenter was held for treason when he told a Negro Army sergeant: 'This is a white man's war, and it's no damn good.'"[22] How could a war for freedom be fought by a Jim Crow military? How could colonialism and freedom co-exist peaceably? And how could South Asians be won to the side of Washington in a conflict with Tokyo—or an impending one with Moscow—as long as Jim Crow reigned?

This discontent about the war was spreading and metastasizing. A correspondent for one Chicago-based Negro journal who had just returned from a tour of the region reported that "West Indians", many of whom had relatives in New York City, were "not behind [the] British war effort" because they felt that "the war is one of the classes not of the masses"" and that "they are not citizens . . . even in the armed forces." In Trinidad and Tobago particularly, "discontent" was widespread, especially since there was "an unwritten law that no Negro can rise above the rank of Sergeant-Major."[23] In London, headquarters of the colonial master of Trinidad and Tobago and India alike, the virus of "racial discrimination which U.S. Army officers and soldiers [were] spreading throughout England was lightly dismissed by the government as 'unfortunate,'" the *Louisiana Weekly* declared. "'[T]here is a necessity of discrimination in connection with Negroes in London,' the Prime Minister declared."[24] Firing back, George Padmore, by then a pre-eminent Pan-Africanist based in London, charged that Prime Minister Winston Churchill "remains fundamentally a die-hard imperialist who has no sympathy with the aspirations of the colored subject races for self-determination."[25] It was also Padmore who informed Black America in the pages of the *Pittsburgh Courier* that "Indian, African and West Indian leaders in London have decided to set up a united front committee to press their claims on the British government for full self-government. . . . [A] committee of 20 has been set up to establish contact with Afro-American leaders to carry out the idea of a world conference of colored peoples."[26]

Of course, all the news about Negroes and the war was not negative from the vantage point of London or Washington. Otherwise, it would have been even more difficult than it was for the Allies to prevail. For example, there was "solid opposition of 500,000 French West Indian Negroes and [the] col-

ored elite against continued Vichy control of the Caribbean isles of Martin-
ique and Guadeloupe,"[27] a figure that presumably included those beyond the
shores of those small islands. And all of the reporting from the Negro press
just seemed to be negative. This was not the case, however. Otherwise, how
can one explain a warm and fuzzy story that appeared in the *Pittsburgh Courier* recounting the tale of "Staff Sgt. Willie Davis, first American Negro soldier to disembark in India"? Davis, who hailed from Port Tampa City, Florida,
reportedly was taken with the horses he saw when he landed. "Horses being
cheap in India, many of our soldiers have availed themselves of the opportunity of owning 'nags,'" the *Courier* reported. "It takes only a rupee—about
32 cents—a day to feed them."[28]

But such tales did not distract African Americans back home from what
they saw as the critical issues facing Black America and India. A. Philip Ran-
dolph argued that "Negroes should back India." The "freedom of the people of
India," he said, "is intimately tied up with the freedom of the Negro people of
America."[29] Not to be outdone, weeks later, in September 1942, a boisterous
crowd of four thousand people, many of whom were from "trade union and
Negro organizations, packed New York's Manhattan Center," the *New York
Age* reported. They "wildly applauded a group of notable speakers including
Paul Robeson and Kumar Goshal . . . when they called for the immediate formation of Indian national government as the best guarantee of defending India against Japan."[30] Max Yergan, the Christian missionary turned Communist
revolutionary, received a most enthusiastic welcome from this "Free India"
rally. A "free India," he asserted, "now is vital to the entire cause of the United
Nations." No doubt thinking of Robeson, he argued that "it makes sense that
many of the speakers here this evening are members of the Negro race [be-
cause] they [the Dixiecrats] withhold freedom from Negroes exactly as British
Tories and fascists deny India her freedom." The Council of African Affairs
(CAA), the organization he and Robeson headed, Yergan proclaimed, "sup-
ports the demand of India for freedom because India's freedom will mark the
beginning of the freedom of all other colonial and subjugated people. A defeat
for fascists and oppressors anywhere," he cried, "is a blow at international fascism and is a step toward world freedom. Freedom for India should speed a
free Africa and would hasten the arming of Africans." Not least, he noted,
"Puerto Rico, America's India," would be a step closer to "self-determination"
if India were to be freed.[31]

It was no surprise that Robeson's CAA was in the vanguard when India
took center stage in Black America. Robeson told the cheering masses in
Manhattan that his interest in India went back to the 1930s, when he had met
Nehru and his sister Vijaya Lakshmi Pandit in London after touring Spain
with Krishna Menon, the dominant force in the India League.[32] One evening

in London, Robeson, to "Nehru's amazement, . . . had recited some classic Hindu poetry in the original Hindi to demonstrate the similarity in rhythm and intonation between Hindu and African-American speech patterns," Robeson recalled. "That evening marked the beginning of a lasting friendship between the Nehru and Robeson families."[33] It was near that time that Robeson also encountered the young Indian student E. S. Reddy, who was matriculating in the United States. Reddy, along with Robeson, Nehru, and others, were part of the budding Afro-Asian International that was exploding in importance under the pressure of war. Reddy went on to become a key figure in this process, toiling for the nascent United Nations for more than four decades as perhaps its leading anti-apartheid official.[34]

Yergan might not have been able to recite Hindu poetry, but his words in English were no less potent. For his public declamations mirrored the words he transmitted to President Roosevelt. "Negro Americans are alarmed over the present situation in India," he told Roosevelt. "We see etched in blood in India the stake in which oppressed people all over the world have in this war of liberation." When Black Americans examined India, he said, it tended to "raise doubts in [their] minds . . . concerning the fate of the Ethiopian, African and other colonial and semi-colonial peoples." Warning the White House, he concluded, "There is yet time to save America by putting the Atlantic Charter into effect in India."[35] Then Yergan told the readers of the *Chicago Defender* that "Negro people" were vitally concerned with "what happens in India. They are concerned first because more than any other section of the American people, they appreciate, understand and feel the humiliating experience [to] which the Indians have been subjected for so many years. The cup from which the Indian masses drink is also pressed to the lips of Negro Americans and its bitter taste lingers."[36]

Yergan's words echoed throughout Black America. The new *Negro Quarterly*, for which Ralph Ellison served as managing editor and the famed former political prisoner Angelo Herndon served as editor, editorialized that "many will argue that it is incorrect to draw parallels between the American Negro–white and the Indian–British situation. But as we see it, what appears in India in an acutely intensified form appears here in confusion. For this reason we must observe the parallels and learn."[37]

Fortunately, the *Negro Quarterly*—and, by implication, African Americans—had excellent teachers. One was Kumar Goshal, whose presence with Robeson and Yergan at the Manhattan Center rally was no accident. He had arrived in the United States from India in 1920 and since that time had become a familiar figure in Black America, writing a column regularly from 1942 to 1947 for the influential *Pittsburgh Courier*. He was a living symbol of the ever closer alliance between Black America and India.[38] Now he was informing readers of the *Negro Quarterly* that, "whether one likes it or not, India and the United States are indissolubly linked, at least for the duration of the war. Thousands of American soldiers, both Negro and white, are in India now to fight any possible Japanese attack on the country." This potential clash was forever transforming conditions for India and Black America alike.[39]

The Black Left had not been indifferent to India over the years, but it certainly did seem that the press of war, and the left's idea that the war could not be won while nations were held in colonial bondage, compelled its voices to become ever more insistent. "It just does not make sense," said Langston Hughes in the fall of 1942, "for allied leaders of the western world to make beautiful speeches about freedom and liberty and democracy with India still enchained and Negroes still Jim-Crowed and neither group permitted to participate with fullness and enthusiasm in the war effort.... Millions of darker people are thus forced to wonder if logic is dead. Freedom for India is not only a military need but a moral need to lift the fighting spirit of all who want to believe in freedom *for all*."[40]

As the war unwound, African Americans found it useful to focus on India, not only for the reasons adduced by the *Negro Quarterly*, but also because the presence of Japan as a U.S. antagonist raised sharply sensitive racial matters and was grounded in a relationship with South Asia that stretched back decades. This was a "world war," after all, and of the major combatants, India and Japan struck the most resonant chords in Black America. Certainly, it was hard to identify with colonizers in London and Paris, and decades of anti–Communist conditioning had made Soviet Russia radioactive for many. Still, it is quite remarkable to recall the energy expended by Black America in lobbying for Indian sovereignty, which at times seemed to be a higher priority than sovereignty for colonized Africa.

The abject refusal of the Indian leadership to back the British in the war without an immediate guarantee of independence had "a powerful influence on black American political consciousness," according to Penny von Eschen. Certainly it contributed to a still consequential pro–Tokyo sentiment in Black America and tempted others correspondingly to withhold support from the war until and unless there was a guarantee of equality. In October 1942, the *Pittsburgh Courier* reported that, "in an October 1942 survey of 10,000 black Americans, 87.8 percent 'responded with a loud 'yes' to the question 'do you believe that India should continue to contend for her rights and her liberty now?'" The survey found no regional bifurcation: "Southern Negroes joined with their Northern brothers [and sisters] in full approval of the Indian struggle for self-rule."[41]

But this anticolonial sentiment was no trifling matter for London. India, after all, was the sparkling jewel in Britain's colonial crown. London was paying attention to unrest about India in the United States and was not pleased. A secret report prepared in London expressed displeasure when an "extremely important union," the United Auto Workers, which had a sizeable African American membership, endorsed Indian sovereignty. "This resolution will receive wide publicity," the report noted sadly. In response, the United Auto Workers wanted Britain's National Council of Labour to issue a statement.[42] "I resent very much the idea that our policy in India shall be governed by the ignorant views of the United Automobile Workers of America," huffed one British bureaucrat. His colleagues, however, were becoming "panicky" in response, particularly since London could hardly absorb the sledgehammer blows from Tokyo and Berlin without Washington coming to the fore. If prime Democratic Party constituencies were bailing out on the key question of India, that was something to worry about.[43]

Many African Americans seemed unwilling to subscribe prematurely to the idea that World War II was the "good war" fought by the "greatest generation." To embrace this notion, they would have to be amnesiac about lynching, Jim Crow, and the rest. At the same time, however, they did not want to appear nonchalant about fascism. A tight focus on India was a way to express unease about the war and unease about the "ally" in London while still pressing for a successful conclusion of the global conflict. "India to Be Topic of Negro Youth War Meet" was just one headline that appeared during the war; Robeson, Yergan, Pearl Buck, and the trade-union leader Ferdinand Smith were slated to appear.[44]

So London did have something to worry about, especially given the constant labor of Kumar Goshal, Krishnalal Shridharani and other figures who garnered wide popularity in Black America. "I want you to know how deeply sympathetic I am, and many other Negroes are, to the point of view you expressed in the India crisis," Pauli Murray told Shridharani in August 1942. "I wish very much I could discuss the entire situation with you before returning to school."[45] But Murray was not so busy with her studies that she failed to protest directly to the State Department its position on Indian freedom. Gordon P. Merriam of the State Department's Near East Division responded, albeit tepidly, to Murray's démarche on "developments in India arising from Mr. Gandhi's fast."[46] The ever busy Murray also elicited a response from the U.S. War Department after she protested angrily the outrage that led to segregated blood banks on the battlefields of Burma and elsewhere. Major F. N. Schwartz of the Blood Plasma Division passed the buck, telling Murray that, "unfortunately, there is a disinclination on the part of many whites . . . to have Negro blood injected into their veins." Besides, he said, "Disregard of that feeling would greatly mitigate [*sic*] against successful conclusion of the program for collecting blood plasma."[47]

Murray's Harlem Ashram continued to plug away, as did she. The idea for the ashram had been foreshadowed in the mid-1930s by P. O. Phillips of the National Christian Council in Nagpur, India. "As illustrations of the kind of institutions under Indian control with which American Negroes might be associated," he said, were ashrams because they provided an institutional way for "Indians and foreigners [to] work on absolute terms of equality." He also thought that Black Americans could become associated with "Christian work in India," and this could provide a foretaste of what could develop in North America.[48]

A few years later, this wish was fulfilled. "We see the beginning of an ashram movement in [the United States] at a time when pacifist circles are being increasingly awakened to our need of a vital American adaptation of that non-violent resistance developed so fully in India," said Jay Holmes Smith. An activist, Smith was given substantial credit for the ashram movement that he was hailing in August 1942—coincidentally, as London had given a jolt to the movement for Indian sovereignty by incarcerating Gandhi and Nehru. Smith himself, however, gave credit to "the pacifist movement of Indians in [the United States] like Krishnalal Shridharani and Haridas Muzumdar. They have helped us to feel with Tagore that 'East and West are but alternate beats of the same heart.'" Smith found it "significant that the American Negro feels a strong bond of sympathy with Gandhi, Nehru and their compatriots." Referring to a "great rally of some 20,000 Negroes in Madison Square Garden" in Manhattan, he found it meaningful that "three of their speakers quoted Gandhi as one with them in the cause of racial solidarity."[49] The ambitious Smith, recalled his comrade, Bayard Rustin, "indicated that he looks to the American Negro to assist in developing along with the people of India, a new dynamic force for the solution of conflict that will not merely free these oppressed people but will set an example that may be the first step in freeing the world."[50]

Buoyed by the energy provided by the Indian independence movement, the Harlem Ashram held a demonstration against the poll tax in Washington, D.C., in May 1944. While in town, they joined with the Free India Committee in picketing the British Embassy.[51] What was striking about the ashram, and what augured well for the future, was its ability to involve Christian pastors who were African American in its activities. One of these pastors, who hailed from Baltimore, was ecstatic after taking a summer course with the ashram. "I don't know any experience in my life that has been so helpful as my two weeks at the Ashram," he said. "My vision of life and the Gospel has been so changed it is inexpressible."[52] But it was not just clerics who were being moved. The Fellowship of Reconciliation "supplied the impetus for CORE," which became one of the stalwarts of the Civil Rights Movement of the 1960s, and in 1942–1943, "certain black FOR and CORE leaders infused [A. Philip] Randolph's March on Washington Movement with a Gandhian thrust," say August Meier and Elliott Rudwick. "By the autumn of 1942, [Randolph] enthusiastically referred to the Gandhian mass movement in India as a model for black Americans and at year's end proposed a week-long civil disobedience campaign against Jim Crow public accommodations."[53] Rustin was not exaggerating when he remarked, "Gandhi had a more direct influence on the development of civil rights strategy than any other individual, here or abroad."[54] "CORE's principles," Rustin stressed, "were Mohandas Gandhi's principles."[55] This direct engagement with India, which had been brewing for years, accelerated during the war, then overflowed afterward as Martin Luther King Jr. was tutored by Rustin.

The growing prestige of India during the war was driven in no small part by the apparent selflessness of the Indian National Congress leaders, who were imprisoned as a direct result of their anticolonial protests. It became difficult for African Americans to back the war in good conscience when such injustices occurred. Then again, Indian nationals in the United States—beyond such stalwarts as Goshal—were speaking up ever more vigorously. Just before war broke out in Europe, Mubarek Ali Khan, president of the India Welfare League in New York City, contacted the White House about the "possibility of enacting a law to permit Indians living in this country to vote. There are more than 3000 natives of India residing in this country."[56] Although Roosevelt had bested the Republican Party rather handily in the 1936 and 1940 elections, he could not be indifferent to such a large cache of votes as he faced the prospect of an unprecedented fourth term in office.

As Indians were thrust forward as the moral symbol of the unrealized promise of the bloody war; as Indians in the United States became more energized as a partial result; as Indian National Congress leaders served time in jail because of their refusal to sheath their anticolonial sword; and as African Americans, inspired by their example, began to clamor more insistently, the momentum toward independence in India and equality for U.S. Negroes became more difficult to stop. The two struggles also became more intertwined. This was reflected in Bombay when, in 1943, the popular-front publication *The Student* featured a "Negro student" proclaiming, "This is our war"—as if there might have been doubt. When the African American Dick Anderson attended the International Student Assembly in Washington, *The Student* reported, he sought to answer the question, "How could he best fight fascism?" The paper published his answer in dramatic italics: *"I heard the answer in the speech of the Indian delegate who, amidst thunderous applause, demanded the immediate freedom of India so that the energies and strength of the Indian people might be thrown against the Japanese aggressors.*" But the sober Anderson was not carried away by the wild enthusiasm. "Call me a dreamer if you will," he said soberly. "But I live in Washington where the best anti-fascist films are shown only at Jim Crow theatres whose thresholds I can cross only if I carry a mop and pail. . . . [B]eatings and lynchings of Negro soldiers and civilians [continue]." So, obviously, not only must India be freed, he said, but Negroes must be freed if the war were to realize its promise.[57]

These two entangled questions, which brought into sharp relief all of the blather about freedom emanating from London and Washington, were also brought directly to the desk of U.S. Secretary of State Cordell Hull. "It will be difficult for you to serve with the full confidence of the British," Hull was told, "when they look at the way we in America treat our Negro brothers, but *perhaps it will quicken our own consciences to do more in that direction.*" That Hull, in reply, pointed the finger of accusation back at British colonialism— notably, in India—only served to indict the Allies. As Ashley Hope has noted, in one of his best-known essays Tagore "compared the difficulties of India and America in trying to solve the problem of racial unity, challenging America's critics of the caste system to improve their treatment of the 'Red Indian' and the Negro before presuming to question India." Gandhi, "in the course of an appeal to [Roosevelt] for the relinquishment of British rule and the defense of the country by allied troops, took occasion to equate Indian and African exploitation by Great Britain with the American treatment of the Negro." He "simultaneously dismissed allied claims to be fighting for individual freedom and democracy, saying India and Africa were being exploited by Great Britain 'and America has the Negro problem in her home.' "[58] It was just such a realization that impelled Private Perry to flee the U.S. military after he was dispatched to the India–Burma Theater.

11

TOWARD INDEPENDENCE AND EQUALITY

Paul Robeson notwithstanding, Walter White of the NAACP continued to command more troops. Therein hangs a tale. The conclusion of World War II was followed by the launching of another conflict—this time, targeting the former ally in Moscow and those, such as Robeson, thought to be within its orbit. Similarly, many of the Black Nationalists who had subscribed to the idea of Japan leading a V-shaped formation of peoples of color that included Black America and India had been imprisoned or otherwise isolated during the war and emerged from this titanic fracas ideologically fragmented and, certainly, less taken with Japan and, to a degree, with India. Fundamentally, this left White's NAACP as the last man standing, but the association was soon to move decisively away from a searching critique of U.S. foreign policy as part of a bargain that led to the granting of civil-rights concessions. In any case, the NAACP found that any friendliness toward an independent India that was decidedly pro–Soviet was not in its perceived best interest. However, as the Negro allies of Tokyo retreated and the Negro allies of Moscow were assaulted, the Negro allies of New Delhi—Rustin, Farmer, and then King—emerged hegemonic in the postwar era.

As noted, the NAACP had more dues-paying members than any of its competitors in Black America. Even as the war was unfolding, it was better positioned than they were to wield influence. Thus, it was White's organization that, in 1942, in the midst of the jailing of the Indian leadership, asked Roosevelt to form a "board for the military defense" of India with General

Douglas MacArthur as the "American member, to act with one Englishman, one Indian and one Chinese." The NAACP was not hesitant about crossing swords with London in the process: "We implore you to act even at the risk of offending our ally, Great Britain." This, White said, was "no longer a question solely of India freedom," but also a question of whether the Allies could ultimately prevail.[1]

The once mighty British Empire not only had trouble in subduing its Japanese counterpart. It could hardly keep Walter White out of its own backyard. Apprehensions arose in London that its even mightier ally in Washington could accomplish this task.[2] "White is of course something of a problem in the present state of mind of the Negroes here," said an analyst in the British Embassy in Washington. "I fear that United States authorities may be unwilling themselves to intervene to prevent his further journey. . . . I am afraid that if we want to keep him out of India or the colonies we shall have to do so ourselves by refusing him a visa." Or, the analyst said, London could "consider telling [White] that you are prepared to let him go anywhere the United States War Department agree[s] to accept him as a correspondent. This would place the onus of opposition on the United States authorities."[3]

London remained adamantly opposed to allowing White within shouting distance of India. "His visit to India and especially his wish to see Gandhi and Nehru raise very considerable misgivings," the British Embassy reported with dismay. "We do not believe that an American with such a desire and working under such journalistic auspices either understands the realities of the Far Eastern war or will give a helpful picture on his return." Moreover, the embassy said with oblique delicacy, "India has, as you know, its own colour questions, and for this and other reasons he would be in a very difficult position." Grasping for straws, the embassy asked with evident frustration, "Might it not be possible to suggest that [former presidential candidate Wendell] Willkie, of whose world tour White's journey is reminiscent, might comment adversely on facilities being [allocated] to White which were denied to Willkie?"[4]

London continued to hope against hope that Washington would shackle White and handicap his ability to travel. A. F. Morley of the India Office prayed in a confidential dispatch that "some part of the U.S. Administration might be willing to withhold from him the necessary facilities for a visit to India." Repeatedly, White was told that "under no circumstances would he be given the opportunity of seeing the Congress leaders while interned," but the "possibility cannot be excluded that Mr. White may arrive in India without previous intimation reaching the Government of India."[5] When White arrived in London in March 1944, the panic was at a fever pitch, as if Gandhi himself had landed. White "did not succeed in getting interviews with the

Secretary of State, the Prime Minister or (he even suggested it!) the King," Neville Butler complained. Instinctively, the London authorities tried to resolve their problem with White by throwing him into conflict with his own government. Still, they remained concerned that "the way in which our public have received the coloured troops has not altogether pleased our Southern friends who think it may lead to trouble for them after the war."[6] This, of course, was correct.

Reverend John Haynes Holmes, a veteran campaigner for Indian freedom who also served on the NAACP's Board of Director, was "excited to know" that White was going to India but sensitive to the brewing controversy over the visit. "I must butt in your plans just enough to say that I hope you are not going to make any mistake in that difficult and highly important country," he cautioned. "For you to make a mistake would be well nigh incredible, but I felt a moment of alarm . . . when you spoke as you did about Gandhi. Don't let anybody fool you with the idea that Gandhi has entered upon his decline. . . . [I]f you went to India and saw others and did not see him, it would never be forgiven you."[7] Holmes was sufficiently reassured to provide White with a letter of introduction, telling "Dear Gandhiji" that White's acquaintanceship "begins with the President and runs straight down through the whole world of public and official life in Washington. . . . [Y]ou will be glad to see Mr. White. You will enjoy meeting him, and will be doing India and America alike a great service in talking with him."[8] Another colleague, J. J. Singh of the India League of America, also intervened, telling Bhulahbai Desai, the leader of the Indian National Congress faction in Delhi's Central Legislative Assembly that White was a "great friend of India and I depend upon him for counsel and guidance in my work here."[9]

The helpful Singh provided "five letters of introduction" and vowed to make arrangements for White to "see Gandhi sometime in the third week of January [1945]." Helpful hints were also provided. "There is hardly anything in Karachi besides some Negro troops," White was told. "It will serve no purpose to go to Lahore or Amritsar. If you want to meet Sikh leaders, you will most likely find them in New Delhi. . . . I would advise you not to be a guest of any one who is prominently connected with either the Moslem League or the Hindu Mahasabha [lest White become ensnared in sectarianism]." Likewise, Singh advised White "not to be a guest of any of the leading industrialists or representatives of big landed interests. Of course, you must see and talk with Jinnah [the influential Muslim leader who became the embodiment of the state to be known as Pakistan]. You must also meet Ambedkar, the self-styled leader of the Untouchables."[10]

African American leaders rejected the idea—which some of their friends on the left propounded—that they should pipe down about India and the Allies' failings, lest they inadvertently give a boost to the Axis. White in particular sailed in the opposite direction. "Our people understand, perhaps more clearly than any other American group," he told Anup Singh of the India League of America, "the conditions forced upon India. They resemble in many respects the proscription suffered by colored Americans. The arguments for not acting upon the Indian question are in many cases a duplicate of the arguments for not recognizing the American Negro as a first class citizen."[11]

White's persistence paid off in the sense that his reluctance to back down on the fraught matter of anticolonialism did not prevent the Allies from prevailing. It also gave a boost to independence forces in India and the battle for equality in the United States.[12] Perhaps London sensed this and thus spent so much time seeking to keep White as far away as possible from the empire—a wish that was not fulfilled, although White did not make a great splash, either. As the war was coming to an end in the spring of 1945, Pauli Murray acknowledged: "I am more hopeful about the future of the American Negro than at any other time in my life. Thinking white people everywhere are beginning to see us in relation to the darker races, the majority of mankind and the minority numbers of white men throughout the world." That, in fact, was the key to the crusade for equality, since African Americans continually had had difficulty in winning a majority of Euro-Americans to their righteous cause, and it was by linking their movement to larger forces globally—in India, in Africa and, yes, in Japan—that this logjam was broken. (Unfortunately, this profound point has been lost in today's struggles.) Murray, for one, was heartened. "The American Negro has become a symbol of dark oppressed peoples throughout the world," she said. "We're no longer a 'problem.' We're an opportunity. We're America's chance to make good abroad." Murray wanted Black Americans to "raise their sights, readjust their focus and feel themselves an integral part of international affairs. Because we blend with so many of the peoples of the world, our contribution during the next 25 years can be tremendous." This was due in part to the inescapable fact that the United States could not "compete with the other great powers in the world arena, and specifically Russia, for a share of the moral leadership over the world, unless she clean[ed] up this Aegean . . . stable of 'race.'"[13]

Thus, as the postwar era commenced, there was considerable optimism in Black America, while in India there was a broad perception that the British Empire—battered and bloodied by its bruising encounter with Japan—could not hold on to its colonial jewel in Asia, even if it tried assiduously. Two years after the war concluded in Asia, India gained sovereignty, and seven years after that, the U.S. Supreme Court felt compelled to rule that Jim Crow could no longer stand. But between these dates was a swirl of complexity that could have delayed both independence and equality.

The NAACP continued its engagement with India, but with the winding down of the U.S. alliance with the former Soviet Union and a rising wave of conservatism, buffeted by anticommunism, it became increasingly difficult for the association to maintain its determined stand on anticolonialism. Indeed, a delicate minuet unfolded in which, in return for tentative steps toward equality, Black America backed away from the status that Pauli Murray and others had envisioned—that is, being an advance guard for the "darker" peoples of the planet. Instead, African Americans fundamentally accepted a kind of formal citizenship that lacked economic and social sinew. Of course, Black Americans made up less than 15 percent of the U.S. population, which limited their options. Nonetheless, the fact remains that the international outlook that characterized Black America in the first half of the twentieth century was barely recognizable afterward. India, meanwhile, remained true, becoming a fierce critic of apartheid, an initiator of the historic Bandung Conference of 1955 that catapulted Asia and Africa into international prominence, a founder of the Non-Aligned Movement, and a leading critic of global anticommunism.

A telling signal was transmitted a scant year before Indian independence when Reverend John Haynes Holmes confided to a conservative columnist his concern about the drift of the NAACP. "I am seriously alarmed by the infiltration of Communists and fellow-travelers into many into many of our liberal groups, reform and religious, and am terribly alarmed by this report of yours on the situation of the NAACP," he said. "I want to do something about it, [such as] force the issue in the Board of Directors."[14] What followed shortly thereafter was the purge of W. E. B. Du Bois, who had returned to the association he had helped to found as a kind of minister of foreign affairs, and ultimately the retreat of the association from its deeply engaged and left-leaning posture on the global stage.

Still, it was not easy to turn the largest organization in Black America away from relationships that stretched back decades. In May 1946, the NAACP announced its "support of legislation to lift immigration bars so as to admit into the United States natives of India and thus allow them to become eligible for American citizenship. Since 1917 immigrants from India and several other Asiatic countries have been prohibited from coming here, [and such] bans on Indians [are] resting 'solely on racial grounds.'" Leslie Perry of the NAACP said there were "approximately 4000 nationals of India resting in the U.S., most of whom have been here from thirty to forty years."[15]

This noble gesture was accompanied by a burst of pro–India activity by the NAACP. White became a member of the Executive Committee of the India League of America, one of the leading groups pushing for Indian sovereignty,[16] which complemented his joining Albert Einstein and Pearl Buck in the leadership of the India Famine Emergency Committee,[17] to which the

NAACP donated funds.[18] Certainly, it appeared that the NAACP and the Indian leadership were becoming closer. It was White who informed the Black newspaper executives John Sengstacke of the *Chicago Defender*, Carl Murphy of the *Afro-American*, and Ira Lewis of the *Pittsburgh Courier* that "Devedas Gandhi, son of Mahatma Gandhi, will telephone you this morning. Please give your most sympathetic help." White confided to them, "Negro assistance now will have wide influence in India and Asia, particularly in view of [the] attitude of some white publishers."[19] In short, in the United States, White was the man to see about India. In late 1946, when V. K. Krishna Menon, general-secretary of the India League of London, and "personal representative" of Nehru visited Manhattan, his colleague J. J. Singh told White that "it would be very interesting for you and your associates to have a talk with Mr. Menon."[20]

But there were potential obstacles to full collaboration between the leaders of South Asia and those of Black America. Kaikhusroo Hormuz of San Francisco, for example, informed the segregationist Senator Richard Russell of Georgia that it was a "miscarriage of justice and degradation to my racial people by being branded as 'not a white person.'" Hormuz described himself as a "disabled veteran of World War I and a citizen of the U.S.A. I am a Parsee (Persian Zorastrian) by race, [which] is the foremost known *White Aryan Race*. . . . I was the one and only Parsee prisoner of war in the Japanese concentration camp in Shanghai, China for three years and seven months. . . . [I]t is clear as daylight that the Parsees have been, and shall remain, Aryan, [and] only insist upon their rights to be treated as a White Race and not to be mixed up with Hindus because their ancestors were born in India," just as Europeans born in South Africa were not Black.[21]

Should the NAACP campaign to prove that some people of South Asian origin were "white"? Was that a judicious use of its scarce resources? Or was it an aspect of the attempt to implode white supremacy? Other substantive issues were entangled with Hormuz's dilemma. For example, the "relevant United States immigration law in the [1940s] stipulated that 'Asiatic and East Indian' women who married American citizens did not automatically become citizens themselves and hence gain admission to the United States," unlike the smoother path laid out for those of European descent. How could the NAACP remain mute?[22]

In a larger sense, the concern expressed by Hormuz was losing potency in the wake of the war. Driven in part by the racial quagmire exploited so adroitly by Tokyo, London and, especially, Washington moved to undermine the de jure value of race, which simultaneously served to checkmate the attempt by the new antagonist in Moscow to mine this rich vein of discontent. In early 1946, the American Friends Services Committee (AFSC), the humanitarian and relief arm of the Quakers, contemplated the "general idea of appointing a Negro or a Negro couple" to its India office. The idea "interests us a good deal," said Eric Johnson, an AFSC official.[23] This was a key post for both India and the AFSC, which was especially competent in famine relief. "There is no other agency but ourselves concerned with emergency relief in India at this time," Johnson reported in the spring of 1946.[24] Moreover, as the future top U.S. diplomat Chester Bowles saw it, despite its size and potential strategic value, India in this pre-independence year was not a high priority in Washington. "Many of us are willing to look the other way when the East is concerned on the general theory that Asia and India are remote and the people there are accustomed to privation," Bowles told Pearl Buck. "I have had some personal experiences with individuals here in Washington along this line which were very shocking indeed."[25] The "great needs of India are often forgotten in the publicity which fills the headlines concerning the needs of Europe," concurred Leah Mills of the AFSC, who was in a position to know.[26] This did not augur well for the time that was soon to come in which independent India would be catered to by Washington in the aftermath of the Communists' coming to power in neighboring China in 1949. Yet India's not being in the spotlight made it simpler to post African Americans there.

India, said Johnson, is "one of the most dangerous tension spots in the world today." Further, in this complex land there is "deep resentment toward the West." Yet due in large measure to the "whole-hearted encouragement and cooperation" of the Congress of Industrial Organizations and labor generally in the United Sates, he reported, the AFSC was able to "work principally in Bengal."[27] As a result, by early 1946 "approximately $650,000 [had] been expended for the emergency program in India," which was considerable, given the logistical barrier of the two months that were needed to "get supplies from the United States to the Indian points of distribution."[28]

Hence, posting African Americans in India was more than symbolic—although it was certainly also that. The importance of such a gesture was not entirely understood within the AFSC, though African Americans had "assurance [that] they [would] be welcome."[29] Against this backdrop, the youthful African American theologian William Stuart Nelson and his spouse, Blanche Wright Nelson, arrived in Calcutta in the fall of 1946. They were slated to stay in Bengal for a year, with the goal of "working toward developing greater inter-racial understanding and goodwill."[30] They arrived amid enormous intercommunal conflict between Hindus and Muslims. "I have talked to several ex-military men, each of them reported that they had never experienced anything in the army to compare with the horror of Calcutta," said Harry Abrahamson of the AFSC. "One of these men was with the U.S. Marines on

Guadalcanal and he said even Guadalcanal could [not] compare with the bloodshed and violence of Calcutta."[31]

The Nelsons tried to apply the skills they had gleaned from traversing the perilous racial divide in the United States to the even more dangerous fissures in India. Soon they were "speaking and meeting with groups [in] South India" and conferring with the top leaders, including Nehru.[32] Nelson also was involved in "placing Negroes in India" in various positions in South Asia.[33] He was seeking to keep his constituency in the United States apprised. Reports of his activities were circulated to P. B. Young of the *Norfolk Journal and Guide*, which had a predominantly African American readership.[34] In a relatively short period, Nelson had become not only a major presence in India, but also a bridge between Black America and India. "I do not contemplate with enthusiasm the shortness of our remaining stay in India," he said with a tinge of dissatisfaction.[35]

William Stuart Nelson was born in Paris, Kentucky, in 1895. He was a graduate of Howard and Yale universities and had also attended the Sorbonne and the University of Berlin. His head of hair that was already showing signs of thinning, and his light skin often made him stand out while he was visiting southwestern India. Nelson eventually became dean of the School of Religion at Howard University and a force in shaping the Civil Rights Movement.[36]

Nelson held the bona fide credential of having conferred with Gandhi. "Dearest Blanche," he wrote his beloved spouse in early December 1946. "By the light of a dimly lit lantern, I have begun this note. . . . [Y]esterday we saw Gandhi and the experience was a benediction. Not only did we hold a most helpful conversation with him but were privileged to attend his prayer meeting." As was his wont, Gandhi "wished me . . . to sing him an American hymn, which we declined to do with regrets."[37] But this was the only note of disagreement in an otherwise mutually enriching session. It was in Noakhali that he "first met Mr. Gandhi," Nelson reported. "After hours of truck travel over impossible roads and a three mile journey by foot, [I] found him in a simple hut of a tiny village."[38] On the lower part of his body, Nelson recalled later, Gandhi wore a "spotless white garment woven probably from cotton which he himself had spun, with the upper part of his frail body looking like a piece of burnished bronze upon a white pedestal. . . . [He was] seated on the floor of a bare room. There were only the floor and the walls and the ceiling."

Nelson was in the trenches, taking a "51 hour ride from Madras to Delhi" in early 1947. He and his spouse reached Lahore on March 5, he recalled. "It was a dismal Lahore that greeted us—riot disturbed, curfew bound and thoroughly frightened. . . . I delivered three talks to the graduate students at

Wilson College, preached at its Sunday morning service and spoke to the faculty and the undergraduate students on Monday morning." This may have been the only idyll experienced by this mutinous metropolis. "There was no one who dared take us, even during the day, to the old part of Lahore," Nelson observed. Even an African American familiar with the pogroms of Tulsa, Oklahoma, and East St. Louis, Illinois, would be stunned by the bloodiness of what was transpiring in British India. "We and the family with which we lived suffered some excitement one evening when partisans began shouting slogans from house tops and beating drums," Nelson wrote. "Fire engines rushed through the streets, and there was every indication that a mob was bearing down upon our section." He found it hard to forget the "utter helplessness which one experiences when faced by a frenzied and hostile crowd, armed or partially armed." This was "exacting a terrific mental toll."

Then it was off to Delhi, where Nelson spoke at the Quaker Centre on "The Race Problem in America." Then he spoke to a Delhi University Teacher's Group and to the Indian Council of World Affairs, which sponsored a conference "The American Negro in Law and in Fact," Nelson reported. "Blanche spoke to a group of women on this same subject. The interest of the Delhi people," he said tellingly "seemed somehow to center on race relations." In Delhi Nelson was a "distinguished guest" and, he added modestly, "accorded courtesies which, I am sure, my actual status did not deserve." He attended receptions for Lord Mountbatten, who was then negotiating London's exit from the subcontinent, and his wife, Lady Mountbatten, who was then embroiled in a passionate tryst with "Pandit Jawaharlal Nehru. Both of these were brilliant affairs," Nelson enthused, referring to the glittering events. Nehru found time to have a "conference" with him. "I expressed to him appreciation for the warm reception which Blanche and I had received everywhere in India," Nelson said, "and for the profound interest which Indians evidenced in the American race problem and their deep sympathy with Negro Americans." Again, he named a major item on his agenda: his "hope that the [Indian] government in search of experts to assist in [their] programme would not overlook competent Negro Americans. [Nehru] responded very favorably to the suggestion and asked that he be presented with a list of Negroes who might be interested in a call to India." Nelson was "deeply desirous of seeing a large number of Negro experts called to the services of foreign lands." Sensing a historic opportunity, he added portentously, "This will help, in a measure, to offset the large denial to them in America of the opportunity to work in Government and industry." The whirlwind journey took the Nelsons next to Bombay, where the topic was again "race relations" and they were again given a rapturous reception. "One seldom sees such a number of virile civic discussion groups as we discovered in Bombay," he observed. But what dominated this tour of pre-independence India were the blood-spattered "riots" and one "strike" after another.[39]

Yet what engaged Nelson's imagination was his conversation with Nehru. A "growing number of Negroes in America [were] prepared technically for numerous forms of work" that Jim Crow forbade, he pointed out. "Many of our men and women who are well trained in the colleges and universities are unable to find work. . . . Coming to the East would be a great experience and through them a significant contribution to the life of the Negro in America," he added with profundity. The idea seemed to appeal to Nehru, according to Nelson, who perhaps sensed that such an initiative could address his nascent nation's dearth of technicians while building a lobby in what had become the planet's most powerful nation.[40] Interestingly, the first concrete step in implementing the program emerged when Howard University "offered Dr. [Amiya] Chakravarty an appointment as Visiting Professor of English."[41]

As it turned out, Nelson was present in India at a decisive moment in the nation's history. He was heavily involved in relief efforts, as British misrule—again—was feeding famine.[42] Hunger does not necessarily create an appetite for comity. Nelson noted days before the moment of India's independence, "The communal situation in Calcutta has deteriorated during the past few days." This was gross understatement, as the situation there was comparable to the distress he had witnessed earlier in Lahore.[43] The weather was fraying nerves, too. The heat in Calcutta, which ranged from "95 . . . to 108 [degrees Fahrenheit]," was punishing. "Rumors are abroad in India," he said, "concerning the likelihood of widespread disturbances upon the announcement of any definite plan for India's future."[44] But as his time in India was winding down, and as India was moving inexorably toward independence, Nelson could only be heartened, despite the gore all around. He and his spouse had been "overwhelmed by the warmth with which they had been received by everyone." Remarkably, he said, amid the turmoil he "could not think of one single unpleasant incident in the whole trip." His focus overwhelmingly was "race relations, especially in America," a bleeding subject all its own that could comfort Indians in the notion that theirs was not the only intercommunal conflict. "There were only two days or three on the entire trip," Nelson said, in which he "did not speak at least once and [his] program had included as many as five talks in one day. In addition, people kept him busy with interviews in between engagements."[45]

A talk he gave at Calcutta University, which was published in India, was typical. Of the many "failures of America," he said, "the greatest [is] its attitude toward the Negro people in its midst. . . . We [had] read recently here in India of the freeing of twenty-eight white men in the state of South Carolina accused of participating in the lynching of a Negro." This was not unique by any means.

In words pregnant with meaning, he referred to African Americans as "international orphans" with "international alienage [*sic*]" and, thus, worthy of international support from the likes of India, a land "destined to be a significant and, perhaps, a dominant factor in future world relations." It was to be hoped that India would "throw the great power of her land and her people constantly and courageously upon the side of the freedom of men everywhere from those conflicts which for so long have darkened and embittered their lives."[46]

As it turned out, the AFSC's apprehensions about the arrival of the Nelsons—or of Negroes generally—in India were misplaced, because Black Americans proved to be exceedingly effective. (Whether they were effective in pushing U.S., as opposed to Black Americans', interests was another question and, perhaps, the core of the original concern about their presence.) As "Race War!" gave way to an effort to sustain racial concord, dispatching African Americans to India seemed to be the thing to do. For it was then, in 1946, that the YMCA posted Lawrence Burr to South Asia for a five-year term. Born in Denton, Texas, in 1913, Burr received a degree from Langston College in 1932. His spouse, Mildred Burr, also was grounded in Black America: She was born in Oklahoma, was a graduate of Wilberforce University, founded by Black religionists, and belonged to the African Methodist Episcopal church. She also read French.[47] The bespectacled Burr, often dressed conservatively in a dark suit and white shirt with a striped tie, had frizzy hair and was somewhat hirsute.[48]

In the postwar era, many religionists thought that sending Negroes to India was putting the best foot forward and, perhaps, an advantage in a nation teeming with dark-skinned people. Initially, the Burrs did not seem to be following this script, and they initially received rebukes. "Their pathetic gratitude simply makes me write," said one colleague. "I have felt so ashamed over their bad start here." Evidently, Burr had somewhat tactlessly "said what he thought of the dirt and the smell," which enraged some of his listeners. "Relationships are strained indeed," the colleague reported in November 1946.[49] But the Burrs quickly regained their footing. Immediately upon his arrival in India, Lawrence Burr charted a new approach to India's waif problem and directed his work among destitute boys for the Madras YMCA. Burr started India's first "Boys Town." The youth belonged to the Sudra, or laboring caste, of Hindus, or "to the even lower Untouchables condemned by birth to the bottom level of human society. . . . Soon after reaching India in 1946, Mr. Burr's activities in the slums of Madras began making newspaper copy at home and abroad." Often he could be found "searching the streets at night for homeless boys" to rescue.[50]

The impending independence of India was bringing to fruition the promise of bilateral cooperation that had been bruited about years earlier. Sadly, Gandhi was not to witness what he had done so much to realize. "The death of Mr. Gandhi bears for me a sorrow deepened by my numerous associations with him of a few months past," said Nelson. "I had come to feel deep affection for him. . . . [He] permitted my stay in his ashram and addressed himself by the hour to questions which I raised. . . . One of Mr. Gandhi's intimates . . . said I could now speak of Gandhi as a friend."[51]

Thus it was that Nelson stood stolidly "at midnight on 15th August 1947" in India and "listened to Mr. Nehru as he spoke of the transfer of power that was then taking place from the British government to India. He referred to Gandhi, who was absent, as one would if he could would wipe every tear from every eye." The "tryst with destiny" of which Nehru spoke also encompassed the lengthy tie that bound Black America and India.[52]

But this epochal moment was bittersweet, because an India whole and free did not emerge. Instead, there was partition and the creation of a Muslim state in Pakistan. In seeking to unravel this intricate religious knot, one Indian National Congress militant pointed to a U.S. example: "When Abraham Lincoln conceived that noble form of government, he excluded from its people the Negroes of America. Many of my Hindu friends who talk of nationalism and freedom and independence exclude the Muslims from its domain."[53] Tensions between Hindus and Muslims were not solely a creation of London, yet articulate African American opinion repeatedly accused the empire of playing the age-old game of divide and conquer to insure that an independent South Asia would be wracked with fissures and unable to realize its immense promise. This opinion was prefigured ominously in the socialist-oriented journal, *The Messenger*,[54] which indicted London, although *Phylon*, a journal founded by W. E. B. Du Bois, took a different tack, arguing that "British racial and cultural distinction has by historic irony served as an influence to weaken caste, even to weaken the distinction between Hindu and Mohammedan. Caste itself does not imply a color distinction, whereas British ascendancy is the ascendancy of the white man over the brown man."[55] Du Bois himself denounced the partition of British India in unwaveringly harsh terms.[56] Still, with independence, a long, hard slog had reached victory. Yet that was not the end of the story of Black America and India.

12

TOWARD EQUALITY/BEYOND
INDEPENDENCE

No!"[1] "No!"[2] "No!"[3] And "no!" again.[4] These were the responses of John Haynes Holmes to, respectively, a request from Paul Robeson to speak out on behalf of leaders of the Communist Party USA who were on trial; a letter to protest an anti-leftist riot at Peekskill, New York; a letter from the attorneys of jailed Communist leaders who were under attack; and a letter from W. E. B. Du Bois, Benjamin Mays, and others concerning a civil-rights rally that did not exclude those on the left. What these adamant rejections reflected was that, at the conclusion of World War II, the United States embarked almost immediately on a Cold War, and the latter conflict had dramatic impact on the longstanding alliance that had existed between Black America and India. Black Nationalists had been compromised—in the eyes of many—by a perception that they were too closely tied to the now discredited foe in Tokyo, while Black leftists, as symbolized by Robeson and Du Bois, fell victim to their refusal to repudiate the Communist Party and Moscow. This left a coterie of leaders with varying ties to New Delhi—for example, A. Philip Randolph, James Farmer, Bayard Rustin, Pauli Murray, and, particularly, the NAACP leadership surrounding Walter White—with various claims to legitimacy and in a unique position to claim credit for the retreat from Jim Crow that followed, perhaps inevitably, from the "Race War!" that characterized the recently concluded conflict.

Like Holmes, these leaders were hardly forthcoming toward the now reviled pro–Soviet sympathizers but, simultaneously, this posture was not advantageous in maintaining an alliance with a nation, India, that turned out to be one of Moscow's more reliable allies in the non–Communist world. Moreover, Washington was hardly in favor of Black America conducting its own foreign policy when a principal objective of this global initiative was to erode the very Jim Crow on which the ruling Democrats relied so heavily to maintain their grip on power. Simultaneously, Washington felt, understandably, that the newly enhanced leadership of Black America could be strategically significant in winning the affections of New Delhi. At the same time, India, justifying the faith that Black America had put in it, emerged as one of the more forceful and articulate opponents of racial bias, be it in newly apartheid South Africa or in the United States.

Pre-eminent, as well, was the fact that in the aftermath of "Race War!" African Americans moved steadily away from their previous polecat status to a form of full citizenship. This necessarily entailed an alteration from the previous posture of maintaining an independent foreign policy for Black America that did not blanch in the face of alliances with Tokyo or Moscow to today's notion of adopting policies that are not radically different from those of dominant elites—albeit those of the liberal persuasion. Walter White, for example, became something of a counselor to President Harry S. Truman on policy to what was now being routinely described as the planet's largest democracy: India.

U ntil recently our eyes were always turned toward Great Britain," said J. J. Singh, president of the Indian League of America in 1948, "but today it is more important that the aspirations of the Indian people be correctly understood by Americans than Englishmen, Russians or any other people." This was not puffery: The war had devastated every major participant except the United States, which proceeded to wield ever greater influence in the international community. Singh had sensed the arrival of this development as he sought to "recall an incident, I think in 1942, some time after the arrest of the Indian leaders, when a real 'Iron Curtain'—and perhaps the first 'Iron Curtain'—was drawn between India and the United States. . . . Do you know how we secured some of this important news [from India?] . . . [W]e would get American soldiers to send us clippings and other material in their letters to this country. American soldiers' letters were handled by the American Army Post Office and were not subject to censorship by the British." This helped to convince Singh of Washington's growing clout, even in the heart of the British Empire.

But if the United States was gaining in influence, so was India, he thought, in light of its newly declared independence. "Before the Second World War," he recalled, "hardly any Indian businessmen, tourists, political leaders or students ever came to the United States. . . . With regard to Indians living in the United States, at no time have there been more than 6000. The first 'immigrant' came in 1899." The figure, as he spoke in 1948, was "in the vicinity of 4000. Almost 95% of the 4000 odd Indians are illiterate. There are about 3000 on the Pacific Coast (2000 Sikhs, 1000 Moslems and Hindus), mostly farmers (some of them very well-to-do). Then we have about 500 in Greater New York, . . . most of whom work in factories, restaurants or garages (large numbers of them are Lascara [or seafarers] who jumped ships). And there are about 300 in Detroit, Michigan, most of whom work in automobile factories." There are "not more than 30 to 40 Indian businessmen in the whole of the United States," he said, a partial result of the fact that Indians "were not eligible for citizenship until the passage in 1946 of the India Immigration and Naturalization Bill," a measure backed avidly in Black America.[5]

Meanwhile, U.S. nationals in India were enduring their own adjustment to the new situation but they were not as upbeat as Singh. Based in Calcutta, a citadel of Hindu and Muslim culture, Eugene Barnett of the YMCA announced none too cheerily days after Indian independence, "This is a new day for Christianity . . . in India. Under British rule it had a preferred, a protected position—whether its adherents have wanted this dubious advantage or not. The end of British rule removes this adventitious prop." But U.S.-based Christians were not without advantages, for Indian independence coincided with a renewed effort by Washington to improve the sorry lot of African Americans. This could provide a further rationale for dispatching Negro missionaries to India, who, in the name of spreading the Good Word of Christianity, also could—coincidentally—be walking display models for Washington's new enlightenment. And this (also coincidentally) would be advantageous in wooing India in the face of Moscow's challenge. For his part, Barnett recognized that "Christian influence" in India was "far greater than the numerical strength of the Church," which augured well. Not auguring well, he thought, were London's colonial religious policies, which set the stage for repetitive sectarian conflict. "Many say that a long step was taken toward the present explosions when in 1909 the policy was established of communal voting, thus magnifying and freezing communal divisions instead of developing a common citizenry." But all was not lost. "This pace is strenuous," he declared. "The weather is atrocious. I am having a wonderful time."[6]

It is not evident that the Burrs, the African American couple dispatched to India, were enjoying themselves similarly. There was a "certain amount of temperamental incompatibility" between them and other YMCA personnel in Madras. "The personal relationship between the Burrs [and the] General Secretary at Madras are still far from what they should be," suggested a mutual colleague.[7] Even the simplest of tasks required profound patience—for example, it was stressed that it took the "Madras bank *60 days* to give [Burr] rupee credits to draw on for his dollar checks after he has deposited them."[8] The Burrs' "quarters . . . were not entirely satisfactory"; the "roof [leaks] likes a sieve whenever it rains hard, and the walls of many of the rooms are in a shabby state." From the other shore, the allegation arose that the heralded work the Burrs were doing with Indian youth was "proving far more expensive than they had anticipated." Still, the colleague noted, "Everyone in Madras recognizes that Burr is a first-class Boys' Work Secretary and they also appreciate the hard work which he and his Boys' Work colleagues have been doing."[9] A YMCA executive in New York City, D. F. McClelland, thought that "it would be unfortunate for many reasons to loss Burr's service. All accounts indicate that he has done an outstanding job." Yet that was not all, as it was thought that Burr had another advantage that would play quite well in India: He was "the first Negro appointed to our foreign staff since Max Yergan, [and] we are very anxious that he should succeed and should have the happiest experience possible."[10] As for Burr himself, he found his work stirring and enriching, with meaning beyond the confines of eastern India. "It was heartening," he said in mid–1948, "to see high school boys of different schools, religions and communities share a common experience in the midst of rising tensions in the world based on religion and race."[11]

Burr's presence was unique in that, by 1949, out of a "total number of YMCA secretaries in the area," including 189 in India, 7 in Pakistan, and 20 in Ceylon, Burr was one of the few Negroes they could find to hold such a post.[12] The YMCA also considered poaching, and it began to eye William Stuart Nelson for recruitment. He "would make a most admirable YMCA Secretary for our staff in India," McClelland was told.[13] "Bihari has been asking for a Physical Director (possibly a Negro) for Lahore and I strongly endorse this request," said T. D. Santwant of Calcutta's YMCA in early 1949.[14]

Yet Burr found himself in the middle of sectarian issues in the city that came to be known as Chennai. Within the inner councils of the YMCA, there were "very prolonged and interesting discussions [about] problems [concerning the] Christian [versus] non-Christian issue as it affected the city of Madras." This "problem" was emphasized because it was "real."[15] This was not the only real problem the increasingly beleaguered Burr was enduring. An underdeveloped India was a tough assignment, and it was not clear that Burr was up to it. His doctor had advised him "to use his jeep as sparingly as possible because it was having an injurious effect on his spine & kidneys, due to the jolting & bumping it caused. . . . [This] seemed to have caused some enlargement of [his] prostate gland," which forced him to sell the vehicle at "considerable loss." Now he was "greatly handicapped," and both he and his spouse had to "depend on riding in buses or walking, as taxis are not available where they live. . . . [A co-worker] could help [Burr] greatly by taking him down to the office in the morning, without any trouble or inconvenience to himself as their houses are less than a block apart on the same street," but "never once" was this easy favor offered. Besides, it was emphasized, "*the Madras* YMCA *is in acute financial straits*" and "under these conditions [could not] give Lawrence any help."[16]

Soon thereafter, the Burrs departed. Still, his impact and those of other African Americans were not for naught. Though certain U.S. elites may have thought they were gaining a propaganda advantage by dispatching Negroes to India, African Americans had their own intentions in deciding to embark on the trans-oceanic journey. When Bayard Rustin arrived in Bombay in late 1948, he reported quickly to the NAACP's Roy Wilkins, "This morning I spoke with [S. T.] Patel of Patel Bros., a large cotton firm. He's interested to know as much as possible (when in New York for which he leaves in a few days) about colored Americans. I have told him that he should see you."[17] Likewise, Burr asked early on "what possibility there is of arranging for [John] Anantharaz" and his Fellowship Training, which was designed with India in mind, to "spend some time with one of the Negro YMCA branches"—for example, the "branch in Chicago from which [Burr] came to India." This globally minded branch, which Burr had started a few years earlier, had "more than 1000 high school boys and girls in active membership" and recently had raised a hefty $4,500 for various global projects.[18] The enhanced contact between Madras and Black Chicago could only redound to the benefit of both.

In the meantime, Burr was toiling valiantly. On one occasion, he told an audience subsequently in Chicago, "At 4 A.M. [in Madras] an Indian 'Y' man and I went out on the streets and rounded up a group of . . . orphans" to provide them shelter.[19] Burr's activism was receiving publicity back in the United States,[20] and for good reason. "It still seems incredible," said his colleague Wilson Hume, that as a partial result of the YMCA's labors, "Muslims began to embrace Hindus & to walk arm-in-arm with them & to garland them—in the very streets where only a day or so previously they had been stabbing one another! It seems to have been an instance of mass-psychology expressing itself in a sort of mass conversion. . . . Calcutta went freedom mad."[21]

This may have been a false dawn, however, as sectarian conflict continued to influence politics in India as the century unfolded. This did not prevent African Americans from continuing to advance the decades-long tie to India, although the postwar situation had altered the relationship decisively. Before the shape of the new Cold War world became clear, which compromised the once promising tie between Black America and India, the idea was still afoot in the NAACP particularly that there was something to be gained by maintaining an alignment with India. Days after the declaration of Indian sovereignty, Du Bois contacted the charismatic Vijaya Lakshmi, Delhi's delegate to the newly created United Nations. "Sending [a] document by the hand of Mr. Walter White," he wrote. It contained a "copy of the petition and statement which [the NAACP is] trying to get before the Assembly of the United Nations, or the Economic and Social Council. I am also enclosing a letter which I have to Mr. Trygve Lie [the body's leader]. . . . I should be under great obligation if you could do anything to see that we get some chance for a hearing." Du Bois was seeking to bring the plight of U.S. Negroes before the august international body, a démarche with potentially far-reaching implications and a maneuver certain to outrage Washington, which was positioning itself as a paragon of human-rights virtue in the ongoing ideological battle with Moscow. Du Bois was also seeking to keep alive the age-old notion that African Americans were part of a larger "colored" community in which India was a constituent element. "The determination of our rulers to conquer Asia and hold Africa," he said, "is but logical prolongation of our despising of Negroes here."[22] As it turned out, Du Bois, who in 1944 had returned to the organization he had founded in a vastly different, left-influenced atmosphere, was ousted from the NAACP in 1948 precisely because of the United Nations initiative for which he had sought Indian aid. This was a telling sign of the newly minted political environment.

The diminutive Du Bois, with his balding pate and generous intellect, had reason to believe that the conclusion of World War II would lead in a direction different from the one that emerged. After all, it was in November 1946, while making one of the rare public appearances that her duty as head of the Indian delegation to the United Nations permitted, that Vijaya Pandit arrived in Harlem to speak under the auspices of the New York branch of the NAACP at the Golden Gate Ballroom alongside Walter White. This climaxed the Gotham drive for 10,000 new members, and the assembled was not disappointed when she made a sharp assault on South Africa's Jan Christian Smuts, complementing "her consistent championing of the rights of colored peoples."[23] Pandit did not disappoint, either, when her office told Du Bois in early 1948 that the government of India had brought his appeal "to the notice of the Indian Council of World Affairs, which is prepared to give publicity in its journal to any contribution on this subject which might be sent them by the [NAACP]."[24]

With Du Bois's ouster, White had the field to himself and tried to execute his own foreign policy, albeit in a direction that was not congruent with past actions. The NAACP's foreign policy devolved from an alliance with India and common goals targeting imperialism and white supremacy to a campaign that aligned with Washington in order to influence India toward anticommunism. But this was not evident immediately, and, as a consequence, White continued to be party to sensitive and important confabs. In early 1948, J. J. Singh invited White to join "as [a] guest at our luncheon . . . to meet Sheikh Mohammad Abdulla, [h]ead of the emergency government of the state of Jammu and Kashmir," a flashpoint that was to complicate India–Pakistan relations for decades to come.[25] In a personal and confidential note to Nehru, White continued to display his familiarity and intimacy with Indian politics when he noted that, "from the point of view of the internal situation now going on in India, it was probably wise of you to select a Muslim as the first Ambassador from India to the United States." But White counseled that Nehru's sister might be the "ideal" choice partly because "the fact that she is a woman would bring her appointment" some welcome publicity.[26] Nehru had developed an intimacy and familiarity of his own, purchasing a "life membership" in the NAACP.[27]

Yet the Cold War soon began to assert itself on NAACP policy. About a year after Du Bois was ousted, White was confiding to Fowler McCormick of International Harvester, "I was asked by a high official of the United States government to make recommendation on what could be done to assist India in solving its problems and thereby affirmatively demonstrat[e] the superiority of democracy to communism. This was based on the very sound premise that if India falls, there is no way whatever of stopping the march of communism through Asia and on the further premise that if Asia falls, democracy in the United States will be in dire peril."[28] Thus, from Black America and India collaborating for mutual advantage against white supremacy and imperialism, White was now seeking to steer Black America toward a collaboration with the U.S. ruling elite against "communism" in India. McCormick, for his part, sought to assure White that "we have been for years as interested as you are in trying to find a solution to the use of farm machinery" in India, as this major corporation sought to secure a lucrative foreign contract with White's judicious assistance.[29]

"I have had several talks with Prime Minister Nehru and Mme. Pandit," White told McCormick, "and know that they look forward to talking with you." Burnishing his own glossy name, he added that he had an "invitation from Dr. Ralph J. Bunche and myself for an off-the-record conference with Prime Minister Nehru here in New York." He also suggested how the old Black America–India tie had morphed into a Black America–U.S. attempt to influence India and how this could still (it was thought) benefit African Americans. He told McCormick, also confidentially, that one of his

> chief difficulties in persuading Asians, and particularly Indians, to have faith in the United States instead of Russia is the playing up not only by Moscow radio but [by] Reuters as well of lynching and racial discrimi-

nation in the United States. Recently in New Delhi Prime Minister Nehru asked me to arrange for him to talk with some leading Negroes about this subject. I told him that I did not want to arrange a segregated meeting and that it was very important for him to see and know that white as well as Negro Americans are interested in this question.[30]

In sum, the United States had to eliminate Jim Crow to gain a propaganda advantage over Moscow in the battle for affections of nations such as India.

White had decided to throw in his lot with the Cold Warriors and was gaining some influence as a result. Washington was well aware of Black America's pre-existing tie to India and thought this could be useful in affecting New Delhi's policies, foreign and otherwise. "Yesterday morning," White told India's United Nations delegate in 1949, "President Truman asked me if I saw any prospect of India and Pakistan solving the Kashmir problem. He also asked me what I believed was responsible for the recent refusal of the Government of India to arbitrate the issue." The diligent White said that he had "read everything I can lay my hands on regarding the Kashmir issue and talked both in India and here with as many authorities on the subject as I could." But like legions of others, past and present, he was flummoxed, adding wanly, "The facts are not clear to me."[31] Independent of White, the White House had worked out a detailed proposal but, apparently, decided to humor the NAACP leader by encouraging his freelance diplomacy.[32]

Besides finding time to advise the White House on Kashmir, White became the man to see when Prime Minister Nehru paid a visit to the United States in the fall of 1949. This was partially due to Nehru's own intervention, as he—at least, initially—tried to keep the alliance between Black America and India alive. For as White informed President Mordecai Johnson of Howard University after conferring with Truman about Kashmir: "Wednesday night at dinner at the Embassy, Mme. Pandit told Mrs. White and me that she and her brother [Nehru] had insisted that arrangements be made for the Prime Minister to meet some of the leaders of Negro life while in the United States." White, ever eager to confirm his own importance, added knowingly, "The Prime Minister expressed the same desire to me when I talked to him recently in New Delhi. But the State Department," which was still unsure about the dimensions and intentions of the Black America–India relationship, "interposed objections." In a real sense, White was more in tune with the long-term interests of the nation as he confirmed that the "presence of a number of distinguished Negroes will be a most effective thing and will be a subtle rebuke to the shortcomings of the State Department." Sensing the import of his remarks, he added, "For obvious reasons, please keep this strictly confidential."[33]

But whether this information leaked or not, the bureaucrats of Foggy Bottom were not enthusiastic about White's continuing the past practice of Black America conducting its own foreign policy, even if its aims were not necessarily inconsistent with Washington's. "The State Department is up to its old shenanigans," he wearily informed the Black journalist Louis Martin. "Since I talked with you, I had dinner that evening with Madame Pandit. She informed [me] that virtually over the State Department's dead body she and Prime Minister Nehru had insisted on a time when a small group of Negro leaders would have the opportunity to meet with Nehru." White was convinced that there would be "a few heart attacks at the State Department when they see the guest list and find Negroes on it," and, naturally, he noted, "the presence of Negroes at the [Indian] Embassy will be a subtle but stinging rebuke to the State Department."[34]

White had visited South Asia in the summer of 1949 and was seeking to become an important go-between in relations between Washington and New Delhi. He was resolute in reminding Truman that it was "impossible to exaggerate [India's] importance" in the battle against communism; the "British proposal to defend Hongkong . . . would be nothing but another Dunkirk if India falls." This was in the aftermath of White's own visit to India, where he had conferred with Nehru and other leaders; the Negro leader was quite concerned about the "Communist agitators" he witnessed, "especially in Bengal." Seemingly more concerned about the struggle against communism than the struggle against white supremacy and a still regnant Jim Crow, White told Truman that, "based upon observations in Pakistan, Delhi and Calcutta," he now "advocated an Asian federation . . . combating communism."[35]

In retrospect, it is evident that White had a point when he lamented the State Department's short-sightedness in seeking to block his attempt to set up a meeting with Nehru and Negro leaders. As White and his fellow host, the black diplomat Ralph Bunche, made clear, a prime goal of their meeting with Nehru was to "end racial injustices [by] withdrawing from the Communists their strongest propaganda weapons."[36] Where was the harm when White, along with Bunche, organized a "small and informal reception" for Nehru at the home of the powerful Robert Lehman at 625 Park Avenue in Manhattan[37] that was attended by, among others, the lawyer William Hastie, the educator Mary McLeod Bethune, and the intellectual Robert Weaver?[38] The harm was in highlighting Jim Crow, which leading members of Truman's party were hesitant to dispense with, and empowering Jim Crow's victims to the detriment of the Dixiecrats. White's second-in-command at the NAACP, Roy Wilkins, was explicit in his aim of leveraging Indian prestige on behalf of the crusade against Jim Crow, telling "Pandit Nehru" that he wished "on this occasion to express his concern over the impairment of American prestige throughout Asia, Africa and the Pacific because of American racial policies. The dinner would serve as an opening effort in a campaign to raise $100,000 in special gifts from the assembled group to support the struggle of the NAACP."[39] Still, White was simply exemplifying the heartfelt desires of Nehru himself; he had spoken with the Indian leader in Delhi before addressing the same issue with Madame Pandit in Paris. She, too, White told the invitees, "expressed to me a desire to meet with a small group of Americans who would be interested in discussing . . . the repercussions in Asia of America's racial prejudice."[40]

The persevering White held his small Park Avenue meeting with Nehru and his entourage. If Washington was concerned about the gathering, it must have been inflamed by White's desire to take his Indian friends on a tour of the hovels to which African Americans in New York City were too often consigned. "We could leave the Waldorf and drive up Park Avenue to 135th Street," White suggested. At "110th Street you will move into an area of markets under the New York Central [railroad] tracks and there see something of the conditions in which Puerto Ricans and Negroes live in very marked contrast to what you will see on lower Park Avenue." At 135th Street, the group could head west and "drive through the so-called 'lung' [tuberculosis] blocks which are more densely populated than any other spot in the world." They could "cross the river into the Bronx and there see one of the housing projects where racial segregation has been broken down," then "stop briefly at Riverton Houses which was built by the Metropolitan Life Insurance Company in an attempted answer to their exclusion of Negroes from Stuyvesant Town, a huge housing project for which [Metropolitan Life] received such benefits as tax exemption from the City of New York but from which they excluded Negroes because of their color."[41] White's anticommunism, as Washington saw it, was insufficient to lessen the damage that would be inflicted by such candid tours.

White continued to try to exert influence on U.S. policy, however. In late 1950, he suggested that President Truman consider asking Ralph Bunche, who was in Norway, to go to India as representative of either the United Nations or the United States to handle a brewing "crisis." Why Bunche? "Anti-white sentiment in Asia today [is] such that [a] Negro American might conceivably counteract suspicion and hostility," White argued.[42] Yet, ironically, when the time came to recommend Pauli Murray for a post in New Delhi, White—though well aware that the State Department was searching for "qualified Negroes"—retreated. He noted that "several Negroes [had already] been assigned to India in posts of varying degrees of importance," and he "question[ed] the wisdom of sending Negroes only to India, Liberia and other so-called colored countries."[43] It was equally striking that India, whose tie to Black America was strong, was now being grouped with Africa and that White would not recommend a woman to go there.

White's aggressive intervention was also complicated by frosty relations between Washington and New Delhi. U.S. Ambassador Loy Henderson was in sync with his government. He "secretly . . . disliked and mistrusted Nehru. He disliked Nehru with a passion . . . [When] we took Nehru to the United States," the U.S. diplomat John M. Stevens recalled later, "he acted as though he wasn't interested at all in going. He didn't look upon it as any great favor. His daughter, Indira, who we had to deal with later . . . carried on the same haughty attitude toward the United States. The attitude was reciprocated." Stevens also said that the ambassador's spouse was a "real 'pain in the neck.' . . . [S]he was terrible . . . she was awful" and was disliked intensely by all sides—including the Indians.[44]

In the early 1950s, Smith Simpson was a consular officer in Bombay, a "very large consular district, the size of France," he said. Unlike in the United States, he continued, "Labor unions were strong [in Bombay]. The principal Communist periodical was published there. So we got severe reactions from all of these sources, government and non-government." Repeatedly, Washington was "accused by the Communists of having our eyes on Goa for a naval base," which did not improve relations between the two nations.[45]

Indian Communists, who were influential in their homeland, repeatedly zeroed in on Jim Crow, and such pressure proved useful in compelling the United States to retreat from the more egregious aspects of the hateful system. Chester Bowles, the influential U.S. Ambassador to India, told Walter White, "I have met up with many questions on racial tolerance in the United States. In fact, it is a sure-fire question every time I speak." Bowles thought it would be "immensely helpful" if White were to write a book that would help him deflect these angry inquiries.[46]

When it came to Communists' influence, however, Bombay paled in comparison to West Bengal. It was "extraordinary," says Alfred Leroy Atherton Jr., who served the United States in Calcutta. The region had "one of the best-organized most effective Communist parties in India." Equally extraordinary was the fact that India developed two separate and similarly influential Communist parties, suggestive of the contrast with the United States, which did not have one in this category.[47] The U.S. diplomat Richard McKee has alleged that India "had never been fond of the United States. She in many ways had both rightist disdain for our sort of humble-jumble society and of course she had a leftist disdain, maybe a socialist disdain for our economic system."[48]

Plus, says the U.S. diplomat Donald Anderson, who served in New Delhi, Indians were a "very prickly people, and have a very strong sense of national dignity. They would get huffy about what we would often times consider minor things. . . . [W]hen the Indians are furious they can [wallow] in their own glorious, pompous self."[49] Charles W. McCaskill, who served in Bombay and Madras, concurred, finding Indians "more than a little self-righteous and insensitive at times." In fact, he said in an interview, Indians could be not only "insensitive" but "rude."[50] The U.S. diplomat Bilha Bryant also agreed. "Their arrogance overshadows their achievements," she has said. Besides, according to Bryant, India's weather was "enervating," and "because of the water we all had stomach problems."[51] Note that, although these are the diplomats' personal opinions, they are also more than that : They reflect the cool but correct relations between an India that was far from hostile to the former Soviet Union and that harbored influential Communists and an officially anti–Soviet United States. When Washington formally embraced Black America in the form of limited citizenship rights, this former ally of New Delhi felt it had no alternative but to turn its back on its long-time friend.

White, in turn, was seeking to trade on his relationship with Nehru to gain an advantage in his relationship with International Harvester's McCormick—perhaps to aid in raising funds for the NAACP or perhaps for personal aggrandizement—who apparently was not as enthusiastic as the NAACP leader in sharing intimacies. "I am distressed we are having so much difficulty in finding a mutually convenient time . . . to talk," White informed McCormick lamentingly, before adding quickly, "Mrs. White and I are taking [Nehru] to the theatre this evening [and] will spend a good part of tomorrow with [him]."[52] A few weeks later, he wrote quizzically, "We are having a hard time getting together, aren't we?[53] Finally, he told "Dear Fowler" that "President Truman asked me to give him a report and recommendations on what we can do to stop communism in Asia and especially in India." Adroitly, White tried to yoke this overriding national objective to his organization's, reminding McCormick that the "counteracting of Russian and British propaganda against us because of lynching and race prejudice" was the key.[54] The problem with this conjoining was that India was not as anti–Soviet as White, and this kind of appeal could lead policymakers there to view the NAACP as no more than a pawn of Washington, thereby vitiating an important alliance.

In the pivotal year of 1949, White complained that the "proposed arrangement between India and the United States providing for an exchange of wheat for mica and manganese is being held up by the State Department because Pandit Nehru refused to sign on the dotted line and commit India without equivocation to support the United States and its allies under any all circumstances as opposed to Russia." White's pledge to "talk with or write the President and also to write a column or article sharply criticizing such a policy" was hardly worth the effort, since his own anticommunism was bolstering an unstoppable national policy that would be sated only with the Soviet Union's demise decades later.[55] "During one of my recent conversations with the President," White said, speaking of Truman, "he asked me about the effect of Paul Robeson on the thinking of Negroes." The legendary performer and activist had refused to yield in his sympathies for Moscow and was in the process of being subjected to official ostracism, a policy that White endorsed, as he informed Truman, evidently oblivious to the impact such a move would have in India, where anti–Sovietism was not necessarily a primary value.[56]

Yet New Delhi could not easily dispense with White, for after all he had the ear of Truman and others who routinely consorted with the powerful. Moreover, White also had close relationships with other leaders who were scrambling to avoid being overtaken by Cold War events. Pre-eminent amongst these were Walter and Victor Reuther, leaders of the United Auto Workers (uaw), whose fracases with Communists were every bit as spirited as those involving the naacp. A broker of no small talent, White tried to meld his ties to the uaw with his ties to the union's bosses at International Harvester, presumably on behalf of India, although the figurative fees he was to receive for this coup would not be negligible. Thus, in late 1949 White spoke with Vijaya Pandit about a conversation he had had with Victor Reuther. According to White, Reuther was considering "asking every member of the union working in plants manufacturing farm equipment [such as International Harvester] to give one day's work to make tractors, ploughs and other machines to be given to India as a gift from the workers of America." White was "enthusiastic about the idea" and upped the ante by deciding to "ask management to match, at least the dollars and cents contribution." Completing the grand scheme, White planned to request that Truman, "through the Maritime Commission, . . . utilize Liberty ships to transport the machinery to India without cost." "What do you think of the idea?" he asked Pandit about the scheme, which was conceived as a Cold War measure to counter Soviet foreign aid to India.[57] "Sounds exciting," she replied, and "worth trying out," though given her nation's foreign-policy bent, she was compelled to add that "recent developments regarding India in this country [the United States] have been depressing." She suggested meeting at the Ritz Carlton in New York to talk further.[58] White, who was also seeking to win over Henry Ford II, tried to include him in the plan, but the auto baron kept dodging him.[59]

Presumably, the Pandit–White tête-à-tête took place. White followed up with his typical mixture of insider access and zest: "I talked with the President for half an hour and with Secretary of State [Dean] Acheson [for] almost an hour yesterday about the proposal [and] both . . . were very enthusiastic about the plan."[60] White told Acheson he had "enjoyed and profited immensely from our talk of yesterday. . . . It was most gratifying that both of you approved the idea."[61] Then White had a "telephone conversation" with the Indian diplomat B. R. Sen, who informed the NAACP leader of "the types of tractors and trucks in India" and underlined the potential importance of the initiative: "If you can arrange to supply us with tractors and trucks in the above specifications, the pace of our land reclamation operations will be correspondingly advanced."[62] White continued to court India—"Thank you for the lovely bunch of violets," Pandit gushed at one point to "dear Walter"[63]—but it is unclear what happened to his grand proposal. In any case, even White's considerable charm had difficulty overcoming the formidable obstacle of India's decision to become a leader of nations that professed non-alignment—and thereby rejected the idea of alignment with Washington—and one of Moscow's closest non–Communist allies.

The Cold War held a fundamental contradiction for White that his tactical skill could not overcome. Many of the African Americans who were the most consumed with global affairs were frightened away from this sphere for fear that the slightest misstep would bring to their doorstep the explosive charge of being "soft on communism." Robeson and Du Bois and their many followers were exemplars of this trend. This meant that, in seeking to become a diplomatic player in Washington, White at best simply positioned himself to be an apologist for the indefensible—for example, the U.S. intervention in Korea and the U.S. overthrow of regimes in Guatemala and Iran, not to mention support for continuing brigandage by London in British Guiana, Malaya, and elsewhere. Of course, there was a considerable payoff for such support: a decisive step toward full citizenship rights for Negroes. But an African American community in which leading lights such as Robeson and Du Bois were isolated was hardly in a position to capitalize on this new situation.

The West Indian National Council, which brought together in New York nationals from the soon-to-be-independent islands of the British Caribbean, "honored" at one of its many postwar celebrations "Mrs. Vijaya Lakshmi Pandit of the Indian delegation and Foreign Minister V.M. Molotov of Soviet Russia."[64] Such an event was not controversial in India or in Jamaica and Trinidad, the leading nations of the West Indian National Council, but African Americans would soon have to think thrice before appearing at such a gathering. The price to be paid for the new relationship with Washington was high: isolation from a good deal of progressive humanity, the world's majority of which they had previously been an important component. U.S. Negroes moved from being an "international orphan" to being taken in—and taken—by a still abusive Washington. The old notion of U.S. Negroes being part of a "colored" global majority aligned with South Asia in particular began to evaporate.

As it became clear that African Americans visiting India were not necessarily members of a besieged minority seeking diplomatic assistance in their embattled struggle against Jim Crow but U.S. nationals lobbying New Delhi on Washington's behalf, their reception became decidedly chillier. P. L. Prattis of the *Pittsburgh Courier* was one of the brightest stars in the black press's constellation. When he visited Delhi in late 1949,[65] he was welcomed into high-level meetings.[66] But his influential newspaper also received a stern lecture on the dynamics of U.S. foreign policy from an India that sought to reclaim African Americans from the U.S. government that now was moving haltingly to claim them. "The world is not divided into two blocks—not the Anglo-American and the Soviet," an unnamed, high-level Indian official instructed the *Courier*. "That is only a superficial and apparent division," the writer said, for "in reality" the basic division was "between the exploiter and the exploited." But what Negro leader could afford to agree with such verbiage, which mirrored Marxist discourses that were now deemed terribly outré? It was "in this context that one [had] to view the entire problem of racial and colour prejudice," the writer said. "By some strange fortunes of history, up to now the advantage of science and industry lay with the white man, even as it lay with the coloured an era earlier." African Americans now in the suffocating embrace of a rudimentarily conservative Cold War definition of citizenship also found it difficult to accept the basics of analysis about the plight of the "coloured."[67]

For a while, White sought to project this old-time religion of the "coloured." "Four centuries of British siphoning off the wealth of India for absentee landlords in England" was devastating, he told J. J. Singh in 1949. "The freedom Great Britain had been forced to grant India was pretty much like an orange sucked dry."[68] So far, so progressive. But when Singh's India League of America (ILA) came under assault by the anti–Communists, White was nowhere to be found. The rout began when the conservative Senator Karl Mundt told Singh that he was vexed by a "growing source of embarrassment" and was "receiving an increasing amount of critical mail and office visitations because I have permitted my name to be used on the [ILA's] National Advisory Board together with that of one Jo Davidson who apparently is either a Communist or has appeared at many Communist rallies." Either Davidson had to be ousted or the senator would resign, which, no doubt, would have spurred an exceedingly invasive investigation of the ILA.[69] The episode also suggests that the diminishing warmth between India and Black America was not all due to the latter. South Asians residing in the United States also had to conform to the Cold War consensus, which led them on a path trod by the nation: distance from Du Bois and his ilk and resultant self-marginalizing.

In response, Singh sought to reassure "Dear Karl," but the senator was having none of it. Still, Singh pressed on. "Jo Davidson joined the National Advisory Board," he explained in words that would have not been accepted with equanimity in Delhi, "when Russia was our war-partner and we hadn't begun to realize the dangers of Russian imperialism and expansionist policies." The ILA, he claimed, did not "seek or accept the support of Communists." In fact, he charged, "We openly and unremittingly fight the Communists and have studiously kept them out of our organization." Moreover, Davidson was "supporting [Yugoslavia's] Tito [and] has now turned against Stalinist Russia." So, "Karl," Singh advised, "how about making private off-the-record inquiries from the State Department as to what they think of Jo Davidson now?"[70]

The senator was unmoved. He did "feel as you do that there may be some temporary advantage in encouraging Tito to oppose Stalin," he told Singh, but, he added with rising concern, "I do not feel that the fact that Jo Davidson may favor the Tito version of Communism over the Stalin version of Communism, in itself, is any definite indication that Jo Davidson is not a Communist sympathizer."[71] Boxed into a posture at odds with that of their ostensible sponsor in New Delhi, whose dearth of hostility to Moscow was no chimera, the ILA soon was obliterated, and along with it departed a lengthy African American engagement with the "coloured."

The conservative British journal *The Economist* captured the dilemma faced by African Americans who refused to follow New Delhi in its decision to disagree with Washington on the rudiments of the Cold War. In doing so, African Americans were turning their backs on what could have been one of their staunchest allies. "Viewed from Delhi," this weekly reported, "the fervour of the West's belief in freedom and democracy is less evident than it appears in London. For Indians, freedom means the end of colonial imperialism, democracy means votes for Negroes too. . . . Indian faith in the American way of life cannot be complete until that way is open to the Negro; every fissure in the Mason-Dixon line strengthens the cause of democracy."[72] Still, Washington could hardly ignore such sentiments emerging from a nation that was destined to play an outsized role on the global stage, exceedingly proportionate to its immense population.

Hence, the NAACP became Washington's emblem of its own good intentions in the minefield that was race relations. Repeatedly, the association was called on by Washington to host visiting South Asian dignitaries and thereby validate that the United States was on the proper path. In 1951, "Mr. and Mrs. Natarajan of Bombay" were in the United States "under the auspices of the State Department. He is editor of the *Bombay Chronicle*," noted the NAACP leader Roy Wilkins, "and she is a member of the staff of the *India Social Reformer*." Most important was that the Narajans were "keenly interested in the

Negro Question," and it was up to the NAACP to put the nation's best foot forward—while Jim Crow continued to fester.[73]

Yet this public-relations offensive was hardly triumphing. Amar Singh, an Indian farmer, visited Carroll County, Georgia, in late 1951 and was decidedly unimpressed. "I think actually we are helping our untouchables learn how to fight for their rights better than you are helping your Negroes," he said. "Certainly in India there are more untouchables in Parliament and in high government positions than there are Negroes [in comparable U.S. posts]." Still, his visit was not in vain, for, speaking of the oppressed African Americans, he asserted, "They used to think they couldn't go where white men went because they had dark skins. But then they saw that I was accepted everywhere." Negroes were predisposed to follow his example, he said, because "they said they always thought that colored people all over the world were united."[74]

But it was not only Negroes who were being influenced by these sojourns. In 1952, Argus J. Tresidder of the U.S. Embassy in Colombo reproved the UAW's journal after it published an article about a "distinguished Ceylonese visitor in the United States who became so embittered because of alleged mistreatment in America that on his return to Ceylon he became active in the Communist Party." This was not true, Tresidder insisted, though it was true that the influential Colonel C. P. Jaywardana, "Chief of the Ceylon Boy Scouts," was "embarrassed on a number of occasions during his visit." And yes, there were "incidents in which he was humiliated because of the color of his skin."[75] But, no, he did not become a Communist as a result, Tresidder said. Still, the fact that such a story could be sufficiently believable to publish suggests that Jim Crow had to go lest the United States run the risk of pushing South Asia into the column of the Communists, thereby validating the continuing vitality of a once thriving tie between the British Empire's former chief asset and the primary victim of what seemed to be a disappearing empire of Jim Crow.

13

THE END OF EMPIRES

The picture that appeared in the 18 May 1954 edition of the *New York Times* said more than a few words could say. At the podium stood Channing Tobias, chairman of the NAACP's Board of Directors. Flanked behind him were Walter White, Roy Wilkins, Ralph Bunche, and a number of other Negro leaders who had played varying roles in a moment of juridical triumph captured on film that was, in its own way, as potently meaningful as Indian independence seven years earlier: the U.S. Supreme Court's decision in *Brown v. Board of Education* that invalidated Jim Crow in the educational system of Topeka, Kansas, striking a figurative death blow to the hateful system nationwide.[1] These men—notably, Tobias and White—also were among the leaders of the decades-long alliance between Black America and India that, ironically, was receding from the historical stage at the peak of its triumph. For as African Americans received a form of full citizenship rights, they—it was thought—had correspondingly less need for foreign entanglements. The high court and the backing of other well-placed elites were thought to be what was needed to vindicate rights.

In fact, the dueling epoch-making moments of 1954 and 1947—like the two peoples of Black America and India—were inextricably linked. The "empire of Jim Crow" found it hard to survive once the British Empire began to disintegrate. Jim Crow could only thrive and flourish in an era dominated by colonialism and its cognate—that certain peoples, mostly the "coloured," did not merit self-determination or the simplest of citizenship rights. India's independence signaled the demise of colonialism not just in

Asia, but in Africa, too, and once that occurred, Washington found it difficult to enlist the newly independent nations in the Cold War conflict with Moscow as long as the "coloured" were treated terribly in the United States itself.

"During the Truman years," asserts Mary Dudziak, "in no country was the focus on American race relations of greater importance than in India."[2] A telling moment occurred a few months after the momentous Supreme Court decision when a visiting Ambassador from India was forced into segregated restaurant facilities on a sojourn to Houston, Texas.[3] New Delhi was not amused, not least since this was not a single, isolated instance. The melanin-richness that allowed some South Asians to melt into Black America also meant that nationals of independent India could fall victim to entrenched white supremacy. Jim Crow was not a hospitable edifice when it came to embracing Asia, Africa, and Latin America and therefore had to go. Just a few years before this chagrin-inducing Texas encounter, an Indian visitor to the United States proclaimed, "American racialism is not logical. Non-American non-whites on their visit to the States are accorded a kind of 'honorary' white status which is embarrassing to them and a source of considerable justified grievance to colored nations. Instances are not uncommon of Negroes donning a turban or an English accent to escape the prejudice which as American citizens they are made to suffer." When Supreme Court Justice William Douglas, a key molder of the majority opinion in the *Brown* case, traveled to India in 1950, the "first question asked of him at his press conference in New Delhi was 'why does America tolerate the lynching of Negroes?'" Douglas was so moved that he later wrote in detail about the "importance of Asian 'color consciousness,'" adding portentously that "the attitude of the United States toward its colored minorities is a powerful factor in our relations with India."[4]

Douglas's insight was not unique to him. Eleanor Roosevelt had a similar encounter in South Asia at the same time. "We have against us the feeling that we, because our skins are white, necessarily looks down upon all peoples whose skins are yellow or black or brown. This thought is never out of their minds," she wrote in 1953. "They always asked me pointedly, however, about our treatment of minorities in our country." While visiting Allahabad, Roosevelt was asked brusquely, "Why in the land of Lincoln and Roosevelt is there still discrimination, color prejudice and Negro lynching?"[5] Washington's position was not aided by its covert and overt support for apartheid South Africa, a land inexorably linked with Gandhi and a matter of no small concern in New Delhi. "When India noted that Great Britain and the United States supported the position taken by the Union of South Africa on the racial discrimination issue" [during crucial United Nations votes] New Delhi was disappointed," according to Shiwaram Krishnarao Kshirsagar. Outraged might be a better description.[6]

In fact, the revolt against Jim Crow was global. Just as the YMCA rushed to recruit African Americans after World War II concluded, so did the State Department, albeit in a limited way. One African American so chosen, Edith Sampson, provided sobering reports to her Cold War supervisors when she returned from a 1950 lecture tour that took her to Germany, France, Finland, Sweden, Norway, Denmark, Holland, and England. "I spoke before thousands," she claimed, and was "prepared to discuss such subjects" as Moscow's alleged perfidy and Washington's stout response. But audiences "waved aside these subjects," she reported. "They were hungry for information regarding the status of the Negro in America. [The] Number One problem which people all around the world discuss is the so-called Negro Problem."[7] Washington found it hard to change the subject to Moscow's human-rights failings as long as its own were so egregious.

Sampson's case was an exemplar of an obvious trend—that is, how the Cold War propelled a passel of African Americans skyward, dispatched abroad as living symbols of how expeditiously Washington was handling problem "Number One." African Americans traveling in India had devolved from seeking solidarity against the pestilence of white supremacy to offering tortured apologias for a government that continued to countenance Jim Crow, particularly as it concerned the basic right to vote. Thus it was that the journalist and future U.S. Ambassador Carl Rowan found himself in 1950s Assam. "My first evening there," said the roly-poly, caramel-colored scribe, "I lectured at B. Barooah College. . . . I talked for half an hour about the press; students questioned me for an hour and a half about international politics and race relations in America." Rowan said he was "startled at one point when a young man asked, 'now, isn't it true that at the train station in Tucson, Arizona there are signs on toilet and water fountains saying: 'for white gentlemen', and 'for colored men?'" Distressed, Rowan could only remark, "I had been in India a month, and hardly for a single day had I been able to forget that I was a Negro." Eager to defend the government that had sent him, Rowan had difficulty grappling with the fact that "college students and principals insisted on introducing me as a heroic character who had dashed to India just a step ahead of Simon Legree, [for] questions never ceased about whether Negroes can own property or vote, whether they are lynched with regularity, permitted to marry white people or allowed to live outside all-Negro neighborhoods." Rowan was thrown off balance when one Indian told him, "'We trust you and we speak to you frankly, because there is a common bond of color. We hate the white man because he is the cause of all the trouble in Asia today. We respect you but we hate white America.' I looked around,'" said the far from bemused Rowan, "to see nods of agreement. . . . [The] meeting lasted an hour and a half," said the stern and balding future diplomat "and when it was over I was filled with a frightening realization that there was an inverse racialism which [was] as much a threat to peace and to man's dignity, to his intellectual being, as was the kind of racism under which I had suffered."[8]

Maybe. But a systemic slave trade that involved the dehumanizing of Europeans might have to occur before Rowan's comparison became valid. Nonetheless, Negro apologists for a still despicable U.S. racism that was far from eliminated by the *Brown* decision continued to arrive in South Asia. This list included federal Judge William Hastie, who was traveling in the same vicinity as Rowan and who made time to visit neighboring Burma. He reassured the skeptical that U.S. racism "would soon become a thing of the past."[9] The African American politician Sterling Tucker took a three month lecture tour of India at the same time and, he said, found "great interest in the subject of race relations in America everywhere I went," though he offered that "none of these problems is as horrible and as fantastic as most Indians imagine them. Most Indians have gotten their information on this subject from materials on the Civil War Reconstruction period." Sounding stunned, Tucker asserted, "From the questions asked by many, one would think that the Negro just landed in America from Africa the day before yesterday." Seeking to inoculate himself against the often heated charges, Tucker preferred "to discuss this subject in detail for it was the subject of greatest interest to my audience and presented to me my greatest challenge." Actually, the questions resonated with thoughtfulness—for example, "How can there be a race problem in a democracy?" "How can you speak in support of a Government which permits lynching"? "Is the Negro problem in America very much like the [H]arijan problem of India?"[10]

These questions also were rather mild compared with the scalding denunciations of Jim Crow that came to characterize the Indian press during this era. Helen Semmerling of the officially sanctioned U.S. Information Service was sufficiently concerned to contact Walter White of the NAACP for counsel. She attached an article from the 27 August 1953 edition of the *Hindustan Standard*, which she regarded as part of the "substantial press" in India and not a fringe publication. It was little wonder she was so concerned, as the *Standard* had reported, "It sounds almost like a paradox that 15 million souls should rot under squalor, misery and degradation in the world's wealthiest and most advanced country." This "habitual complex of racialism," the paper said, explained why the United States "refused to side with India in the [United Nations] against the apartheid laws. . . . [For] the history of the Negroes is nothing but a sad chronicle of slavery, debt, chronic land hunger,

dependence and inequality." Even now, the journal said, "The fate of the Negroes in the South is determined by plantation masters and capitalists who
'act as the outpost command for the real masters—the financial dynasty of
Wall Street.' The economy [in the Deep South] resembles that of a colony."
Citing V.I. Lenin, the fiery article concluded, "It is high time that the
peace-loving people all over the world should come forward with a concerted
move through the [United Nations] to eradicate the social evil of racial segregation in South Africa and the USA."[11]

White did not need to be reminded about the often scorching Indian assessments of Jim Crow. During his journey to India, he found, as he informed
Ralph Bunche distressingly, that not "only Moscow radio but Reuters and
other news distributing agencies feature riots, filibusters and racial segregation in the United States to such an extent that in many places we found the
opinion that the Negro in the United States occupies as low or lower a status
than the Untouchables in India prior to the abolition of Untouchability by
Nehru's government."[12]

Countering this negative Indian assessment of the United States motivated many of White's maneuvers to provide aid to India—for example, his
attempts to have agricultural machinery shipped from International Harvester. But just as paying ransom can encourage hostage taking, when it became evident that negative publicity about the United States was driving
attempts by White and others to increase aid to India, the Indian press may
have been motivated to publish even more downbeat stories about Jim Crow.
Undeterred, the creative White approached the U.S. diplomat Raymond Hare
about a proposal involving the "exchange of American wheat for Indian mica
and manganese."[13] He went straight to the top with his next scheme, contact-
ing his now frequent advisee, President Truman, to tell him that a "means
[must be] found to give surplus food and send grains purchased by
government . . . to India and other non-Communist Asian countries to relieve famine conditions."[14] Combating communism by "lessening the hunger
and misery and despair upon which Communist propaganda thrives" was
another goal.[15] So motivated, in 1951 NAACP branches throughout the United
States were asked, at White's initiative, by the association's Board of Directors
to urge their "Congressmen and Senators to support the proposal to send
2,000,000 tons of surplus wheat to India in order to avert mass starvation."
This, he said, would be "not only . . . an act of great humanitarianism," but
also "one which would give part of the answer to Communist propaganda
that only they are willing and able to help the unfortunate."[16]

As one who straddled the dual concerns of Communist encroachment
and Jim Crow, White was peculiarly situated to become a major influence on
the battleground where these two issues converged: U.S. policy toward India.

However, at times it appeared that White was more concerned about the former concern than the latter—that is, the reason his association was called into being. "It is quite true that Nehru has done a number of things which have irritated Americans," he said at one juncture, but, he accentuated, "the sole hope of stopping Communism in Asia is in the present government of India, [as] the strategic materials of Asia are absolutely essential to our own survival."[17]

But White was to find that it would not be simple to maintain sound ties to a government in New Delhi that was not unfriendly to Moscow while spouting anticommunism at home and—all the while—not losing sight of his ostensible chief goal: the eradication of Jim Crow. He continued to maintain positive relations with Vijaya L. Pandit, who by 1955 was complaining that "the exaggerated stories" about India in the press were "enough to drive a saint crazy!" She reassured White that he would be "welcome" if he desired to revisit India and offered him a "holiday" at her place in London, where she was now to be found quite frequently. "I would so love to have you [and your spouse] stay with me as long as you like," she said.[18] But by 1955, White was not long for this earth, which was probably for the best, as his relationship with Pandit and India itself were beginning to sour. In a personal and confidential note, he found it "painfully necessary" to apprise her of his concerns. There was "increasing and harmful opinion spreading around important places in New York and Washington that the Indian Embassy is interested only in getting what it can out of individuals and groups and then promptly forgetting them. . . . [This] has not been an easy letter to write," he said, "but I would be less a friend of yours and India were I to remain silent."[19]

Soon thereafter, White was no more. Perishing with him, in a sense, was the once proud alliance between Black America and India, sabotaged by contrasting interests, particularly concerning communism and the nature of Indian criticism of the government that now purported to claim and represent African Americans.

Channing Tobias, who had visited Gandhi in the 1930s and presided over the NAACP at the moment of its greatest triumph, was born in Augusta, Georgia, in 1882. His visage also betrayed another striking connection in that his mother was "partly Indian," or Native American—possibly Cherokee—and his own face had "Indian characteristics."[20] He was an ordained minister of what was referred to as the "Colored Methodist Church" and a close friend of Fiorello LaGuardia, in whose Republican Party he had also served.[21] He was also subjected to a vicious anticommunist attack by the conservative columnist Westbrook Pegler.[22] In other words, he was no neophyte.

Thus, worthy of recitation are his words about the importance of India to the new stage of the freedom movement of African Americans marked by the 1954 Supreme Court opinion. In 1951, in the pages of *Ebony* magazine, then as now an important arbiter of Negro opinion, he asserted that "the situation Negroes face in the U.S. is completely different [in that] Gandhi was striving to throw off the control of a foreign power. We Negroes here are seeking integration."[23] Earlier, it had been reported that "Gandhi's pacifism and way of procedure do not appeal to [Tobias] as being the proper course in all circumstances. [Tobias] favors the more aggressive way of Jawaharlal Nehru. 'I think as Nehru thinks,' he said. 'His autobiography has had a profound influence on me.' "[24]

Tobias's viewpoints, which seem all the more striking because they came as a profoundly Gandhi-influenced upsurge in the Negroes' battle for equality was commencing, were not unique to him. As early as 1924, the famed sociologist E. Franklin Frazier had dismissed the idea of Negroes' turning the other cheek and seeking to apply Gandhi's methods to the U.S. South. Frazier was responding partially to an idea propagated by the NAACP leader, diplomat, and intellectual James Weldon Johnson, who had argued in 1922: "It will be of absorbing interest to know whether the means and methods advocated by Gandhi can be as effective as the methods of violence used by the Irish. . . . [I]f non-cooperation brings the British to their knees in India, there is no reason why it should not bring the white man to his knees in the South.' " Frazier was dumbfounded by this notion. "If a Gandhian type of movement ever emerged in the South," he observed, "I fear we would witness an unprecedented massacre of defenseless black men and women in the name of Law and Order."[25] It was "a strange attitude," he opined, to pursue such a strategy "in the name of Christian humility," which was premised on the idea that "hatred may have a positive moral value." Frazier was baffled that "colored people who talk glibly of the white man's love [can] forget that a man may love his dog" and beat him, too.[26]

Such opinions from such movement veterans as Tobias and Frazier should erode the teleological conceit that the advent and rise of Dr. Martin Luther King Jr. was somehow preordained or inexorable. Actually, Frazier was correct—in 1924 when he uttered these words—but by the 1950s, an increasingly influential sector of the U.S. ruling elite was seeking a way out of the dilemma brought by Jim Crow—that is, how it compromised the basic tenets of the Cold War. Actually, Tobias and Frazier and others may have underestimated the extent to which the Indian experience had seeped into the marrow of African American culture, thereby conditioning many Negroes to accept King as it bent King himself in the direction of Gandhi. One of King's confederates, the Reverend James Lawson, attended Baldwin-Wallace College in

Ohio in the late 1940s, where he "read Gandhi's autobiography." He was so inspired that he traveled to India in the 1950s, where he toiled for three years as a Methodist missionary.[27] He was following in the wake of Tobias, Howard Thurman, Sue Bailey Thurman, Benjamin Mays, William Stuart Nelson, Lawrence Burr, and others who had lubricated the path for the arrival of Gandhian stratagems in the United States. Following in their wake was the man who spearheaded the trailblazing sit-in demonstrations in Greensboro, North Carolina, in February 1960, Ezell Blair Jr., who "said that the non-violent method was agreed upon, since a year before he had seen a documentary film on television depicting Gandhi leaving jail and thus revealing the price the Indian leader was willing to pay for India's freedom."[28]

King himself conceded, "Even as a child the entire Orient held a strange fascination for me—the elephants, the tigers, the temples, the snake charmers and all the other storybook characters." Not surprisingly, he noted that, "while the Montgomery Bus Boycott was going on [in the mid-1950s], India's Gandhi was the guiding light of our technique of non-violent social change. We spoke of him often."[29] "I gained a great deal of inspiration from Mahatma Gandhi," King emphasized.[30]

Thus, Dr. King's 1959 visit to India was something of a homecoming. "We received a most enthusiastic reception and the most generous hospitality imaginable," he recounted. "Almost every door was open." That was not all, as the kernel of the earlier alliance between Black America and India resurfaced. "We were looked upon as brothers with the color of our skins as something of an asset," he declared. "The strongest bond of fraternity was the common cause of minority and colonial peoples in America, Africa and Asia struggling to throw off racialism and imperialism." As the Thurmans had discovered decades earlier during their encounter with Gandhi, Dr. King found that "Indian people love to listen to the Negro spirituals" and that this brought the two peoples closer together. He marveled at the powerful expressions of solidarity emanating from this vast land. "Indian publications perhaps gave a better continuity of our 381-day bus strike than did most of our papers in the United States," he observed.[31]

"For a long time I had wanted to take a trip to India," King said. When Nehru made a short visit to the United States in 1956, "He was gracious enough to say that he wished that he and I had met." Dr. King compared President Dwight D. Eisenhower unfavorably to Gandhi, remarking that the latter "not only spoke against the caste system but he acted against it. He took 'untouchables' by the hand and led them into the temples from which they had been excluded. To equal that, President Eisenhower would take a Negro child by the hand and lead her into Central High School in Little Rock," a concept then seen as impossibly absurd.[32]

Figure 13.1   The civil-rights organizer Bayard Rustin confers with Prime Minister Nehru. Just as African Americans campaigned relentlessly against British rule in India, they also successfully emulated Gandhian tactics of nonviolent resistance. (*Records of the Fellowship of Reconciliation, Swarthmore College Peace Collection; photographer unknown.*)

As time passed, however, the bonds between Black America and India became more attenuated. The promise of nonviolence was battered by the assassination of King himself in 1968, and it became more difficult for African Americans to unite with a nation that was a tribune of non-alignment—a concept typically derided in the United States—and an ally of the Soviet Union, a nation viewed widely on this side of the Atlantic as an "evil empire." Recently revealed conversations between President Richard M. Nixon and his close adviser Henry Kissinger have exposed rather unkind statements made about the political leadership in New Delhi. Nehru's daughter, Prime Minister Indira Gandhi, was called a "witch" and a "bitch," while her compatriots in general were variously labeled " 'treacherous', 'cowards', vicious bastards', 'sons of bitches' and for good measure 'cannibals.' "[33] As African Americans were granted a theoretical complement of citizenship rights, it became more difficult for them to adopt foreign-policy postures at odds with that of the political leadership in Washington.

This was of consequence for the bilateral relationship between Black America and India. Tellingly, when a literary critic analyzed representations of the United States in Hindi literature, it was pointed out that, "First, the hero is astonished with the number of black Americans in New York . . . ; kale (blacks) are the only people he is capable of noticing in the first moment: 'he had thought of going to the country of whites but there it proved not to be such. Wherever you turned only blacks and blacks: black porters, black checkers, black taxi-drivers. In the streets most people were also black.' "[34]

The hero's astonishment was symbolic of the distance that had grown between Black America and India. This occurred for many reasons, but one often neglected reason was the rather difficult relationship that had developed, with saddening frequency, between Africans and Indians throughout the former British Empire, including Tanzania, Uganda, Kenya, Guyana, and Trinidad. As migration of Africans from these regions to the United States increased in the latter part of the twentieth century, some of their attitudes inevitably arrived with them. The leading civil-rights activist once known as Stokely Carmichael, who was born in Trinidad, was thus exceptional in recalling, "My impression is that, with the exception of a few demagogic bigots on both sides (V. S. and Shiva Naipul come to mind), the relationship between these two very different peoples [Africans and Indians]was reasonably civil and tolerant."[35]

This developing rift may have been more of a class phenomenon than a "race" or ethnic one. When Africans and Indians encountered each other in East Africa and the Caribbean, the South Asians often held a more elevated socioeconomic position as shopkeepers and entrepreneurs. Something similar was occurring in the United States itself as an influx of nationals from India powered the economy from Silicon Valley to Cambridge. "Indian Americans have surged forward as the most successful Asian minority in the United States," asserted the *Los Angeles Times* in late 2004, "reporting top levels of income, education, professional job status and English language ability."[36] According to the analyst Ashutosh Sheshabalaya, "Already by the 1990 Census in the U.S., the average household income of Indian-Americans was about $60,000—more than Japanese or Chinese-Americans and considerably above the national average of about $39,000. By 1996, Indian-Americans had America's highest median household income and highest proportion of college graduates, according to a Harvard study." According to a "recent Merrill-Lynch survey, there are no fewer than 200,000 Indian millionaires in the U.S.," Sheshabalaya notes, and the United States has seen the "emergence of the Indian-American community as one of the [its] most powerful lobby groups."[37]

By the mid-1990s, the largest concentration of Indian migrants to the United States had come from northern India, according to Johanna Lessinger, "Particularly from highly industrialized states such as Gujarat, Haharashtra or Uttar Pradesh." They were "more likely to come from large cities and towns [and] to be from middle and upper castes," all of which may have predisposed them to various levels of success in their new homeland. Still, their transition was not always easy. A "non-Indian school teacher in a well-off New York suburb was extremely distressed about the discussions about racial identity she heard from her first-graders," Lessinger writes. "She said her white students taunted the Indian, Korean and Chinese: 'you're not white, you're black!' and 'see how dark you are!' Every year this teacher said, tearful Asian children approached her to ask, 'teacher who am I? Am I black? Am I white?'"[38]

These children's parents were also being compelled to endure a more severe form of harassment. Consider the case of Neelima Tirumalasetti, who recently filed a lawsuit in Texas. Tirumalasetti, an information analyst, accused her employer of tolerating an environment replete with "racial harassment" after this company, Caremark decided to send some jobs to India, the nation from which she hailed, although she had since become a U.S. national. Tirumalasetti alleged that she had been called a "brown-skinned bitch," a "dirty Indian," and worse. This was akin to the harassment unleashed on Indians who answered telephone inquiries from the United States and were subjected to "abusive and racist outpourings by . . . customers angry over jobs being outsourced." Even PepsiCo's president, Indra Nooyi, who is of Indian origin and is one of the most important corporate leaders in North America, was subjected to harassment after she gave a speech that was deemed controversial. Said an Indian newspaper in response, "No matter how many years she has lived in the U.S. and how much she professes her loyalty to the country, to a bigot she is a brown foreigner." Nooyi did not have to endure the fate of the unfortunate Tirumalasetti, however, who "suffered a final emotional breakdown."[39] It seemed that the kind of taunting that had welcomed South Asian migrants to the U.S. West Coast a century ago had yet to disappear totally.

Some African Americans had done fairly well also, but the self-selection process that migration brings vitiated the possibility that as a group they could have, or would have, done as well as Indian Americans. Moreover, unlike in the nineteenth century, it would have been contrary to the self-interest of Indian Americans to seek to integrate themselves silently into the larger African American community. In fact, some Indian Americans held the opinion that "colour prejudice against Indians is not as strong in the United States" as elsewhere, such as Europe. One commentator has argued, "The colour bar which applies to Indians in Britain or, for that matter, Canada, does not exist in any significant degree in the United States." In most cases and on most continents, the degree to which South Asians faced discrimination often turned on how dark they were, suggesting the continuing resonance of the white supremacy that had helped to bring

Black America and India together in the first place. Danuta Stasik has suggested that "the problems related to the hero's skin colour emerging from the literary context testify to [its] greater significance in Great Britain than in North America," which was a testament to the fierce contestation of white supremacy spearheaded over the decades by African Americans—which served to open doors of opportunity for many others, including Indian Americans.[40]

The relatively positive attitudes toward South Asians in the United States (compared with Great Britain) also suggested that, with the demise of the Soviet Union and Washington's concomitant apprehension about China's rise, New Delhi might be played off against Beijing, just as Beijing had been played off against Moscow during the Cold War. As former Reagan administration official Clyde Prestowitz put it, "For the United States, an alliance with India may be the only way in the long run to preserve its own place at the top table as Asia regains its historically dominant weight in the global economy."[41] Likewise, the *Financial Times* reported in July 2005, "Indo–U.S. relations, U.S. diplomats insist, are on the cusp of a profound transformation." There is "certainly no higher priority than expanding and broadening our relationship with India," the paper quoted a U.S. official as saying. "You will see this relationship grow very dramatically."[42]

The diplomat in question did not go on to suggest that an offshoot of the improved relationship between Washington and New Delhi might be a revival of the tattered alliance between Black America and India, although this is a distinct possibility. Of course, there are barriers to overcome—for example, the growing hysteria in the United States over the "outsourcing" of jobs to India. In 2005, the financial-services firm JPMorgan Chase announced that it planned to hire thousands of Indians, with the aim of moving 30 percent of its back office and support staff offshore by the end of 2007.[43] As a writer in the *New York Times* put it, "Stories [about outsourcing] have aroused a primal fear in the Western public: that they might soon need to line up outside the Indian Embassy for work visas and their children will have to learn Hindi."[44] If this were to occur, the African American working class would be compelled to move to the front of the line to gain the opportunity to migrate to India. And if this were to occur, it is to be hoped Black Americans could revive and capitalize on a historic and friendly relationship with India, a tie that was revealed once more when the Hollywood star Will Smith, an African American, brokered a lucrative deal with the planet's largest film industry, sited in India.[45]

More than this, friendly relations between the former jewel of the British Empire and the primary victims of the empire of Jim Crow were revealed when the tennis player Serena Williams, who is also African American, defeated the Indian national Sania Mirza at the 2005 Australian Open in Melbourne. "I told her to keep up the good work, because it was good to see someone from India for the first time do so well," said the amply muscled and dark-hued Williams. "I told her to keep fighting."[46]

NOTES

INTRODUCTION

1. See, e.g., Shashi Tharoor, Nehru: The Invention of India (Boston: Little, Brown, 2004); idem, *India: From Midnight to the Millennium* (New York: HarperCollins, 1998).

2. For a biography of Nelson, see the unprocessed William S. Nelson Papers, Howard University, Washington, D.C.

3. *New York Amsterdam News*, 26 February 1944.

4. *The Crisis*, vol. 54, October 1947, 301–304, 316–317.

5. Martin Luther King Jr. to William Stuart Nelson, 7 April 1959, in Clayborne Carson, ed., *The Papers of Martin Luther King, Jr., Volume 5: Threshold of a New Decade, January 1959–December 1960* (Berkeley: University of California Press, 2005), 181–182.

6. Statement by Martin Luther King Jr., 18 March 1959, in ibid., 142–143.

7. David J. Garrow, *Bearing the Cross: Martin Luther King, Jr., and the Southern Christian Leadership Conference* (New York: William Morrow, 1986), 43.

8. *New York Times*, 6 October 2005. See also Anthony Read and David Fisher, *The Proudest Day: India's Long Road to Independence* (New York: W. W. Norton, 1998, 146. Gandhi's relationship to people of African descent has been bathed in controversy. "Oddly, he was never bothered by the oppression suffered by a black and coloured people" during his long stint in South Africa, according to Read and Fisher "never considering them equal to his fellow Indians." The question of "Aryan" ideology and its impact on Gandhi and caste and India itself are beyond the purview of this work, but see, e.g., Fazlul Huq, *Gandhi: Saint or Sinner?* (Bangalore: Dalit Sahitya Akademy, 1992); N. K. Dutt, *Origin and Growth of Caste in India* (Calcutta: Mukhopadhyay, 1968); idem, *The Aryanisation of India* (Calcutta: Mukhopadhyay, 1970). Of course, just as France could pursue racist policies in Haiti and West Africa and still embrace African Americans, problems of color and caste in India or problematic views held by prominent Indians do not automatically vitiate the possibility of fruitful bilateral ties with Black America. See,

e.g., Michel Fabre, *From Harlem to Paris: Black American Writers in France, 1840–1980* (Urbana: University of Illinois Press, 1991).

9. James Merriwether, *Proudly We Can Be Africans: Black Americans and Africa, 1935–1961* (Chapel Hill: University of North Carolina Press, 2002).

10. Vijay Prashad, *Everybody Was Kung-Fu Fighting: Afro-Asian Connections and the Myth of Cultural Purity* (Boston: Beacon Press, 2001), 144.

11. Gary Y. Okihiro, *Margins and Mainstreams: Asians in American History and Culture* (Seattle: University of Washington Press, 1994), 34.

12. *Honolulu Record*, 6 October 1955.

13. Manoranjan Jha, *Civil Disobedience and After: The American Reaction to Political Developments in India during 1930–1935* (Delhi: Meenakshi Prakashan, 1973), 1.

14. Alfred P. Wadsworth and Julia De Lacy Mann, *The Cotton Trade and Industrial Lancashire, 1600–1780* (Manchester: Manchester University Press, 1931), 16.

15. P. J. Marshall, *The Making and Unmaking of Empires: Britain, India and America, c. 1750–1783* (Oxford: Oxford University Press, 2005), 137.

16. See "The Importance of the British Dominion in India Compared with That in America," J. Almon, London, 1770, 5, Huntington Library, San Marino, California. See also James Wilbert Snyder, "The First American Voyage to India," *Americana* 32, no. 2 (April 1938): 1–22.

17. D. A. Farnie, *The English Cotton Industry and the World Market, 1815–1896* (Oxford: Clarendon Press, 1979, 100).

18. J. T. Sunderland, "Mrs. Naidu and Mr. Andrews in America," n.d. (ca. 1920s), box 22, J. T. Sunderland Papers, University of Michigan, Ann Arbor.

19. *New York Times Book Review*, 5 January 1930. For a contrary view, see Joan M. Jensen, *Passage from India: Asian Indian Migrants in North America* (New Haven, Conn.: Yale University Press, 1988), 278, who writes, "In 1942 only 40 percent of Americans could locate India on a map."

20. Susan Bean, *Yankee India: American Commercial and Cultural Encounters with India in the Age of Sail, 1784–1860* (Salem, Mass.: Peabody Essex, 2001), 21.

21. Ben Macintyre, *The Man Who Would Be King: The First American in Afghanistan* (New York: Farrar, Straus, Giroux, 2004), 264–265.

22. Sven Beckert, "Emancipation and Empire: Reconstructing the Worldwide Web of Cotton Production in the Age of the American Civil War," *American Historical Review* 109, no. 5 (December 2004): 1405, 1413, 1415, 1421.

23. Dwijendra Tripathi, "A Shot from Afar: India and the Failure of Confederate Diplomacy," *Indian Journal of American Studies* 10, no. 2 (1980): 75.

24. Olive Risley Seward, ed., *William Seward's Travels Round the World* (New York: D. Appleton, 1873), 401–402.

25. Marshall, *The Making and Unmaking of Empires*, 57.

26. Jensen, *Passage from India*, 13.

27. Dhan Gopal Mukerji, *Caste and Outcast* (Stanford, Calif.: Stanford University Press, 2002), 6.

28. Rayvon Fouché, *Black Inventors in the Age of Segregation: Granville T. Woods, Lewis Latimer and Shelby J. Davidson* (Baltimore: Johns Hopkins University Press, 2003), 28, 214.

29. Ben Vinson III, *Flight: The Story of Virgil Richardson, a Tuskegee Airman in Mexico* (New York: Palgrave, 2004), 9.

30. Prashad, *Everybody Was Kung-Fu Fighting*, 122–123.

31. See, e.g., Gerald Horne, *Red Seas: Ferdinand Smith and Radical Black Sailors in the U.S. and Jamaica* (New York: New York University Press, 2005), passim.

32. Farah J. Griffin and Cheryl J. Fish, eds., *A Stranger in the Village: Two Centuries of African-American Travel Writing* (Boston: Beacon Press, 1998), 56, 77, 84, 86.

33. Seward, *William H. Seward's Travels Round the World*, 329.

34. *New York Times*, 26 October 1901.

35. Mrinalini Sinha, *Specters of Mother India: The Global Restructuring of an Empire* (Durham, N.C.: Duke University Press, 2006), 33.

36. Bill V. Mullen and Cathryn V. Watson, eds., *W. E. B. Du Bois on Asia: Crossing the World Color Line* (Jackson: University Press of Mississippi, 2005), 69.

37. Michael A. Gomez, *Black Crescent: The Experience and Legacy of African Muslims in the Americas* (New York: Cambridge University Press, 2005), 250, 285–286.

38. Prashad, *Everybody Was Kung-Fu Fighting*, 110.

39. *Moslem Sunrise*, October 1939, New York Public Library.

40. Ibid., July 1921.

41. Ibid., October 1922.

42. Surendra Nath Kaushik, *Ahmadiya Community in Pakistan: Discrimination, Travail and Alienation* (New Delhi: South Asian Publishers, 1996), 12.

43. Proceedings of the Asiatic Exclusion League, Council Hall, 316 14th Street, 8 December 1907, Asiatic Exclusion League Papers, Urban Archives, San Francisco State University.

44. Vivek Bald, "Overlapping Diaspora, Multiracial Lives: South Asian Muslims in U.S. Communities of Color, 1880–1950," *Souls: A Critical Journal of Black Politics, Culture and Society* 8, no. 4 (Fall 2006): 6–8, 12.

45. See, e.g., Gerald Horne, *The Deepest South: The U.S., Brazil and the African Slave Trade* (New York: New York University Press, 2007), passim; idem, *The White Pacific: U.S. Imperialism and Black Slavery in the South Seas after the Civil War* (Honolulu: University of Hawaii Press, 2007), passim.

46. J. J. Hannigan to the Director, Office of Naval Intelligence, San Francisco, 4 February 1922, in Robert Hill, ed., *Marcus Garvey and Universal Negro Improvement Association Papers, Volume IV, September 1921–2 September 1922* (Berkeley: University of California Press, 1985), 477.

47. Naval Records Collection, subject file, 1911–1927, in ibid., 338. For comparisons of Gandhi and Garvey, see Tony Martin, *African Fundamentalism: A Literary and Cultural Anthology of Garvey's Harlem Renaissance* (Dover, Mass.: Majority Press, 1991), 137.

48. Tony Martin, *The Pan-African Connection: From Slavery to Garvey and Beyond* (Dover, Mass.: Majority Press, 1983), 81.

49. Ibrahim Sundiata, *Brothers and Strangers: Black Zion, Black Slavery, 1914–1940* (Durham, N.C.: Duke University Press, 2003), 309.

50. Sobhag Mathur, *Echoes of Indian National Movement in America* (Jodhpur: Kusumanjali Book World, 1996), 14.

51. Mukerji, *Caste and Outcast*, 152.

52. Juliette A. Derricotte, "The Student Conference at Mysore, India," *The Crisis*, vol. 36, no. 3, August 1929, 267, 280–282.

53. K. A. Abbas, *An Indian Looks at America* (Bombay: Thacker, 1943), 61.

54. Cedric Dover to Jawaharlal Nehru, n.d., Acc. No. R-8605, R. No. 44, file no. fd8/1936, All India Congress Committee Papers, Nehru Library, New Delhi.

55. Robert O. Jordan to Nehru, 13 April 1936, All India Congress Committee Papers.

56. Guy Hope, *America and Swaraj: The U.S. Role in Indian Independence* (Washington, D.C.: Public Affairs, 1968), 29.

57. Homer Jack, "Mohandas Karamchand Gandhi and Martin Luther King, Jr.," n.d., box 6, M. K. Gandhi Papers, Swarthmore College, Swarthmore, PA.

58. *The People* (Lahore), 23 May 1926.

59. Ibid., 13 April 1929.

60. Lala Lajpat Rai to W. E. B. Du Bois, 6 October 1927, in Joginder Singh Dhanki, ed., *Perspectives on Indian National Movement: Selected Correspondence of Lala Lajpat Rai* (Delhi: National Book Organization, 1998), 409–410.

61. See, e.g., Gerald Horne, *Race War! White Supremacy and the Japanese Attack on the British Empire* (New York: New York University Press, 2004), passim.

62. Charles V. Hamilton, *Adam Clayton Powell: The Political Biography of an American Dilemma* (New York: Athenaeum, 1991), 160–161.

63. David Anderson, *Histories of the Hanged: The Dirty War in Kenya and the End of Empire* (New York: W. W. Norton, 2005), 231.

64. Denis Judd, *The Lion and the Tiger: The Rise and Fall of the British Raj* (New York: Oxford University Press, 2004), 2.

65. J. T. Sunderland, article, January 1927, box 30, J. T. Sunderland Papers.

66. Judd, *The Lion and the Tiger*, 101.

67. Ibid., 67.

68. Ashutosh Sheshabalaya, *Rising Elephant: The Growing Clash with India over White-Collar Jobs and Its Challenge to America and the World* (Monroe, Me.: Common Courage Press, 2005), 201.

69. Niall Ferguson, *Colossus: The Price of America's Empire* (New York: Penguin, 2004); Andrew J. Bacevich, *American Empire* (Cambridge, Mass.: Harvard University Press, 2002); Victoria de Grazia, *The Irresistible Empire: America's Advance through Twentieth-Century Europe* (Cambridge, Mass.: Harvard University Press, 2005).

70. Michael Dawson, *Black Visions: The Roots of Contemporary African-American Political Ideologies* (Chicago: University of Chicago Press, 2001).

71. *New York Times*, 22 October 2005.

CHAPTER 1: PASSAGE TO—AND FROM—INDIA

1. *New York Times*, 11 December 2002.

2. *The Crisis*, vol. 18, no. 2, June 1919, 62.

3. W. E. B. Du Bois, *The World and Africa* (New York: International, 1965), 176–178.

4. See, e.g., Joseph E. Harris, *African Presence in Asia: Consequences of the East African Slave Trade* (Evanston, Ill.: Northwestern University Press, 1971); Graham Irwin, *Africans Abroad* (New York: Columbia University Press, 1977); Runoko Rashidi and Ivan Van Sertima, eds., *African Presence in Early Asia* (New Brunswick, N.J.: Transaction Press, 1995); K. N. Chaudhuri, *Asia before Europe: Economy and Civilization of the Indian Ocean from the Rise of Islam to 1750* (Cambridge: Cambridge University Press, 1990); Fitzroy Baptiste, "The African Presence in India," *African Quarterly* 38, no. 2 (1998): 92–126; V. T. Rajshekhar, *Dalit: The Black Untouchables of India* (Atlanta: Clarity Press, 1995); Dutt, *Origin and Growth of Caste in India*.

5. Michael A. Gomez, *Reversing Sail: A History of the African Diaspora* (Cambridge: Cambridge University Press, 2005), 44.

6. Frenise Logan, "The British East India Company and African Slavery in Benkulen, Sumatra, 1687–1792," *Journal of Negro History* 41, no. 4 (October 1956): 339.

7. R. R. S. Chauhan, *Africans in India: From Slavery to Royalty* (New Delhi: Asian Publication Services, 1995), 2. See also Benedicte Hjejle, "Slavery and Agricultural Bondage in South India in the Nineteenth Century," *Scandinavian Economic History Review* 15, nos. 1–2 (1967): 72–126.

8. Okihiro, *Margins and Mainstreams*, 39.

9. Jeanette Pinto, *Slavery in Portuguese India, 1510–1842* (Bombay: Himalaya Publishing House, 1992), 37. See also D. R. Banaji, *Slavery in British India* (Bombay: D. B. Taraporevala Sons, c. 1933).

10. Bean, *Yankee India*, 29, 34, 75.

11. Marshall, *The Making and Unmaking of Empires*, 331.

12. Gretchen Holbrook Gerzina, *Black London: Life before Emancipation* (New Brunswick, N.J.: Rutgers University Press, 1995), 145.

13. Angela Lakwete, *Inventing the Cotton Gin: Machine and Myth in Antebellum America* (Baltimore: Johns Hopkins University Press, 2003).

14. G. Bhagat, *Americans in India, 1784–1860* (New York: New York University Press, 1970), vii.

15. Adrienne Moore, *Rammohun Roy and America* (Calcutta: Brahmo Mission Press, 1942), vii, 10. See also Bruce Carlisle Robertson, *Raja Rammohan Ray: The Father of Modern India* (New York: Oxford University Press, 2001); S. R. Sharma, *Life and Works of Raja Rammohun Roy* (Jaipur: Book Enclave, 2003).

16. Mrs. Hofland, *The Young Cadet; or, Henry Delamere's Voyage to India, His Travels in Hindostan, His Account of the Burmese War and the Wonders of Elora* (New York: Orville A. Roorbach, 1828), 52, 55. See also *Memoir of Brevet Major-General Robert Ogden Tyler, U.S. Army, Together with his Journal of Two Month's Travel in British and Farther India* (Philadelphia: J. B. Lippincott, 1878).

17. From the Journal of the Belisarius, 1799–1800, in Bean, *Yankee India*, 104.

18. William Maxwell Wood, "The Indolent Effeminacy of East Indian Life," in H. A. I. Goontetileke, *Images of Sri Lanka through American Eyes: Travellers in Ceylon in the Nineteenth and Twentieth Centuries* (n.d., n.p.), British Library, London.

19. Account by William Seward, in ibid., 133.

20. Account by Mary Thorn Carpenter, in ibid., 206.

21. Account by Harry A. Frank, in ibid., 262.

22. Bernard Saul Stern, "American Views of India and Indians, 1857–1900," Ph.D. diss., University of Pennsylvania, 1956, 50, 53–54, 61–62, 87, 246.

23. I. G. Collins, *Scinde and the Punjab, the Gems of India, in Respect to Their Vast and Unparalleled Capabilities of Supplanting the Slave States of America in the Cotton Markets of the World; or, An Appeal to the English Nation on Behalf of Its Great Cotton Interest, Threatened with Inadequate Supplies of the Raw Material* (Manchester: A. Ireland, 1858), 11–12. See also Indian Civil Servant, *Usurers and Ryots: An Answer to the Question of Why Does Not India Produce More Cotton?* (London: Smith, Elder, 1856).

24. Idem, *An Essay in Favour of the Colonization of the North and Northwest Provinces of India, with Regard to the Question of Increased Cotton Supply and Its Bearing on the Slave Trade* (London: W. H. Allen, 1858), 9. See also James Montgomery, *A Practical Detail of the Cotton Manufacture of the United States of America and the State of the Cotton Manufacture of That Country Contrasted and Compared with That of Great Britain* (Glasgow: John Niven, 1840); *How to Abolish Slavery in America and to Prevent a Cotton Famine in England with Remarks upon Coolie and African Emigration by a Slave-Driver* (London: Alfred W. Bennett, 1858).

25. Anthony Howe, *The Cotton Masters, 1830–1860* (Oxford: Clarendon Press, 1984).

26. Edward Baines, *History of the Cotton Manufacture in Great Britain* (London: Fisher and Jackson, 1835), 9. See also James A. Mann, *The Cotton Trade of Great Britain: Its Rise, Progress and Present Extent* (London: Frank Cass, 1968).

27. *Christian Recorder* (Philadelphia), 17 September 1864.

28. Judd, *The Lion and the Tiger*, 78.

29. Roger Norman Buckley, *Slaves in Red Coats: The British West India Regiments, 1795–1815* (New Haven, Conn.: Yale University Press, 1979), 95.

30. William Butler, *The Land of the Veda: Being Personal Reminiscences of India; Its People, Castes, Thugs and Fakirs; Its Religions, Mythology, Principal Monuments, Palaces and Mausoleums; Together with the Incidents of the Great Sepoy Rebellion and Its Results to Christianity and Civilization* (New York: Carlton and Lanham, 1872), 293.

31. Farnie, *The English Cotton Industry and the World Market*, 5, 14–15. See also *The Cotton Question: An Inquiry into the Standing and Prospects of the Cotton States of America, in Comparison with the Production of Cotton in the Rest of the World, Especially India* (Richmond, Va.: Southern Fertilizing Company, 1876).

32. Tripathi, "A Shot from Afar," 74–89.

33. Letter to the editor, ca. 1862, *Despatches from U.S. Consuls in Bombay, India*, microfilm, roll 2, National Archives and Records Administration, College Park, Md.

34. Clipping, Bombay, 9 January 1862, in ibid.

35. Vice-Consul Healy to Secretary of State William Seward, 12 August 1862, in ibid.

36. Butler, *The Land of the Veda*, 222.

37. Tripathi, "A Shot from Afar," 74.

38. Idem, "India's Challenge to America in European Markets, 1876–1900," *Indian Journal of American Studies* 1, no. 1 (1969): 62–63.

39. "How to Make India the Place of America as Our Cotton Field," ca. 1863, British Library, London. See also Robert Crunden, ed., *Traffic of Ideas between India and America* (Delhi: Chanakya, 1985).

40. Earl Robert Schmidt, "American Relations with South Asia," Ph.D. diss., University of Pennsylvania, 1955, 15.

41. Farnie, *The English Cotton Industry and the World Market*, 164, 174.

42. Jensen, *Passage from India*, 17.

43. Ibid., 17, 37, 40–41, 113, 118.

44. Andrew Carnegie, *Round the World* (London: Sampson Low, Marston, Searle and Rivington, 1879), 227, 239, 297.

45. Amanda Berry Smith, *An Autobiography* (New York: Oxford University Press, 1988), xxxiii, 300–301, 317, 325, 328–329. See also Alasdair Pettinger, ed., *Always Elsewhere: Travels of the Black Atlantic* (London: Cassell, 1998).

46. Robert Eric Frykenberg, ed., *Pandita Ramabai's America: Conditions of Life in the United States* (Grand Rapids, Mich.: William B. Eerdmans, 2003), ix, 28.

CHAPTER 2: THE COLOR LINE

1. Read and Fisher, *The Proudest Day*, 34, 98.

2. Proceedings of Asiatic Exclusion League, 16 January 1910, Asiatic Exclusion League Papers.

3. Gary R. Hess, "The Forgotten Asian Americans: The East Indian Community in the United States," *Pacific Historical Review* 53 (November 1974): 576.

4. Emily C. Brown, *Har Dayal* (Tucson: University of Arizona Press, 1975), 82, 88, 102.

5. Nayan Shah, *Contagious Divides: Epidemics and Race in San Francisco's Chinatown* (Berkeley: University of California Press, 2001), 188, 191–192. U.S. medics, Shah writes, "freely used hospital patients as laboratory specimens, in one case administering an anthelmintic drug to extract 'a hundred or more of the worms themselves' from one Asian patient. This use of detainees for medical experimentation without their consent was a standard practice in the formation of medical disciplines and demonstrated how bodies were made instrumental for medical data prior to the advent of patient's rights.... Asian and Middle Eastern immigrants were far more frequently diagnosed with trachoma and deported than the European immigrants. In a study of trachoma diagnosis at all immigration stations from 1908 to 1910 in the United States, the ... officer Victor Safford concluded that Chinese, Japanese, Syrian, and Asian Indian immigrants were more likely to be certified for trachoma than the most 'susceptible' southern and eastern European 'races.'" See also James Jones, *Bad Blood: The Tuskegee Syphilis Experiment* (New York: Free Press, 1981).

6. State Board of Control, *California and the Oriental* (Sacramento: State Printing Office, 1922), 115, Urban Archives, San Francisco State University.

7. *The People*, 25 January 1931.

8. *White Man*, vol. 1, no. 2, August 1910, 1, Urban Archives, San Francisco State University.

9. Proceedings of the Asiatic Exclusion League, 16 February 1908. See also Herman Scheffauer, "Tide of Turbans," *The Forum* (New York), vol. 43, June 1910, 616–618.

10. "Third Annual Meeting," 10 May 1908, Asiatic Exclusion League Papers.

11. Danvers Osborn, "Asiatic Immigration and British Columbia: An Imperial Problem of Pressing Importance," *Empire Review*, vol. 25, no. 148, May 1913, 235–246, 242. See also Robert E. Wynne, "American Labor Leaders and the Vancouver Anti-Oriental Riot," *Pacific Northwest Quarterly* 57 (October 1966): 172–179.

12. *Colored American Magazine*, vol. 7, no. 7, July 1904, 465.

13. *Voice of the Negro*, January 1905.

14. Horne, *Race War!* 45, 187. See also Eldon R. Penrose, *California Nativism: Organized Opposition to the Japanese, 1890–1913* (San Francisco: R and E Research Associates, 1973).

15. R. P. Dua, *The Impact of the Russo-Japanese (1905) War on Indian Politics* (Delhi: S. Chand, 1966), 22–23.

16. Governor Hiram Johnson to Secretary of State Philander Knox, 16 January 1911, part 2, box 41, Hiram Johnson Papers, University of California, Berkeley. See also Karen Leonard, "The Pakhar Singh Murders: A Punjabi Response to California's Alien Land Law," *Amerasia Journal* 11 (1984): 75–86.

17. "Democratic Platform—1900," part 2, box 41, Hiram Johnson Papers.

18. "Democratic State Platform, adopted at Fresno, May 20, 1908," part 2, box 41, in ibid.

19. "Committee Substitute for Assembly Bills Nos. 10, 113, 183, and 194, Assembly Bill No. 2064, Introduced by Committee on Judiciary, April 4, 1913," part 2, box 41, in ibid.

20. Patriotic Order of Sons of America to Governor Johnson, 2 June 1913, part 2, box 38, in ibid. See also Milton R. Konvitz, *The Alien and the Asiatic in American Law* (Ithaca, N.Y.: Cornell University Press, 1946).

21. Edward Hungerford, article in *Harper's Weekly*, n.d., part 2, box 41, Hiram Johnson Papers.

22. See clipping dated 16 May 1913, part 2, box 41, in ibid. "The race problem is the burning question of the day. It is now 30 years since the writer first raised the problem down in New Zealand," the clipping's author states. "[A] fear stole into his soul that the savage races of Africa and Asia might creep in and fill the vast solitudes with a mongrel race. . . . [T]hen he drafted the Alien Law, which has since been adopted first in New Zealand and then in Australia. That, whether they shall have been born in this land or beyond, no one of Asiatic or of African blood can ever be a citizen of this land, or even can hold any land freehold or leasehold, or ever can conduct any business, or do any work in this land. . . . [T]his law has saved Australia from becoming [an Asian] land in the North and a nigger land in the West." See also Robert Huttenback, *Racism and Empire: White Settlers and Colored Immigrants in the British Self-Governing Colonies, 1830–1910* (Ithaca, N.Y.: Cornell University Press, 1976).

23. Testimony, "In the Assembly Chamber, State Capitol Building, Sacramento, California, Monday, April 28th, 1913, 11:30 o'clock A.M., Senate and Assembly in Executive Session, Honorable A. J. Wallace, Lieutenant Governor of the State of California, in the chair on the platform, Honorable Hiram W. Johnson, Governor, Honorable William Jennings Bryan, Secretary of State, Honorable C. C. Young, Speaker of the Assembly of the State of California," part 2, box 41, Hiram Johnson Papers. See also U.S. House of Representatives, Committee on Immigration and Naturalization, "Hearing on Restriction of Immigration of Hindu Laborers," 63rd Cong., 2nd sess., 13 February–30 April 1914, Government Printing Office, Washington, D.C., 1914; U.S. Senate, Immigration Commission, 1907–1910, "Abstracts of Reports of the Immigration Commission with Conclusions and Recommendations and View of the Minority," 61st Cong., 3rd sess., doc. 747,1911 (see esp. 676–682); P. Kodanda Rao, "Indians Overseas," *Annals of the American Academy of Political and Social Science* 233 (May 1944): 200–207.

24. Jensen, *Passage from India*, 145.

25. *New York Times*, 19 January 1909; *Some American Opinions on the Indian Empire* (London: T. Fisher, n.d.).

26. Sydney Brooks, "British Rule in India: A Reply to a Recent American Manifesto on the Subject," pamphlet no. 5 (ca. 1909), East India Association, London, British Library.

27. India National Party, *America on British Rule in India* (New York: India National Party, 1912n.d.), British Library.

28. Proceedings of Asiatic Exclusion League, 15 November 1908, Asiatic Exclusion League Papers.

29. Ibid., 16 January 1910.

30. Proceedings of the First International Convention of the Asiatic Exclusion League of North America, February 1908, Asiatic Exclusion League Papers.

31. *White Man*, vol. 1, no. 2, August 1910.

32. Jaideep Singh Alag, "Racism, Violence and Exclusion: Historical Factors in the Demographics of the South Asian American Community," in *The Repeal and Its Legacy: Proceedings of the Conference on the 50th Anniversary of the Repeal of the Exclusion Acts*," 12–14 November 1993, San Francisco State University, 149–153, Urban Archives, San Francisco State University.

33. *New York Times*, 8 October 2005.

34. See, e.g., Gerald Horne, *Black Liberation/Red Scare: Ben Davis and the Communist Party* (Newark: University of Delaware Press, 1994; idem, *Race War!*

35. Richard Brent Turner, *Islam in the African American Experience* (Bloomington: Indiana University Press, 1997), 124, 127, 134, 139.

36. Kaushik, *Ahmadiya Community in Pakistan*, vii, 12, 14. "Anti–Ahmadiya sectarian violence engulfed Pakistan soon after its emergence," Kaushik writes. "In 1974 the Ahmadiya Muslims were excommunicated through a constitutional amendment and brought at par with other non-Muslim minority communities." Although they "claim to be the true followers of Islam," Kaushik notes, they continue to be "denigrated as apostates by fundamentalist forces." See also H. A. Walter, *The Ahmadiya Movement* (London: Oxford University Press, 1918).

37. *Swami Vivekananda and His Guru with Letters from Prominent Americans on the Alleged Progress of Vedantism in the United States* (London: Christian Literature Society for India, 1897), iv, xxiii, British Library.

38. *New York Times*, 11 October 2005.

39. Ibid., 15 January 2006.

40. *Moslem Sunrise*, October 1921.

41. Ibid., April 1923.

42. Ibid., October 1923.

43. Ibid., January 1922.

44. Watson L. Johns, "The Hindu in California," paper, University of Oregon, Eugene, 1941, box 6, folder 5, South Asians in North America Collection, University of California, Berkeley.

45. *Moslem Sunrise*, January 1923.

46. *The Messenger*, May 1927.

47. Ibid., August 1927, September 1927.

48. *Negro World*, 21 June 1924.

49. Ibid., 2 August 1924.

50. Ibid., 27 September 1924.

51. Ibid., 7 November 1925.

52. Ibid., 15 May 1926.

53. Ibid., 4 August 1923.See also ibid., 8 September 1923.

54. Ibid., 14 March 1925.

55. Ibid., 6 February 1926.

56. *The Crusader*, August 1921.

57. Ibid., November 1921.

58. *The Crisis*, vol. 25, no. 6, April 1923, 278–279.

59. João José Reis, *Slave Rebellion in Brazil: The Muslim Uprising of 1835 in Brazil* (Baltimore: Johns Hopkins University Press, 1993); Wilson Jeremiah Moses, *Afrotopia: The Roots of African American Popular History* (New York: Cambridge University Press, 1998).

CHAPTER 3: REVOLUTION?

1. *Young India*, February 1920, Nehru Library, New Delhi.

2. Anil Baran Ganguly, *Ghadar Revolution in America* (Delhi: Metropolitan Book Company, 1980); Harish K. Puri, *Ghadar Movement: Ideology, Organization and Strategy* (Amritsar: Guru Nanak Dev University, 1993); G. S. Deol, *The Role of the Ghadar Party in the National Movement* (Delhi: Sterling, 1969); Giles Tyler Brown, "The Hindu Conspiracy, 1914–1917," *Pacific Historical Review* 17 (August 1948): 299–310; Don K. Dignan, "The Hindu Conspiracy in Anglo-American Relations during World War II," *Pacific Historical Review* 40 (February 1971): 57–76; Mark Naidis, "Propaganda of the Ghadr Party," *Pacific Historical Review* 20 (August 1951): 251–260.

3. Khushwant Singh and Satindra Singh, *Ghadar 1915: India's First Armed Revolution* (New Delhi: R and K Publishing, 1966), n.p.

4. See *U.S.A. v. M. N. Roy*, 1917, before Samuel M. Hitchcock, U.S. Commissioner for the Southern District of New York, Misc/1, M. N. Roy Papers, Nehru Library, New Delhi. The defendants sought to "prepare the means for a certain military enterprise to be carried on from and within the territory and jurisdiction of the United States against the King of Great Britain." See also Horst Kruger, *Indian Nationalists and the World Proletariat: The National Liberation Struggle in India and the International Labour Movement before 1914* (New Delhi: Indian Council of Historical Research, 2002).

5. Ram Chandra, letter, *New York Times*, 14 September 1916, box 1, folder 31, South Asians in North America Collection.

6. *Literary Digest*, ca. 1923, box 1, folder 3, in ibid.

7. Herman Scheffauer, "The Tide of Turbans," *The Forum*, vol. 53, June 1910, 616, box 1, folder 6, in ibid.

8. Ram Chandra, "The Appeal of India to the President," 26 February 1918, in ibid.; see in same box another letter, box 1, folder 30, in ibid.

9. Interview with Padmanati Chandra, 18 November 1972, box 4, folder 1, in ibid.

10. Darisi Chenchiah, "History of the Freedom Movement in India: The Ghadar Movement, 1913–1918," box 3, folder 3, in ibid.

11. Mark Juergensmeyer, "The Ghadar Syndrome: Nationalism in an Immigrant Community," *Punjab Journal of Politics* 1, no. 1 (October 1977): 1, box 3, folder 4, in ibid.

12. Randhir Singh, *The Ghadar Heroes: Forgotten Story of the Punjab Revolutionaries of 1914–1915* (Bombay: People's Publishing House, 1945), box 3, folder 11, in ibid.

13. Har Dayal, "Meaning of Equality," published by Hindustan Gadar Party, 5 Wood Street, San Francisco, box 2, folder 3, in ibid.

14. "India's Voice at Last: India's Reply to British Propagandists and Christian Missionaries, Rev. James L. Gordon, D.D., Especially," n.d., box 2, folder 27, in ibid.

15. *The People*, 13 April 1929.

16. U.S. Attorney to James A. Finch, 17 August 1918, record group (RG) 118, box 2, U.S. Attorneys and Marshals, U.S. Attorney: Northern California Neutrality Case Files, 1913–1920, National Archives and Records Administration, San Bruno, Calif. (hereafter, Ghadar Papers).

17. See, e.g., Gerald Horne, *Black and Brown: African-Americans and the Mexican Revolution, 1910–1920* (New York: New York University Press, 2005), passim.

18. "John" to Franz Bopp, 17 January 1917, box 1, Ghadar Papers.

19. Interrogation of Franz Kasper Schnitzler and R. L. Clay, ca. 1915, box 11, Ghadar Papers. See also John Price Jones and Paul Merrick Hollister, *The German Secret Service in America, 1914–1918* (Boston: Small, Maynard, 1918); *United States v. Franz Bopp*, transcript of trial in U.S. District Court for the Northern Division of California, 20 November 1917–23 April 1918, mss. Eur.C. 138, British Library, London.

20. C. G. Crick, collector of customs, Manila, to the insular collector of customs, Manila, 23 August 1915, box 6, Ghadar Papers.

21. Statement made by Quintin Bilarmino, quartermaster of the schooner *Henry S*, c. 1915, box 11, in ibid.

22. British ambassador to Secretary of State Robert Lansing, 16 September 1915, box 11, in ibid.

23. Interview with R. L. Clay, 13 September 1915, box 11, in ibid.

24. Sworn statement by R. L. Clay, ca. 1915, box 11, in ibid.

25. Testimony of the engineer of the schooner *Henry S*, Isidro Avillado, ca. 1915, box 11, in ibid.

26. U.S. Attorney to U.S. Attorney-General, 3 June 1918, box 3, in ibid.

27. Statement, 23 July 1917, box 7, in ibid.

28. Report made by Don S. Rathbun, 30 October 1916, box 7, in ibid.

29. From "Zimmerman," "Berlin to Washington," 4 January 1917, box 9, in ibid.

30. Report made by Don Rathbun, 30 October 1916, box 7, in ibid.

31. John Hilliard, E. F. Hutton, to John W. Preston, U.S. Attorney, 14 December 1917, box 1, in ibid.

32. Sworn statement by Thomas J. Vitaich, 30 August 1913, box 6, in ibid.

33. Sworn statement by Fran B. Briare, 30 August 1913, box 6, in ibid.

34. Sworn statement by William Johnson, 29 August 1913, box 6, in ibid.

35. H. Hamer, Office of Immigrant Inspector, to Commissioner of Immigration, San Francisco, 30 August 1913, box 6, in ibid.

36. Sworn statement by George E. Gee, 28 August 1913, box 6, in ibid.

37. Sworn statement by M. C. Polk, 26 August 1913, box 6, in ibid.

38. Amy Dudley to Mrs. Hamilton, ca. 1915, box 7, in ibid.

39. Folder on case of Gopal Singh, box 3, folder 9, South Asians in North America Collection. See also Naeem Gul Rathore, "Indian Nationalist Agitation in the U.S.: A Study of Lal Lajpat Rai and the India Home Rule League of America, 1914–1920," Ph.D. diss., Columbia University, New York, 1965; Alan Raucher, "American Anti-Imperialists and the Pro-Indian Movement," *Pacific Historical Review* 43 (February 1984): 83–110. For insight on the trial, see, e.g., David Machado, "The Ghadr Party and the Hindu–German Conspiracy," 1973, box 5, folder 1, South Asians in North America Collection. See also *San Francisco Chronicle*, 28 February 1918.

40. Hess, "The Forgotten Asian-Americans," 586.

41. *The Crisis*, vol. 19, no. 2, November 1919, 78.

42. *The Messenger*, March 1920.

43. Ibid., April 1922.

44. Ibid., June 1922.

45. Geoffrey C. Ward, *Unforgivable Blackness: The Rise and Fall of Jack Johnson* (New York: Knopf, 2004), 231.

46. Barbara Foley, *Spectres of 1919: Class and Nation in the Making of the New Negro* (Champaign-Urbana: University of Illinois Press, 2003), 34.

47. Joyce Moore Turner, *Caribbean Crusaders and the Harlem Renaissance* (Champaign-Urbana: University of Illinois Press, 2005), 145.

48. Jonathan Rosenberg, *How Far the Promised Land? World Affairs and the American Civil Rights Movement* (Princeton, N.J.: Princeton University Press, 2005), 84.

49. Read and Fisher, *The Proudest Day*, 208.

50. *The Crisis*, vol. 36, no. 10, October 1929, 350.

51. *Negro World*, 30 April 1927.

52. Ibid., 19 December 1925.

53. Speech by Marcus Garvey, 11 September 1921, in Hill, *Marcus Garvey and Universal Negro Improvement Association Papers*, 4:51.

54. Speech by Marcus Garvey, 12 March 1922, in ibid..

55. *Negro World*, 29 March 1924.

56. Ibid., 19 December 1925.

57. Ibid., 19 April 1924.

58. Ibid., 12 July 1924.
59. Ibid., 9 January 1926.
60. See, e.g., ibid., 27 February 1926.
61. Ibid., 10 May 1924.
62. Ibid., 25 April 1925.
63. Ibid., 17 April 1926.
64. Ibid., 13 October 1923.
65. Ibid., 25 August 1923.
66. Ibid., 14 July 1923.
67. Ibid., 9 November 1932. Another commentator, this one from New York, who had visited the West Coast of Africa less than ten months earlier, asserted that British "rule is the most infamous, oppressive and destructive of all the white nations of the earth": see ibid., 17 January 1925.
68. Ibid., 10 October 1925.
69. Ibid., 26 September 1925.
70. Ibid., 12 September 1925.
71. Ibid., 2 February 1924.
72. Ibid., 18 July 1925.
73. *The Crisis*, vol. 21, no. 2, December 1920, 74.
74. *The Crusader*, July 1921.
75. *The Messenger*, November 1920.
76. J. J. Hannigan, commander, Twelfth Naval District, to the director, Office of Naval Intelligence, San Francisco, 3 December 1921, in Hill, *Marcus Garvey and Universal Negro Improvement Association Papers*, 4:233.
77. See memorandum, 18 March 1922, reel 22, no. 686, and memorandum, 18 March 1922, reel 22, no. 689, in Theodore Kornweibel, ed., *Federal Surveillance of Afro-Americans, 1917–1925: The First World War, the Red Scare and the Garvey Movement*, Frederick (Frederick, Md.: University Publications of America, 1985).

CHAPTER 4: NOT QUITE "WHITE"

1. Charles J. McClain, "The Asian Quest for Citizenship," *Asian Law Journal* 2 (May 1995): 33–60, 47–48.
2. Suzanne A. Kim, "'Yellow' Skin, 'White' Masks: Asian American 'Impersonations' of Whiteness and the Feminist Critique of Liberal Equality," *Asian Law Journal* 8 (May 2001): 93–94. See also *Ozawa v. United States*, 260 U.S. 178 (1922); Ian Haney Lopez, *White by Law: The Legal Construction of Race* (New York: New York University Press, 1996).
3. *United States v. Bhaghat Singh Thind*, 261 U.S. 204, 208.
4. Karen McBeth Chopra, "A Forgotten Minority, an American Perspective: Historical and Current Discrimination against Asians from the Indian Subcontinent," *Detroit College of Law Review* (Winter 1995): 1287.
5. Royal Copeland, "Hindus Are White," 4 May 1927, folder 4, box 3, South Asians in North America Collection.
6. *Portland Oregonian*, 1 February 1927, OrFiche 655, fiche 413, "Indian Political Intelligence Files, 1912–1950: North America," Oriental and Indian Office, British Library, London.
7. H. W. Brooks, British Embassy, to "Dear Sir," 11 November 1925, fiche 415, in ibid.
8. Memorandum, n.d. (ca. 1926), in ibid.

9. Flyer, 24 March 1926, in ibid.

10. Confidential memorandum from British Consulate in Detroit, 15 February 1927, in ibid. See also Don Dignan, *The Indian Revolutionary Problem in British Diplomacy, 1914–1919* (New Delhi: Allied Publishing, 1983); Crunden, *Traffic of Ideas between India and America*; Sulochana Raghavan Glazer and Nathan Glazer, eds., *Conflicting Images: India and the United States* (Glenn Dale, Md.: Riverdale, 1990).

11. Clipping, 1923, box 30, J. T. Sunderland Pap*ers*.

12. Flyer on Sudhindra Bose, n.d., box 30, in ibid.

13. S. Bose, "Unity," 19 April 1923, box 30, in ibid.

14. J. T. Sunderland to *Modern Review*, 10 March 1926, box 5, in ibid.

15. Idem to the editor of *The Nation*, 2 September 1926, in ibid.

16. See *The People*, 13 April 1929, 11 July 1929.

17. Daniel Argov, *Moderates and Extremists in the Indian National Movement, 1883–1920* (London: Asia Publishing House, 1967), 59–60, 164, 172. Rai's "early identification with Hindus and his attachment to Hinduism stemmed from a rejection of his Islamic upbringing. In his own words: 'the respect for Islam that I had acquired from early training changed into hatred.'"

18. N. S. Hardikar, *Lala Lajpat Rai in America* (New Delhi: Servants of the People Society, 1977), 3–5, 7, 13, 16, 21, 25, 30.

19. *The People*, 13 April 1929.

20. Ibid., 13 April 1929.

21. Rathore, "Indian Nationalist Agitation in the United States," 48.

22. Lala Lajpat Rai, *The United States of America*, 2nd ed. (Calcutta: Sri Gouranga Press, ca. 1919), v, 88, 101, 137, 436–437, 439, 443, 445, 447–448, 464. Rai added, "There is another feature of the education of the Negro which puts an Indian to indescribable shame, viz., the education of the Negro women. The facilities which exist in this country for the higher education of Negro women, are decidedly larger, better and more liberal than those that exist in India for the education of Indian women." After visiting Tuskegee, he wrote, "On the whole I enjoyed my visit considerably and learned a good many practical lessons therefrom, but what the visit principally did for me was to raise the [Dayanand Anglo-Vedic] College of Lahore and its first Principal, and the Gurukula of Kangri and its first Governor, at least 100 times more in my estimation than before. In endowments, in actual expenditure, in buildings, in grounds, in the extensiveness of its operations, the vastness of the industrial and educational activities. . . . Tuskegee is far, far ahead of and very much larger than either of the Arya Samajic institutions in the Pubjab . . . but in the solitary fact that the two institutions of the Arya have been conceived, built, reared, provided for, by Hindus exclusively and that insofar they have been managed and staffed by them only, they stand on a higher level than the Negro Institute of Tuskegee."

23. Idem, *Unhappy India* (Calcutta: Banna Publishing, 1928), 104. See also Rathore, "Indian Nationalist Agitation in the United States."

24. *The Crisis*, vol. 14, no. 4, August 1917, 163–164.

25. Ibid., vol. 26, no. 2, June 1923, 84.

26. Lala Lajpat Rai to W. E. B. Du Bois, 6 October 1927, reel 22, no. 1261, W. E. B. Du Bois Papers, Columbia University, New York City.

27. *Young India*, April 1920, Nehru Library, New Delhi.

28. *Independent Hindustan*, October 1920, in ibid.

29. *Young India*, December 1920.

30. *The People*, 30 May 1926.

31. Schmidt, "American Relations with South Asia," 352–355.

32. *The People*, 12 July 1925.

33. Ibid., 21 March 1926.

34. Ibid., 27 September 1925.

35. Ibid., 4 July 1929.

36. Ibid., 26 July 1925.

37. Ibid., 21 March 1926.

38. Ibid., 23 August 1929.

39. Ibid., 25 January 1931.

40. Read and Fisher, *The Proudest Day*, 217.

41. *The People*, 13 April 1929.

42. Ibid., 14 June 1927.

43. Ibid., 18 August 1927.

44. Ibid., 2 January 1927.

CHAPTER 5: BLACK AMERICANS AND INDIA

1. David Levering Lewis, *W. E. B. Du Bois: The Fight for Equality in the American Century, 1919–1963* (New York: Holt, 2000), 219.

2. W. E. B. Du Bois, *Dark Princess* (Jackson: University Press of Mississippi, 1995), 150–151, 262, 297.

3. Robert Gregg and Madhavi Kale, "The Negro and the 'Dark Princess': Two Legacies of the Universal Races Congress," *Radical History Review*, no. 92 (Spring 2005): 133. See also Maia Ramnath, "Two Revolutions: The Ghadar Movement and India's Radical Diaspora, 1913–1918," *Radical History Review*, no. 92 (Spring 2005): 7–30; Sean Chabot, "Framing, Transnational Diffusion and African American Intellectuals in the Land of Gandhi," *International Review of Social History* 49, supp. 12 (2004): 19–40; idem, "Crossing the Great Divide: The Gandhian Repertoire's Transnational Diffusion to the American Civil Rights Movement," Ph.D. diss., University of Amsterdam, 2003; J. S. Dhanki, *Lala Lajpat Rai and Indian Nationalism* (Jalandhar: ABS Publications, 1990), 200

4. W. E. B. Du Bois to L. L. Rai, 9 November 1927, reel 22, no. 1261, W. E. B. Du Bois Papers.

5. Vijay Prashad, *The Karma of Brown Folk* (Minneapolis: University of Minnesota Press, 2000), 39.

6. Bill V. Mullen, "W. E. B. Du Bois, 'Dark Princess' and the Afro-Asian International," in *Left of the Color Line: Race, Radicalism and Twentieth Century Literature of the United States*, ed. James Smethurst et al. (Chapel Hill: University of North Carolina Press, 2003), 99.

7. Ibid.

8. *The Crusader*, June 1919.

9. *The Messenger*, May–June 1919. Later it was said, "America is the hypocrite on the Negro Question. Japan is the hypocrite on the Korea Question. Italy is the hypocrite on the Fiume Question."

10. *The Messenger*, July 1919.

11. *The Crusader*, June 1919.

12. Ibid., January 1920.

13. Ibid., July 1920.

14. Ibid., March 1921.

15. Ibid., February 1921.

16. *Negro World*, 4 December 1920.

17. Ibid., 28 May 1921.

18. Ibid.; memorandum, 23 March 1922, Federal Surveillance of Afro-Americans, reel 18, no. 0835, University of North Carolina, Chapel Hill.

19. Colonel R. H. Van Deman, General Staff, Chief, Military Intelligence Branch, Executive Division, to Major Nicholas Biddle, 18 March 1918, reel 19, no. 524, in ibid.

20. *Negro World*, 19 November 1921.

21. A. K. Das to W. E. B. Du Bois, ca. 1931, reel 16, no. 1193, W. E. B. Du Bois Papers.

22. A. R. Malik to W. E. B. Du Bois, 1927, reel 22, no. 740, in ibid.

23. K. D. Shastri to W. E. B. Du Bois, 22 January 1918, reel 6, no. 591, in ibid.

24. W. E. B. Du Bois to K. D. Shastri, 17 February 198, reel 6, no. 592, in ibid.

25. N. A. Khan to W. E. B. Du Bois, 29 September 1927, reel 23, no. 855, in ibid.

26. B. Chatuwedi to W. E. B. Du Bois, 9 November 1924, reel 13, no. 389, in ibid. Note that in *The Crisis* (vol. 30, no. 2, June 1925, 93), this letter is printed and cited as coming from "Benarn Da Matiovedi."

27. Shripad R. Tikekar to W. E. B. Du Bois, 23 December 1927, reel 23, no. 319, W. E. B. Du Bois Papers.

28. *The Crisis*, vol. 31, no. 6, April 1926, 297.

29. Ibid., vol. 32, no. 3, July 1926, 146.

30. Ibid., vol. 39, no. 4, April 1931, 138.

31. Ibid., vol. 37, no. 6, June 1930, 210.

32. *The People*, 23 May 1926.

33. *The Crisis*, 37, no. 7, July 1930, 246.

34. International Committee of the YMCA, "Foreign Department," YMCA Archives, University of Minnesota, Minneapolis.

35. Max Yergan to Jesse Moorland, 30 August 1916, box 126-64, Jesse Moorland Papers, Howard University, Washington, D.C..

36. Ibid., 17 October 1916.

37. Ibid., 8 December 1916.

38. Walter Loving to Director of Military Intelligence, 6 August 1919, box 113-1, Walter Loving Papers, Howard University, Washington, D.C.

39. Newsletter, May 1918, Max Yergan Personal Papers, YMCA Archives.

40. George Crawford to J. E. Moorland, 25 November 1921, box 3, Channing Tobias Papers, University of Minnesota, Minneapolis.

41. *The Crisis*, vol. 36, no. 8, August 1929, 267, 280.

42. See, e.g., Gerald Horne, *Black and Red: W. E. B. Du Bois and the Afro-American Response to the Cold War, 1944–1963* (Albany: State University of New York Press, 1986), passim.

43. W. E. B. Du Bois to L. L. Rai, 11 October 1928, reel 26, no. 284, W. E. B. Du Bois Papers.

44. *Inter-Collegian News-Letter*, March 1928, YMCA Archives.

45. See *Student Association News-Letter*, March 1927, in ibid. Frank T. Wilson, an African American, was "one of the ten American delegates chosen to represent the students of the United States in the Pan-Pacific Student Conference" in August in China. The well-traveled Wilson also attended the conference in Mysore. See ibid., November–December 1928.

46. Ibid., February–March 1930.

47. *Open Forum* (Los Angeles), 29 November 1930, box 30, J. T. Sunderland Papers.

48. *Modern Review*, December 1930, in ibid.

49. *New India*, 15 January 1931, in ibid.

50. S. Bose to J. T. Sunderland, 27 February 1927, in ibid.

51. Dr. B. R. Dewan to "Dear Sir," 8 January 1924, box 5, in ibid.

52. Letter to L. L. Rai, 22 November 1926, in ibid.

53. T. Das to J. T. Sunderland, 13 November 1930, in ibid.

54. "Information Obtained from Dr. Legrand Coleman," n.d., box 154-41, Kwame Nkrumah Papers, Howard University, Washington, D.C.

55. Ivor Holm to Dorothy Padmore, 4 April 1962, box 154-41, in ibid.

56. Memorandum, 10 November 1924, box 102-12, Mary Church Terrell Papers, Howard University, Washington, D.C.

57. Janie Porter Barrett to Mrs. Booker T. Washington, 12 February 1925, in ibid.

58. M. E. Josenberger, treasurer, International Council of Women of the Darker Races, to "Dear Maggie," 20 December 1924, in ibid.

59. Elizabeth Ross Haynes to Mrs. Booker T. Washington, 8 March 1925, in ibid.

60. *Opportunity*, vol. 7, no. 1, January 1929, 30.

CHAPTER 6: MISSION TO INDIA

1. "D. O.", 7 October 1950, File on Wilmeth Sidat-Singh, Syracuse University, Syracuse, N.Y.

2. *New York Daily News*, 28 April 2003.

3. *Syracusan*, December 1937, in File on Wilmeth Sidat-Singh.

4. James Roland Coates, "Gentleman's Agreement: The 1937 Maryland–Syracuse Football Controversy," M.A. thesis, University of Maryland, College Park, 1982, 30.

5. *Syracuse Herald-American*, 26 July 1998.

6. *New York Daily News*, 28 April 2003.

7. *Houston Chronicle*, 11 February 2005.

8. Coates, "Gentleman's Agreement," 76.

9. *Syracuse Post-Standard*, 5 April 2003.

10. See, e.g., Gerald Horne, *The Color of Fascism: Lawrence Dennis, Racial Passing and the Rise of Right-Wing Extremism in the United States* (New York: New York University Press, 2007).

11. Prashad, *The Karma of Brown Folk*, 38; Dizzy Gillespie, *To Be or Not to Bop: Memoirs* (Garden City, N.Y.: Doubleday, 1979), 291–293.

12. Flyer, ca. 1935, box 136, Howard Thurman Papers, Boston University. (Much of the foregoing was gleaned from prefatory material in this vast collection.)

13. Howard Thurman, *With Head and Heart: The Autobiography of Howard Thurman* (New York: Harcourt Brace Jovanovich, 1979), 106–107.

14. Howard Thurman to Mabel Simpson, 14 June 1935, box 136, Howard Thurman Papers.

15. Ticket issued on "French Line," 23 March 1936, in ibid.

16. Trudi Smith, "Sue Bailey Thurman: Building Bridges to Common Ground," box 5, folder 24, Bailey–Thurman Papers, Emory University, Atlanta.

17. Thurman, *With Head and Heart*, 130.

18. Edward Nolting to Howard Thurman, 18 November 1935, box 136, Howard Thurman Papers.

19. Mother of Sue Thurman to "Dear Children," 1 November 1935, box 3, folder 1, Bailey–Thurman Papers.

20. Remarks by Howard Thurman, n.d., box 179, Howard Thurman Papers.

21. Mrs. Wells Harrington, national student secretary, National Student Council, YWCA, to Howard Thurman, 5 February 1935, box 136, in ibid.

22. Benedict Williams, general-secretary of YWCA, to Howard Thurman, 14 November 1935, in ibid.

23. Thurman, *With Head and Heart*, 103–104, 107, 112–127. For an account of the delegation's confrontation in Ceylon, see Walter Earl Fluker and Catherine Tumber, *A Strange Freedom: The Best of Howard Thurman on Religious Experience and Public Life* (Boston: Beacon Press, 1998), 200, 205. The preceding paragraphs are all adapted from these sources.

24. *The Guardian, a Christian Weekly Journal of Public Affairs* (Madras), 12 December 1935, box 136, Howard Thurman Papers.

25. P. O. Phillips to Howard Thurman, 14 January 1937, 1 October 1937, in ibid.

26. Henrietta Wise to Howard Thurman, 14 January 1936, in ibid.

27. Letter to Howard Thurman from Colombo, 28 October 1935, in ibid.

28. C. T. Eapen, principal, Sasthamkotta Residential High School, Travancore, to Howard Thurman, 19 November 1935, in ibid.

29. P. V. Radhakrishnan to Howard Thurman, 6 January 1936, in ibid.

30. Remarks by Howard Thurman, n.d., box 179, in ibid.

31. *Daily News* (Colombo), 29 October 1935, box 136, in ibid.

32. Letter to Howard Thurman from Judson College, 13 January 1936, in ibid.

33. Remarks by Howard Thurman, in ibid.

34. Edward Nolting to Howard Thurman, 23 October 1935, box 136, in ibid.

35. Letter to Howard Thurman from Judson College-Rangoon, 18 December 1935, in ibid.

36. Fluker and Tumber, *A Strange Freedom*, 200, 207.

37. Ibid., 206.

38. Russell Friend, "Howard Thurman: American Gandhi," *United Church of Christ Newsletter*, December 1981, box 190, Howard Thurman Papers.

39. Orville Burton, "'Born to Rebel,'" in *Walking Integrity: Benjamin Elijah Mays, Mentor to Martin Luther King, Jr.*, ed. Lawrence Edward Carter Sr. (Macon, Ga.: Mercer University Press, 1998), 55.

40. Benjamin E. Mays, *Born to Rebel: An Autobiography* (Athens: University of Georgia Press, 1987), 155–157, 159.

41. "Interview with Benjamin Mays," 10 January 1937, in *The Collected Works of Mahatma Gandhi* (New Delhi: Ministry of Information, 1974), 64:221–222.

42. Benjamin E. Mays, "The Color Line around the World," *Journal of Negro Education* 6, no. 2 (April 1937): 136–138, 140–142.

43. Idem, *Born to Rebel*, 158–159.

44. *New York Post*, 20 September 1945.

45. "Interview with Channing Tobias," 10 January 1937, in *The Collected Works of Mahatma Gandhi*, 64:229–230.

46. "Travel Notes of Channing Tobias," 30 April 1937, box 1, Channing Tobias Papers.

47. See notes, 2 February 1937, in ibid.

48. Jean Toomer, "This Is Not India," n.d., box 48, Jean Toomer Papers, Yale University, New Haven, Conn.

49. Benjamin Mays, "1959 Commencement Address," in *Benjamin E. Mays Speaks: Representative Speeches of a Great American Orator*, ed. Freddie C. Colston (Lanham, Md.: University Press of America, 2002), 143.

CHAPTER 7: INDIA AND BLACK AMERICA

1. Thurman, *With Head and Heart*, 131.

2. "Interview" with "Harijan Workers," 1934, in *Collected Works of Mahatma Gandhi*, 58:102.

3. Remarks by M. K. Gandhi, 29 July 1933, in the same interview, 55:323.

4. Ibid., ca. 15 June 1935, 61:159.

5. Ibid., 1926, 29:78.

6. Ibid., ca. 1933, 56:89.

7. Ibid., 31 May 1936, in 62:44.

8. *The Crisis*, vol. 36, no. 7, July 1929, 225.

9. Earl Robert Schmidt, "American Relations with South Asia," PhD diss., University of Pennsylvania, 1955, 359, 361–362.

10. *Indian Social Reformer* (Bombay), 2 February 1935.

11. *Independent India* (Bombay), 4 July 1937. See also Reeta Sinha, *Political Ideas of M. N. Roy* (New Delhi: National Book Organization, 1991).

12. Mullen and Watson, *W. E. B. Du Bois on Asia*, 155.

13. M. K. Gandhi to Amy Jacques Garvey, 12 May 1926, in *Mahatma Gandhi: Letters to Americans*, ed. E. S. Reddy (Mumbai: Bharatiya Vidya Ghavan, 1998), 251.

14. Newspaper (Poona), 14 March 1936, box 136, Howard Thurman Papers.

15. Thurman, *With Head and Heart*, 132.

16. "Interview [with] American Negro Delegation," 21 February 1936, in *Collected Works of Mahatma Gandhi*, vol. 64.

17. Smith, "Sue Bailey Thurman."

18. *Harijan* (Poona), 14 March 1936, box 136, Howard Thurman Papers.

19. Ibid., 14 March 1936, in *Collected Works of Mahatma Gandhi*, 62:198.

20. Thurman, *With Head and Heart*, 134.

21. Mary King, *Mahatma Gandhi and Martin Luther King, Jr.: The Power of Nonviolent Action* (Paris: United Nations Education, Scientific and Cultural Organization, 1999), 178.

22. See interview with Channing Tobias and interview with Benjamin Mays, 1936–1937, in *Collected Works*, 64:229–230, 65:221–222, respectively.

23. B. R. Ambedkar to E.R. Seligman, n.d., E. R. Seligman Papers, Columbia University, New York.

24. Ibid., 21 December 1920.

25. Mohan Dass Namishray, *Caste and Race: Comparative Study of B. R. Ambedkar and Martin Luther King* (Jaipur: Rawat Publications, 2003), 77, 126, 129, 136, 138–139.

26. A. M. Rajasekhriah, *B. R. Ambedkar: The Quest for Social Justice* (New Delhi: Uppal Publishers, 1989), 11, 125. See also Dhananjay Keer, *Dr. Ambedkar: Life and Mission* (Bombay: Popular Prakashan, 1971), 31.

27. D. R. Jatava, *B. R. Ambedkar: Unique and Versatile* (New Delhi: Blumoon Books, 1998), 3, 6–7, 37.

28. Edward Luce, *In Spite of the Gods: The Strange Rise of Modern India* (New York: Doubleday, 2007), 13, 113.

29. *National Front* (organ of the Communist Party of India published in Bombay), 11 September 1938, Nehru Library, New Delhi. See also Darshan S. Tatla, *A Guide to Sources: Ghadar Movement* (Amritsar: Guru Nanak Dev University, 2003); Kalyan Kumar Banerjee, *Indian Freedom Movement Revolutionaries in America* (Calcutta: Jijnasa, 1969); L. P. Mathur,

Indian Revolutionary Movement in the United States of America (New Delhi: S. Chand, 1970).

30. Abbas, *An Indian Looks at America*, 31, 33, 37, 55, 61, 67–69.

31. Joseph Kip Kosek, "Spectacles of Conscience: Christian Non-Violence and the Transformation of American Democracy, 1914–1956," Ph.D. diss., Yale University, New Haven, Conn., 2004, 261.

32. John D'Emilio, *Lost Prophet: The Life and Times of Bayard Rustin* (New York: Free Press, 2003), 51–53.

33. Krishnalal Shridharani, *My India, My America* (New York: Duell, Sloan and Pearce, 1941), 269–270. During the same decade, Shridharani notes, the African American historian Lorenzo Green "met a Mr. Moses, a Hindu working for a doctor's degree in psychology at the University of Pennsylvania. Is a brilliant student. Likes Negroes. Naturally! Oppression makes brothers of us all." See Lorenzo Green, *Selling Black History for Carter G. Woodson: A Diary, 1930–1933*, ed. Arvah Strickland (Columbia: University of Missouri Press, 1996, 274). At times, the encounters between India and Black America on this side of the Atlantic were a bit more enthralling—for example, in pre–World War II Atlanta when "an occasional circus came to town with East Indian snake charmers and elephants in tents." See Tera Hunter, *To 'Joy My Freedom: Southern Black Women's Lives and Labors after the Civil War* (Cambridge, Mass.: Harvard University Press, 1997), 151.

34. Cedric Dover to Jawaharlal Nehru, n.d., file no. FD8, All India Congress Committee Papers.

35. Jawaharlal Nehru to Cedric Dover, 22 April 1936, in ibid.

36. "Head of Foreign Department" to Cedric Dover, 20 May 1936, in ibid.

37. Robert O. Jordan to Jawaharlal Nehru, 13 April 1936, in ibid.

38. Robert Jordan to Cordell Hull, 19 September 1936, in ibid.

39. Idem to Secretary-General of League of Nations, 19 September 1936, in ibid.

40. Idem to Jawaharlal Nehru, 28 September 1936, in ibid.

41. Idem to Swaraj Bhawan, 28 September 1936, in ibid.

42. Rammanchar Lohia to Robert Jordan, 12 November 1936, in ibid.

43. George Padmore to Rammanchar Lohia, head of Foreign Department, 5 August 1935, in ibid.

44. Jawaharlal Nehru to Robert Jordan, ca. 1936, in ibid.

45. "Notes for Negro Contacts," n.d., in ibid.

46. Claude Barnett to Cedric Dover, 4 August 1936, in ibid.

47. Cedric Dover to Rammanchar Lohia, 17 August 1936, in ibid.

48. Rammanchar Lohia to Charles Johnson, 20 July 1936, in ibid.

49. Charles Johnson to Rammanchar Lohia, 2 September 1936, in ibid.

50. Max Yergan to Indian National Congress, 9 September 1936, in ibid.

51. Idem to Rammanchar Lohia, 13 August 1937, in ibid.

52. Idem to "Excellency," 3 December 1937, in ibid.

53. Rammanchar Lohia to Max Yergan, 6 September 1936, in ibid.

54. Cedric Dover, memorandum, n.d., in ibid.

55. Idem to Jawaharlal Nehru, ca. 1938, reel 48, no. 902, W.E.B. Du Bois Papers.

56. Rammanchar Lohia to Roger Baldwin, file no. 9/1936, 27 July 1936, All India Congress Committee Papers.

57. W. E. B. Du Bois to M. K. Gandhi, 19 August 1931, reel 36, no. 49, W. E. B. Du Bois Papers.

58. Dennis Kux, *Estranged Democracies: India and the United States, 1941–1991* (New Delhi: Sage, 1993), 92. See also Kenton J. Clymer, *Quest for Freedom: The United States and India's Independence* (New York: Columbia University Press, 1995); Glazer and Glazer, *Conflicting Images*; Harnam Singh, *The Indian National Movement and American Opinion* (New Delhi: Rama Krishna and Sons, 1964); Robert M. Crunden, Manoj Joshi, and R. V. R. Chandrasekhar Rao, eds., *New Perspectives on America and South Asia* (Delhi: Chanakya, 1984); Ranju Bezbaruah, *America and India in Global and South Asian Settings* (Calcutta: Punthi Pustak, 1999); S. L. Poplai and Phillips Talbot, *India and America: A Study of Their Relations* (Bombay: Oxford University Press, [ca. 1956]); Sidney Verba et al., *Caste, Race and Politics: A Comparative Study of India and the United States* (Beverly Hills,.: Sage, 1971); Charles Chatfield, *The Americanization of Gandhi: Images of the Mahatma* (New York: Garland, 1976).

59. Cedric Dover, *Half-Caste* (London: Martin Secker and Warburg, 1937), 60, 284. See also Penny von Eschen, *Satchmo Blows Up the World: Jazz Ambassadors Play the Cold War* (Cambridge.: Harvard University Press, 2004), 181: Robeson's "signature song 'Old Man River' had inspired a Bengali song about the Ganges, which, like the Mississippi was said to be indifferent to the suffering of those who lived on its banks."

60. *The Crisis*, vol. 40, no. 12, December 1933, 292–294.

61. *Pittsburgh Courier*, 19 July 1930, 28 February 1931, 1 October 1932, 4 November 1939.

62. See also *Chicago Defender*, 10 May 1930; *Savannah Tribune*, 5 March 1930, 29 September 1930.

63. *Pittsburgh Courier*, 17 May 1930.

CHAPTER 8: THE UNITED STATES VERSUS INDIA

1. Kanhaya Lal Gauba, *Uncle Sham: The Strange Tale of Civilization Run Amuck* (New York: Claude Kendall, 1929), ix.

2. Katherine Mayo, *Mother India* (Delhi: Anmol Publications, 1986), 24–25, 267, 331, 337.

3. Idem, *Mother India* (New York: Harcourt Brace, 1927), 11.

4. Idem, *The Face of Mother India* (New York: Harper and Brothers, 1935), 46.

5. Gauba, *Uncle Sham*, 37, 39, 42–43, 61.

6. *Bombay Chronicle*, 29 June 1930. See also Schmidt, "American Relations with South Asia," 257.

7. See, e.g., C. S. Ranga Iyer, *Father India: A Reply to "Mother India"* (London: Selwyn and Blount, 1927).

8. Paul Teed, "Race against Memory: Katherine Mayo, Jabez Sutherland and Indian Independence," *American Studies* 44, nos. 1–2 (Spring–Summer 2003): 46.

9. *Yorkshire Post*, 5 September 1928, box 41, Katherine Mayo Papers.

10. *Nottingham Guardian*, 5 September 1928, box 41, in ibid.

11. Undated clipping, box 19, in ibid.

12. *New Masses*, November 1927, box 41, in ibid.

13. *Era*, 9 January 1935, in ibid.

14. *New York Times*, 6 October 1927.

15. See her picture in *Buffalo News*, 27 October 1927.

16. Clipping, 14 February 1928, box 46, in ibid.

17. *Houston Chronicle*, 11 October 1927.

18. Essay by Mayo, ca. 1920s, box 19, in ibid.

19. Story by Mayo, ca. 1918–1922, in ibid.

20. *Independent Hindustan,* November 1920. See also James Campbell Ker, *Political Trouble in India, 1907–1919* (Delhi: Oriental Publishing, 1973); Don Dignan, *The Indian Revolutionary Problem in British Diplomacy, 1914–1919* (New Delhi: Allied Publishing, 1983); H. W. Hale, *Political Trouble in India, 1917–1937* (Allahabad: Chugh Publishing, 1974).

21. International Committee for Political Prisoners to Secretary of State, India, 27 October 1931, reel 34, no. 1202, W.E.B. Du Bois Papers.

22. *Negro World,* 13 November 1926.

23. Speech, 3 June 1938, box 1, Channing Tobias Papers.

24. Remarks by Channing Tobias, 9 October 1932, in ibid.

25. Document on International Committee of YMCA, n.d., Max Yergan Papers.

26. J. T. Sunderland to L. L. Rai, 21 April 1925, box 5, J. T. Sunderland Papers. See also the letter from Sunderland to Rai in *The People,* 5 July 1925: "I only wish I could speak more encouragingly of our propaganda work. For want of funds we have been obliged to close our India Office, which you opened at 1400 Broadway and also to suspend operations in connection with our India Information Bureau as well as to discontinue the monthly magazine which you started."

27. J. T. Sunderland, *Eminent Americans Whom India Should Know* (Calcutta: R. Chatterjee, 1935), 2. See also idem, *India, America and World Brotherhood* (Madras: Ganesh, ca. 1924). Here the author draws analogies between Negroes and India.

28. Idem, *India in Bondage: Her Right to Freedom* (Calcutta: R. Chatterjee, 1929), 25.

29. *New Age* (Madras), May 1937.

30. Taraknath Das to J. T. Sunderland, box 5, J.T. Sunderland Papers.

31. *Time,* 26 August 1929.

32. Report, 30 April 1925, 1/P&J/12/248, India Office, British Library, London. This report can also be found in "Indian Political Intelligence Files, 1912–1950: North America," OrFiche 655, fiche 414, at the same site.

33. Taraknath Das to J. T. Sunderland, 10 October 1925, box 5, J.T. Sunderland Papers.

34. Mary Das to J. T. Sunderland, 2 September 1926, in ibid.

35. A. C. Chakravarty to W. E. B. Du Bois, n.d., reel 30, no. 489, W. E. B. Du Bois Papers.

36. *Independent India,* 22 August 1937.

37. *The People,* 6 October 1927.

38. *Indian Social Reformer,* 27 August 1899: "I will be as harsh as truth and as uncompromising as justice. I am in earnest—I will not equivocate—I will not excuse, I will not retreat a single inch—and I will be heard."

39. J. N. Uppal, *Gandhi Ordained in South Africa* (New Delhi: Ministry of Information, 1995), 234.

40. Chester Bowles, *Ambassador's Report* (New York: Harper and Brothers, 1954), 62.

41. M. S. Venkataramani and B. K. Shrivastava, *Roosevelt, Gandhi, Churchill: America and the Last Phase of India's Freedom Struggle* (New Delhi: Radiant, 1983), 297.

42. *The People,* 7 March 1926.

43. Diary, 12 August 1941, box 1, folder 5, Thomas Murray Wilson Papers, Georgetown University, Washington, D.C.

44. John Haynes Holmes to J. Holmes Smith, 6 December 1940, box 21, John Haynes Holmes Papers, Library of Congress, Washington, D.C. See also S. P. K. Gupta, *Apostle John and Gandhi: The Mission of John Haynes Holmes for Mahatma Gandhi in the United States of America* (Ahmedabad: Navajivan Publishing House, 2000).

45. See, e.g., Christine Rosen, *Preaching Eugenics: Religious Leaders and the American Eugenics Movement* (New York: Oxford University Press, 2004), passim.

46. Walter White to John Haynes Holmes, 8 September 1941, box 31, John Haynes Holmes Papers.

47. John Haynes Holmes, *I Speak for Myself: The Autobiography of John Haynes Holmes* (New York: Harper, 1959), 196.

48. Hemendra K. Rakhi, president, Sirdar J. J. Singh, treasurer, and Dr. Anup Singh, editor, India League of America, to "Dear Friend," 23 September 1941, box 29, John Haynes Holmes Papers.

49. Letter from Sir Alfred Watson, 31 July 1941, box 29, John Haynes Holmes Papers. See also William Archibald Dunning, *The British Empire and the United States: A Review of Their Relations during the Century of Peace Following the Treaty of Ghent* (New York: Scribner's, 1914).

50. August Meier and Elliott Rudwick, *CORE: A Study in the Civil Rights Movement, 1942–1968* (New York: Oxford University Press, 1973), 6–7, 10.

51. Memorandum, n.d., DG 13, sec. II, box 13, Fellowship of Reconciliation Papers, Swarthmore College, Swarthmore, Penn.

52. Harlem Ashram to members of Board of Directors, YMCA, 12 August 1941, in ibid.

53. "Documents for the Use of Delegates and Commissions at the Twenty-First World's Conference of the YMCAS, Mysore, India, January 2–10, 1937," YMCA PAPERS. (This collection was being reorganized during my Summer 2005 research visit.) See also Jensen, *Passage from India,* 171: "When traveling in the Southeast, Indians had to wear their turbans lest they be taken for black Americans and encounter even more discrimination."

54. Harlem Ashram to "Fellowship Friend," 4 October 1941, DG 13, sec. II, box 13, Fellowship of Reconciliation Papers.

55. James Farmer to A. J. Muste, 8 January 1942, series A, sub-series A3, box 2, Fellowship of Reconciliation Papers. On the influence of Japan in India and Black America, see, e.g., Horne, *Race War!*

56. Meier and Rudwick, *CORE,* 14.

57. Haridas T. Muzumdar, *America's Contribution to India's Freedom* (Allahabad: Central Book Depot, 1962), 7.

58. Undated memorandum, ca. 1942, DG 13, sec. II, box 13, Fellowship of Reconciliation Papers.

59. Interview with Pauli Murray, 1975, box 1, Pauli Murray Papers, Harvard University, Cambridge, Mass.

60. Interview with Pauli Murray, 1978, in ibid.

61. Ibid., 1975.

62. Kosek, "Spectacles of Conscience," 144.

63. Diary of Pauli Murray, January 1941, box 1, Pauli Murray Papers.

64. Sinha, *Specters of Mother India,* 291.

65. *New York Amsterdam News,* 29 November 1926.

66. Diary, 25 November 1941, 8 December 1941, 12 March 1942, box 1, folder 5, Thomas Murray Wilson Papers.

CHAPTER 9: RACE WAR!

1. See Horne, *Race War!*

2. *African Times and Orient Review,* ca. 15 January 1917.

3. Ibid., July 1912.

4. Ibid., February 1913.

5. Ibid., July 1912.

6. Ibid., June 1913.

7. Ibid., July 1913.

8. Ibid., October 1913.

9. *Negro World*, 28 February 1925.

10. Ibid., 30 July 1927.

11. Ibid., 3 September 1927.

12. See, e.g., ibid., 21 April 1923: "British Rule Bad for Black People"; ibid., 31 March 1923: "The spirit of hate on the part of the Englishman for the Negro in his country"; ibid., 10 November 1923: "Decline of the British Empire. . . . [T]he death knell of the British Empire was sounded on the declaration of war in 1914. . . . [A]t the present time India is seething with revolt [while] American propaganda aids and abets British imperialism"; ibid., 12 September 1925: "Effrontery of British knows no boundary"; ibid., 2 October 1926: "England doomed as world power."

13. Ibid., 13 November 1926: "Asiatics change attitude toward Africans. . . . [G]ulf which in the past has divided the peoples of Asia from the peoples of Africa is being bridged. . . . [T]he struggles which emigrants from India have had in various parts of Africa with the white races, which dominate those parts, have especially served to bring home the community of interest which exists between colored people"; ibid., 23 October 1926: "India a hotbed of unrest against brutal British rule"; ibid., 19 June 1926: "India developing as spiritual world leader. All the great religions came from Asia."

14. Ibid., 12 September 1925.

15. Ibid., 6 September 1924.

16. Ibid., 17 November 1923.

17. *The Messenger*, May–June 1919.

18. Ibid., August 1921.

19. Speech by Langston Hughes, *Japan Advertiser* (Tokyo), 1 July 1933, box 479, Langston Hughes Papers, Yale University, New Haven, Conn.

20. J. T. Sunderland, "Rising Japan: Is She a Menace?" ca. 1928, box 25, J. T. Sunderland Papers.

21. *Inter-Collegiate Newsletter*, March 1928, Max Yergan Personal Papers.

22. *Student Association Newsletter*, March 1927, in ibid.

23. *The Independent*, 20 April 1919.

24. Ibid., 15 April 1919.

25. *The People*, 13 April 1929.

26. Ibid., 12 April 1931.

27. Ibid., 3 October 1926.

28. Ibid., 4 October 1925.

29. Ibid., 2 May 1929. See also Sujit Mukherjee, *Passage to America: The Reception of Rabindranath Tagore in the United States, 1912–1941* (Calcutta: Bookland Private, 1964); J. L. Dees, *Tagore in America* (Calcutta: N.K. Gossaini, n.d.).

30. See Horne, *Race War!*

31. J. T. Sunderland, *India in Bondage: Her Right to Freedom* (Calcutta: R. Chatterjee, 1929), 25, 32, 191.

32. M. S. Venkataramani and B. K. Shrivastava, *Quit India: The American Response to the 1942 Struggle* (New Delhi: Vikas Publishing House, 1979), 295.

33. "Message to the All India Trade Union Congress," 8 May 1943, box 1, Krishnabai Nimbkar Papers, University of California, Berkeley.

34. Report, 8 May 1942, File of Moorish Science Temple of America, Reading Room, Federal Bureau of Investigation, Washington, D.C.

35. Confidential report from Army Services Forces of Chicago, 9 March 1944, in ibid.

36. Report from Chicago, 18 August 1945, in ibid.

37. FBI to special agent, New York, 11 February 1943, in ibid.

38. Prashad, *Everybody Was Kung-fu Fighting*, 107.

39. *People's Voice*, 21 March 1942, in ibid.

40. Report from FBI Indianapolis, 20 November 1942, in ibid.

41. Confidential report from U.S. Naval Intelligence Service, 28 May 1943, in ibid.

42. Confidential report, Chicago, 16 February 1944, in ibid.

43. Report to FBI director, Chicago, 18 August 1942, in ibid.

44. Report from FBI office in Chicago, 6 July 1944, in ibid.

45. Report from War Department, Headquarters Sixth Service Command, Chicago, 25 May 1943, in ibid.

46. Walter White to All India Nationalist Congress, 16 April 1942, reel 9, no. 10, NAACP Papers, Duke University, Durham, N.C.

47. War Cabinet to Harry Hopkins, 21 July 1942, box 136, Harry Hopkins Papers, Franklin D. Roosevelt Library, Hyde Park, N.Y.

48. Confidential memorandum, 24 April 1942, part 14, reel 9, no. 17, NAACP Papers.

49. Walter White to W. E. B. Du Bois, 28 April 1942, reel 54, no. 1, W. E. B. Du Bois Papers.

50. Gary R. Hess, *America Encounters India* (Baltimore: Johns Hopkins University Press, 1971), 63, 122.

51. Walter White to President Franklin D. Roosevelt, 4 May 1942, reel 54, no. 1, W. E. B. Du Bois Papers.

52. Column by Drew Pearson, 31 March 1943, part 14, reel 9, no. 392, NAACP Papers.

53. Memorandum, 11 January 1944, FO371/38609, Public Records Office, London.

54. Ibid., January 1944, FO371/38609.

55. R. J. Cruikshank to Neville Butler, 18 January 1944, FO371/38609, in ibid.

56. Walter White to James Fly, 23 May 1942, part 14, reel 9, no. 124, NAACP Papers.

57. See Alan R. Murray to Walter White, 3 August 1942, and Walter White to Alan Murray, n.d., part 14, reel 9, no. 193, in ibid.

58. Walter White to President Franklin D. Roosevelt, 10 August 1942, part 14, reel 9, no. 203, in ibid.

59. Ibid., 31 August 1942, no. 223.

60. Venkataramani and Shrivastava, *Quit India*, 296.

61. Anson Phelps Stokes to Walter White, 29 May 1942, part 14, reel 9, no. 124, NAACP Papers.

62. Walter White to Pearl Buck, 5 June 1942, part 14, reel 9, no. 129, in ibid. See Venkataramani and Shrivastava, *Quit India*, 295–296. When White went to the State Department to meet with A. A. Berle, according to Venkataramani and Shrivastava, Berle "made some comments on colour prejudice in India and its influence on the attitude of Indian leaders toward the Negro problem. . . . Negroes like White were unwilling to swallow 'horror stories' from any quarter concerning the attitude of Indian leaders towards the problem of discrimination."

63. H. W. Sewing to Walter White, ca. 1942, part 14, reel 9, no. 215, NAACP Papers.

64. *People's World*, 14 August 1942.

65. *The Call*, 4 September 1942, part 14, reel 9, no. 226, NAACP Papers.

66. R. Lal Singh, editor of *India News* and member of the Indian National Congress, 11 September 1942, part 14, reel 9, no. 234, in ibid.

67. "Minutes of Coordinating Committee on Indian Freedom," 19 October 1942, in ibid.

68. Homer Jack, memorandum, n.d., Miscellaneous Series, ACC. 03A, 082, box 2, Homer Jack Papers, Swarthmore College, Swarthmore, Penn.

69. *Newsletter of the Coordinating Committee for Democratic Action*, New York City, 25 August 1942, part 14, reel 9, no. 218, NAACP Papers.

CHAPTER 10: AFRICAN AMERICANS WAGING WAR IN INDIA

1. *New York Amsterdam-Star News*, 7 April 1945.

2. Secret report from Headquarters, U.S. Forces, India–Burma Theater, 28 August 1945, RG 493, box 57, Records of U.S. Army Forces in the China–Burma–India Theaters of Operations, Adjutant General, General Correspondence, National Archives and Records Administration (NARA), College Park, Md.

3. *Michigan Chronicle*, 19 May 1945. See Leslie Anders, *The Ledo Road: General Joseph Stilwell's Highway to India* (Norman: University of Oklahoma Press, 1965); Nathan N. Prefer, *Vinegar Joe's War: Stilwell's Campaigns for Burma* (Novato, Calif.: Presidio, 2000).

4. *Afro-American*, 31 July 1943.

5. Report from Headquarters, Intermediate Section, India–Burma Theater, 16 July 1945, RG 493, box 57, Records of U.S. Army Forces in the China-Burma-India Theaters of Operations, Adjutant General, General Correspondence.

6. Secret report, Headquarters, 47. Quartermasters Battalion (Mobile), 13 July 1945.

7. Secret memorandum, Headquarters Base Section, India–Burma Theater, 27 July 1945.

8. Secret report from Lieutenant-Colonel Edwin O. Shaw, 17 January 1945, NARA, College Park, Md.

9. *Oklahoma Black Dispatch*, 19 September 1942.

10. Letter from Negro Troops, n.d., in *Taps for a Jim Crow Army: Letters from Black Soldiers in World War II*, ed. Phillip Maguire (Santa Barbara, Calif.: ABC-CLIO, 1983), 227.

11. *Chicago Defender*, 21 April 1945.

12. Charles F. Romanus and Riley Sunderland, *United States Army in World War II: China–Burma–India Theater: Time Runs Out in CBI* (Washington, D.C.: Office of the Chief of Military History, Department of the Army, 1959), 297.

13. *Afro-American*, 29 January 1944.

14. *New York Times*, ca. August 1942, part III, reel 8, no. 53, National Negro Congress Papers, Schomburg Center for Research in Black Culture, New York Public Library.

15. Report, 1 September 1944, External Affairs, file 741 (9)-FE/44, 1944, National Archives of India, New Delhi.

16. Romanus and Sunderland, *United States Army in World War II*, 297.

17. Confidential report, 17 February 1942, box 57-5, Campbell C. Johnson Papers, Howard University, Washington, D.C.

18. President Franklin D. Roosevelt to William John, 1 July 1943, OF93, box 5, President's Official File, Franklin D. Roosevelt Library, Hyde Park, N.Y.

19. Attorney J. C. Ross to Hon. William Colmer, 3 February 1943, in ibid.

20. Clipping, 2 March 1944, FO371/38609, Public Records Office, London.

21. *Afro-American*, 26 June 1943, box 173-14, Leon Ransom Papers, Howard University, Washington, D.C.

22. Clipping, n.d., box 173-14, in ibid.

23. *Chicago Bee*, 13 September 1942.

24. *Louisiana Weekly*, 3 October 1942.

25. *Pittsburgh Courier*, 10 October 1942.

26. Ibid., 9 January 1943.

27. Clipping, 28 November 1942, box 57-8, Campbell C. Johnson Papers.

28. *Pittsburgh Courier*, 28 November 1942.

29. *Chicago Bee*, 30 August 1942; *New York Age*, 22 August 1942.

30. *New York Age*, 12 September 1942.

31. Speech by Max Yergan, 2 September 1942, part III, reel 8, no. 53, National Negro Congress Papers.

32. Penny von Eschen, *Race against Empire: Black Americans and Anticolonialism, 1937–1957* (Ithaca, N.Y.: Cornell University Press, 1997), 28–29.

33. Paul Robeson Jr., *The Undiscovered Paul Robeson: An Artist's Journey, 1898–1939* (New York: John Wiley, 2001), 309.

34. E. S. Reddy to Gerald Horne, 14 May 2007, in possession of the author.

35. Max Yergan to President Franklin D. Roosevelt, 12 August 1942, part III, reel 8, no. 80, National Negro Congress Papers.

36. *Chicago Defender*, 26 September 1942.

37. "Editorial Comment," *Negro Quarterly* 1, no. 2 (Summer 1942): iv.

38. Sandya Shukla, *India Abroad: Diasporic Cultures of Postwar America and England* (Princeton, N.J.: Princeton University Press, 2003), 41.

39. Kumar Goshal, "The Crisis in India," *Negro Quarterly* 1, no. 3 (Fall 1942): 219.

40. Speech by Langston Hughes, 24 October 1942, box 479, Langston Hughes Papers.

41. Von Eschen, *Race against Empire*, 28.

42. Secret report, 12 August 1942, L/PO/6/102a, India Office, British Library. See also *London Times*, 13 August 1942.

43. Secret report, 12 August 1942. See also a thick file of reports—L/PI3/3b—reflecting increasing British trepidation about how U.S. nationals, supposedly, do not understand the British view of India.

44. *Michigan Chronicle*, 22 August 1942.

45. Pauli Murray to Krishnalal Shridharani, 24 August 1942, box 102, Pauli Murray Papers.

46. Gordon P. Merriam, assistant chief, Division of Near Eastern Affairs, to Pauli Murray, 26 February 1943, in ibid.

47. Major F. N. Schwartz, Medical Administration C, Blood Plasma Division, Surgery Division, Assistant, U.S. War Department, Services Supply Office of the Surgeon General, to Pauli Murray, 2 August 1944, in ibid.

48. P. O. Phillips to Charles J. Ewald, 30 September 1936, box 136, Howard Thurman Papers.

49. J. Holmes Smith, "The Conscientious Objector," August 1942, box 4, M. K. Gandhi Papers. See also Chatfield, *The Americanization of Gandhi.*

50. Bayard Rustin, *Down the Line: The Collected Writings of Bayard Rustin* (Chicago: Quadrangle, 1971), 11. See also Pettinger, *Always Elsewhere.*

51. Undated Memo on "The Work of the Harlem Ashram," ca. 1944, DG 13, sec. II, box 13, Fellowship of Reconciliation Papers: "There are three peoples in the world today whom

we regard as having specially redemptive possibilities. They are the peoples of India and Puerto Rico struggling for freedom from imperialistic exploitation and the Negro people of America striving to be free from that white domination which is akin to it. Like the 'suffering servant' of Judaism, they can show the powerful peoples who dominate them the way to a free and just godly social order. . . . [One] of our most heartening adventures in the way of Jesus and Gandhi to the struggle for racial justice in America was our recent public protest against the sham battle on the poll tax issue in the U.S. Senate. One of the best things about it, quite unprecedented, was the participation of eighteen Negro ministers from around the Capitol."

52. J. Holmes Smith to A. J. Muste, 18 November 1944, box 4, in ibid.

53. August Meier and Elliott Rudwick, *Along the Color Line: Explorations in the Black Experience* (Champaign-Urbana: University of Illinois Press, 1976), 348.

54. David Chappell, *A Stone of Hope: Prophetic Religion and the Death of Jim Crow* (Chapel Hill: University of North Carolina Press, 2004), 227.

55. Bayard Rustin, *Strategies for Freedom: The Changing Patterns of Black Protest* (New York: Columbia University Press, 1976), 20–21.

56. Mubarek Ali Khan to Stephen Early, 26 May 1939, Of48h, President's Official File, Franklin D. Roosevelt Library. Attached to this appeal was a petition noting that Indians were "denied the right to become naturalized citizens by the Exclusion Act of 1917 and by Supreme Court decision. . . . [T]here are now over 12,000 Indians living in the United States."

57. *The Student* (Bombay), July 1943, Nehru Library.

58. Ashley Hope, "The American Role in Indian Independence, 1940–1947," Ph.D. diss., Syracuse University, Syracuse, N.Y., 1967, 43–44, 84–86, 198–199. See also R. C. Jauhri, *American Diplomacy and Independence for India* (Bombay: Vora, 1970).

CHAPTER 11: TOWARD INDEPENDENCE AND EQUALITY

1. *Memphis World*, 14 August 1942.

2. Memorandum, 21 January 1944, FO971/38609, *Public Records Office-London*.

3. Ibid.

4. Memorandum, 27 November 1943, in ibid.

5. A. F. Morley to "My Dear Bozman," 22 February 1944, in ibid.

6. Neville Butler to "Dear Michael," 14 March 1944, FO371/38609, in ibid.

7. John Haynes Holmes to Walter White, 14 November 1944, box 3, Walter White Papers, Yale University

8. Idem to "Dear Gandhiji," 21 November 1944, in ibid.

9. J. J. Singh to Bhulahbai Desai, 28 November 1944, in ibid.

10. Idem to Walter White, 28 November 1944, in ibid.

11. Walter White to Anup Singh, 24 January 1944, part 14, reel 11, no. 521, NAACP Papers.

12. See, e.g., Thomas Hachey, "Walter White and the American Negro Soldier in World War II: A Diplomatic Dilemma for Britain," in *Race and U.S. Foreign Policy from the Colonial Period to the Present: A Collection of Essays*, ed. Michael Krenn (New York: Garland, 1998), 331–341.

13. Pauli Murray to Ruth and Augusta, 25 April 1945, box 102, Pauli Murray Papers.

14. John Hayes Holmes to George Schuyler, 23 August 1946, box 66, John Haynes Holmes Papers.

15. NAACP Statement, 18 May 1946, part 14, reel 11, no. 636, NAACP Papers.

16. Hemendra K. Rakhit, secretary, India League of America, to Walter White, 28 March 1946, part 14, reel 11, no. 584, in ibid.

17. See announcement, ca. 1946, part 14, reel 11, no. 634, in ibid.

18. Memorandum from NAACP Board, 24 July 1946, in ibid.

19. Walter White to John Sengstacke, Carl Murphy, and Ira Lewis, 3 June 1946, part 14, reel 11, no. 638, in ibid.

20. J. J. Singh to Walter White, 6 November 1946, part 14, reel 11, no. 706, in ibid.

21. Kaikhusroo Hormuz to Senator Richard Russell, 1 July 1946, part 14, reel 11, no. 658, in ibid. See also H. K. Rakhit, India League of America, to Walter White, 28 December 1945, part 14, reel 11, no. 559, in ibid.: "Advise us how we can obtain information concerning the laws of New York State covering inter-racial marriage, such as Negroes and whites."

22. Harvey Neptune, "Forging Trinidad, Facing America: Colonial Trinidad and the United States Occupation, 1930–1947," Ph.D. diss., New York University, 2002, 387.

23. Eric Johnson to Harry Abrahamson, 11 February 1946, "Foreign Service 1946 Country India," American Friend Services Committee Archives, Philadelphia. (hereafter, AFSC Archives)

24. Eric Johnson to Leonard Jacob II, 20 May 1946, in ibid.

25. Chester Bowles, U.S. Office of Economic Stabilization, to Pearl Buck, 10 April 1946, in ibid.

26. Lela Mills, associate secretary, AFSC, to Mark Mills, 29 October 1946, in ibid.

27. Eric Johnson to John Pierce, National CIO, Community Services Committee, 5 February 1946, in ibid.

28. Gilbert F. White, secretary to Ralph T. Shaw, assistant secretary, Los Angeles War Chest, 25 February 1946, in ibid.

29. Lela Mills, associate secretary, AFSC, to Kamala V. Nimbkar, 18 October 1946, in ibid.

30. "Periodic Summary No. 1," 18 July 1946, in ibid.

31. Harry Abrahamson to Roderick Ede, 24 August 1946, in ibid.

32. "Periodic Summary No. 3," 9 April 1947, in ibid.

33. Roderick Ede, Friends of U.K., to William Stuart Nelson, 4 June 1947, in ibid.

34. William Stuart Nelson to Ruth Bosworth, 11 June 1947, in ibid.

35. Idem to Colin Bell, 6 June 1947, in ibid.

36. Biography of William Stuart Nelson, n.d., William Stuart Nelson Papers, Howard University, Washington, D.C.

37. William Stuart Nelson to "Dearest Blanche," 4 December 1946, in ibid.

38. Idem, "The Gandhi I Knew," *Friends Intelligencer*, May 1948, in ibid.

39. Idem to Colin Bell, 26 May 1947, in ibid.

40. Ibid., 20 May 1947.

41. Idem to Colin Bell and Ruth Bosworth, 4 August 1947, in ibid.

42. Idem to Ruth Bosworth, 22 July 1947, in ibid.

43. Letter from William Stuart Nelson, 10 July 1947, in ibid.

44. Ibid., 2 June 1947.

45. Minutes of Unit Meeting, 14 April 1947, in ibid.

46. William Stuart Nelson, *Bases of World Understanding* (Calcutta: Calcutta University Lectures, 1949), 68–70.

47. *Chicago Tribune*, 5 May 1946; *Chicago Sun*, 9 May 1946.

48. "Biographical Records," n.d., box 28, YMCA Archives.

49. "Marie," writing from Calcutta YMCA, to "Dear Pat," 26 November 1946, in ibid.

50. "Biographical Records."

51. Nelson, "The Gandhi I Knew."

52. William Stuart Nelson, "The Tradition of Non-Violence and its Underlying Forces," n.d., William Stuart Nelson Papers.

53. "Some Notes on the General Approach and the Propaganda Methods of the All India Muslim League with Special Reference to Inter-Communal Relations,' n.d., file no. 40, All India Congress Committee Papers.

54. *The Messenger*, October 1922: "Look out! England is up to her old tricks again! . . . Hindus and Mohammedans had divided and spent their strength upon one the other while the shrewd English manipulator stood by in the role of shocked and aggrieved benefactor of both—and filled her pockets during the engagement! . . . England's two problems, how to keep the East subjugated, and how to stem the tide of Bolshevism in the West, has become a more or less related and vastly complicated one . . . but no matter how it comes England depends upon a war of color. Already a righteous cry has gone up: 'The Moslems are threatening Europe! Christianity is in danger!'"

55. Rushton Coulborn, "Race, Culture and the War in Asia," *Phylon* 3 (1942): 388.

56. *Chicago Defender*, 3 August 1946.

CHAPTER 12: TOWARD EQUALITY/BEYOND INDEPENDENCE

1. Letter from Non-Partisan Committee to Defend the Rights of the Twelve Communist Leaders, 22 September 1949, box 97, John Haynes Holmes Papers.

2. Letter on Peekskill, 15 September 1949, in ibid.

3. Letter from Lawyers' Defense Committee, 13 January 1950, in ibid.

4. Letter from W. E. B. Du Bois, Benjamin Mays, et al., 24 December 1948, box 89, in ibid.

5. Statement by J. J. Singh, 10 September 1948, part 14, reel 12, no. 0080, NAACP Papers.

6. Eugene Barnett to Harper Sibley, 21 September 1947, YMCA Archives.

7. Wilson Hume, Calcutta YMCA, to D. F. McClelland, New York City, 29 November 1947, in ibid.

8. Wilson Hume to Mary Porter, 7 December 1948, in ibid.

9. Idem to D. F. McClelland, 15 January 1948, in ibid.

10. D. F. McClelland to Wilson Hume, 4 March 1949, in ibid.

11. Report by Lawrence Burr, 14 June 1948, in ibid.

12. Publicity report, 1949, in ibid.

13. Wilson Hume to D. F. McClelland, 13 February 1948, in ibid.

14. T. D. Santwan to D. F. McClelland, 21 February 1949, in ibid.

15. Minutes of the Meeting of the National Boys' Work Committee, 11 September 1948, in ibid.

16. Wilson Hume to D. F. McClelland, 5 February 1949, in ibid.

17. Bayard Rustin to Roy Wilkins, 20 December 1948, part 14, reel 12, no. 0124, NAACP Papers.

18. Wilson Hume to D. F. McClelland, 23 June 1948, YMCA Archives.

19. "Chicago Recorded Talk" by Lawrence Burr, 15 April 1949, in ibid.

20. *New York Times*, 9 April 1952.

21. Wilson Hume to D. F. McClelland, 17 August 1947, YMCA Archives.

22. W. E. B. Du Bois to Vijaya L. Pandit, 18 September 1947, reel 60, no. 125, W. E. B. Du Bois Papers.

23. Press release, 27 November 1946, part 14, reel 12, no. 569, NAACP Papers.

24. Delegation of India to the United Nations to Du Bois, circa September 1947, Reel 60, #no. 126, W.E.B. Du Bois Papers.

25. J. J. Singh, president, India League of America, to Walter White, 20 January 1948, part 14, reel 12, no. 0002, NAACP Papers.

26. Walter White to Prime Minister Jawaharlal Nehru, 9 December 1947, part 14, reel 12, no. 671, in ibid.

27. Undated clipping, part 14, reel 12, no. 0118, in ibid.

28. Walter White to Fowler McCormick, 16 September 1949, box 4, Walter White Papers.

29. Fowler McCormick to Walter White, 23 September 1949, in ibid.

30. Walter White to Fowler McCormick, 25 October 1949, in ibid.

31. Idem to Vijaya L. Pandit, 29 September 1949, box 5, in ibid.

32. Memorandum, 27 January 1950, Stephen Spingarn Papers, Harry S. Truman Library, Independence, Mo. A deal was floated whereby, in exchange for France and Portugal relinquishing territory in India (Goa, etc.), India would settle the Kashmir question in a way favorable to Pakistan. See the attached handwritten response on White House stationery with an unclear date: "I shy away from propositions that we should put pressure on European nations to liquidate their empires. Pondicherry et al. might make India happy; what would the French say? A feeble Indian promise to look with favor on Bao Dai [the Vietnamese leader] is small payment for the loss the French would feel. I don't see how the President can become involved in this."

33. Walter White to Mordecai Johnson, 30 September 1949, box 4, Walter White Papers.

34. Idem to Louis Martin, 3 October 1949, box 5, in ibid.

35. Idem to President Harry S. Truman, 23 August 1949, box 6, in ibid.

36. Letter, October 1949, part 14, reel 12, no. 0206, NAACP Papers.

37. Invitation, 5 November 1949, box 5, Walter White Papers.

38. List of attendees at "Meeting with Prime Minister Nehru," 5 November 1949, in ibid.

39. Roy Wilkins to "Your Excellency," 16 September 1949, part 14, reel 12, no. 0193, NAACP Papers.

40. Draft letter, October 1949, box 5, Walter White Papers.

41. Walter White to Vijaya L. Pandit, 19 October 1949, in ibid.

42. Idem to Harry S. Truman, 11 December 1950, part 14, reel 12, no. 0318, NAACP Papers.

43. Walter White to Roger Baldwin, 30 October 1951, part 14, reel 12, no. 470, in ibid.

44. John M. Stevens, oral history, 1996, Georgetown University, Washington, D.C.

45. Smith Simpson, oral history, 1996, in ibid.

46. Chester Bowles to Walter White, 15 November 1951, part 14, reel 12, no. 483, NAACP Papers.

47. Alfred Leroy Atherton Jr., oral history, 1996, Georgetown University.

48. Richard McKee, oral history, 2003, Georgetown University.

49. Donald Anderson, oral history, 1996, Georgetown University.

50. Charles W. McCaskill, oral history, 1996, Georgetown University.

51. Bilha Bryant, oral history, 1998, Georgetown University.

52. Walter White to Fowler McCormick, 4 November 1949, box 4, Walter White Papers.

53. Ibid., 10 December 1949, in ibid.

54. Idem to "Dear Fowler," 28 March 1950, in ibid.

55. Idem to "Dear Nan," 19 October 1949, in ibid.

56. Idem to Matthew J. Connelly, 23 February 1950, box 6, in ibid.

57. Idem to Vijaya L. Pandit, 21 December 1949, box 5, in ibid.

58. Vijaya L. Pandit to Walter White, 27 December 1949, in ibid.

59. See, e.g., Walter White to Henry Ford II, 25 January 1950; Henry Ford II to Walter White, 7 February 1950; Walter White to Henry Ford II, 11 February 1950; all in box 2, in ibid.

60. Idem to Vijaya L. Pandit, 10 February 1950, box 5, in ibid.

61. Idem to Dean Acheson, 10 February 1950, box 1, in ibid.

62. B. R. Sen, minister and charge d'affaires, to Walter White, 15 February 1950, box 2, in ibid.

63. Vijaya L. Pandit to Walter White, 17 December 1953, box 5, in ibid.

64. *New York Amsterdam News*, 14 December 1946.

65. Shri S. Krishnamurti to P. L. Prattis, 14 June 1949, box 144-21, P. L. Prattis Papers, Howard University, Washington, D.C.

66. "Visitor's Card," 12 June 1949, in ibid.

67. Letter to *Pittsburgh Courier*, 15 June 1949, in ibid.

68. Walter White to J. J. Singh, 1 November 1949, box 2, Walter White Papers.

69. Senator Karl Mundt to J. J. Singh, 10 February 1950, in ibid.

70. J. J. Singh to Senator Karl Mundt, 15 February 1950, in ibid.

71. Karl Mundt to J. J. Singh, 20 February 1950, in ibid.

72. *The Economist*, 5 August 1950.

73. Roy Wilkins to Franklin Williams, 31 August 1951, part 14, reel 9, no. 557, NAACP Papers.

74. "Amar Singh Discovers America," November–December 1951, part 14, reel 9, no. 561, in ibid.

75. Argus J. Tresidder, public affairs officer, U.S. Embassy, Colombo, to UAW-CIO newspaper, 4 August 1952, part 14, reel 9, no. 632, in ibid.

CHAPTER 13: THE END OF EMPIRES

1. *New York Times*, 18 May 1954.

2. Mary Dudziak, *Cold War Civil Rights: Race and the Image of American Democracy* (Princeton, N.J.: Princeton University Press, 2000), 33. See also M. N. Gaulati, *What America Did for India's Independence* (New Delhi: Manas Publications, 2004).

3. George Lewis, *The White South and the Red Menace: Segregationists, Anticommunism and Massive Resistance, 1945–1965* (Gainesville: University Press of Florida, 2004), 132.

4. Dudziak, *Cold War Civil Rights*, 42,105.

5. Eleanor Roosevelt, *India and the Awakening East* (New York: Harper and Row, 1953), 115, 189. See also Naresh Chandra Roy, *India and the United States of America* (Calcutta: Mukherjee, n.d.).

6. Shiwaram Krishnarao Kshirsagar, "Development of Relations between India and the United States, 1941–1952," Ph.D. diss., American University, 1957, 146–147.

7. Edith Sampson, "The Negro's Role in America's Fight for a Free World," ca. 1950, box 100, Pauli Murray Papers.

8. See Farah J. Griffin and Cheryl J. Fish, eds., *A Stranger in the Village: Two Centuries of African-American Travel Writing* (Boston: Beacon Press, 1998), 292–294, 297.

9. Remarks, ca. 1956, reel 11, no. 839, William Hastie Papers, Library of Congress, Washington, D.C.

10. Sterling Tucker, "Report of Three Month Lecture Tour of India," 1955, reel 11, no. 936, in ibid.

11. Helen Semmerling to Walter White, 1 September 1953, box 3, Walter White Papers.

12. Walter White to Ralph Bunche, 11 November 1949, box 1, in ibid.

13. Raymond Hare to Walter White, 13 March 1950, box 2, in ibid.

14. Walter White to President Harry S. Truman, 11 August 1950, part 14, reel 8, no. 608, NAACP Papers.

15. Idem to President Harry S. Truman, 23 August 1949, part 14, reel 8, no. 609, in ibid.

16. Press release, 6 March 1951, part 14, reel 8, no. 746, in ibid.

17. Walter White to Hon. John Vorys, 4 April 1951, part 14, reel 8, no. 752, in ibid.

18. Vijaya L. Pandit to Walter White, 30 January 1955, box 5, Walter White Papers.

19. Walter White to Vijaya L. Pandit, n.d., box 5, in ibid. See also Anne Guthrie, *Madame Ambassador: The Life of Vijaya Lakshmi Pandit* (London: Macmillan, 1963).

20. *New York Post*, 20 September 1945.

21. "Hearings before a Subcommittee of the Committee on Foreign Relations," U.S. Senate, 82nd Cong., sess. 1, 18 October 1951, box 5, Channing Tobias Papers.

22. Column, 16 October 1951, in ibid.

23. *Ebony*, ca. February 1951, box 1, in ibid.

24. *New York Post*, 20 September 1945.

25. Meier and Rudwick, *Along the Color Line*, 348.

26. E. Franklin Frazier, "The Negro and Non-Resistance," *The Crisis*, vol. 27, no. 5, March 1924, 213–214.

27. Chappell, *A Stone of Hope*, 68.

28. Jack, "Mohandas Karamchand Gandhi and Martin Luther King, Jr."

29. Martin Luther King article in *Ebony*, July 1959, in Carson, *The Papers of Martin Luther King, Jr.*, 5:231.

30. Martin Luther King Jr. to Richard Gregg, 18 December 1958, in ibid. See also Richard Gregg, *The Power of Nonviolence* (Nyack, N.Y.: Fellowship Publications, 1959); Joseph Kip Kosek, "Richard Gregg, Mohandas Gandhi and the Strategy of Nonviolence," *Journal of American History* 91, no. 4 (March 2005): 1318–1348.

31. Carson, *The Papers of Martin Luther King, Jr.*, 5:142–143, 233.

32. Remarks of Martin Luther King Jr. in 1959, in Griffin and Fish, *A Stranger in the Village*, 281, 284, 287.

33. *Financial Times*, 18 July 2005.

34. Danuta Stasik, *Out of India: Image of the West in Hindi Literature* (New Delhi: Manohar Publishers, 1994), 52–53.

35. Stokely Carmichael with Ekwueme Michael Thelwell, *Ready for Revolution: The Life and Struggles of Stokely Carmichael* (New York: Scribner's, 2003), 37.

36. *Los Angeles Times*, 16 December 2004.

37. Sheshabalaya, *Rising Elephant*, 144–146.

38. Johanna Lessinger, *From the Ganges to the Hudson: Indian Immigrants in New York City* (Boston: Allyn and Bacon, 1995), 10, 135.

39. *Asia Times*, 14 December 2005.

40. Stasik, *Out of India*, 60.

41. Clyde Prestowitz, *Three Billion New Capitalists: The Great Shift of Wealth and Power to the East* (New York: Basic Books, 2005), 233.

42. *Financial Times*, 18 July 2005.

43. Ibid., 5 December 2005.

44. *New York Times*, 12 July 2005.

45. Ibid., 21 August 2006.

46. Ibid., 22 January 2005. In that same vein, note the Hollywood film directed by the South Asian Mira Nair and starring Denzel Washington, *Mississippi Masala*, which portrayed a love affair between an African American man and a woman of Indian ancestry: see *New York Times*, 5 February 1992. But in contrast, note the election of Bobby Jindal as governor of Louisiana in 2007, the nation's first Indian American chief executive, an event that was not embraced by all in South Asia: see *Times of India*, 28 October 2007. Shashi Tharoor, an eminent Indian national who formerly served at the highest level at the United Nations, pointed out that "there is no record of Bobby identifying himself with the needs or issues of his state's black people." Indeed, he "cultivated the most conservative elements of white Louisiana society"—a society that would have elected a Nazi and Ku Klux Klansman, David Duke, as governor years earlier but for the massive vote against him by Black Americans. Jindal was contrasted with Vinita Gupta of Oklahoma, a woman of South Asian origin who "won her reputation as a crusading lawyer by taking up the case of illegal immigrants exploited by a factory owner (her story will shortly be depicted by Hollywood, with Halle Berry playing the Indian heroine)."

INDEX